BRITISH GEOLOGICAL SURVEY

R. A. EDWARDS and
E. C. FRESHNEY

CONTRIBUTORS

Geophysics
I. F. Smith

Palaeontology
M. C. Boulter, R. D. Clark,
J. Cooper, R. Harland,
M. J. Hughes and C. King

Petrography
R. J. Merriman and A. C. Morton

Stratigraphy
M. T. Holder, C. King and
R. C. Scrivener

Water supply
R. A. Monkhouse

Geology of the country around Southampton

Memoir for 1:50 000 geological sheet 315
(England & Wales)

Natural Environment Research Council

LONDON: HER MAJESTY'S STATIONERY OFFICE   1987

First published 1987

ISBN 0 11 884396 6

Bibliographical reference

EDWARDS, R. A. and FRESHNEY, E. C. 1987. Geology of the country around Southampton. *Mem. Br. Geol. Surv.*, Sheet 315 (England & Wales).

Authors

R. A. EDWARDS, BSc, PhD
E. C. FRESHNEY, BSc, PhD
British Geological Survey, Exeter

Contributors

M. T. Holder, BSc, PhD, and R. C. Scrivener, BSc, PhD
British Geological Survey, Exeter

R. D. Clark, BSc, R. Harland, BSc, PhD, M. J. Hughes, MSc, R. J. Merriman, BSc, A. C. Morton, MA, and I. F. Smith, BSc, MSc
British Geological Survey, Keyworth

R. A. Monkhouse, BA, MSc
British Geological Survey, Wallingford

J. Cooper, BSc, PhD
British Museum (Natural History)

M. C. Boulter, BSc, PhD
North East London Polytechnic

C. King, BSc
Paleoservices Ltd, Watford

Produced in the United Kingdom for HMSO
Dd 240402 C20 3/87

Other publications of the Survey dealing with this district and adjoining districts

BOOKS

British Regional Geology
The Hampshire Basin and adjoining areas, 4th Edition, 1982

Mineral Assessment Reports
No. 50 (Fordingbridge), 1980
No. 122 (Lymington and Beaulieu), 1982

Water Supply
The Water Supply of Hampshire, published 1910*

Metric Well Inventories
Sheet 299 (Winchester), 1982
Sheet 300 (Alresford), 1976
Sheet 316 (Fareham), 1983

1:50 000 MAPS AND EXPLANATORY SHEET MEMOIRS

Sheet 298 (Salisbury); Memoir published 1903*
Sheet 299 (Winchester); Memoir published 1912*
Sheet 300 (Alresford); Memoir published 1910*
Sheet 314 (Ringwood); Memoir published 1902*
Sheet 316 (Fareham); Memoir published 1913*
Sheet 329 (Bournemouth); Memoir published 1898*
Sheet 330 (Lymington); Memoir for sheets 330 and 331 published 1915*
Sheet 331 (Portsmouth)
Isle of Wight Special Sheet; District Memoir published 1921 (reprinted 1975)

OTHER GEOLOGICAL MAPS

1:1 584 000
Tectonic map of Great Britain and Northern Ireland

1:625 000
South Sheet (Geological)
South Sheet (Quaternary)
South Sheet (Aeromagnetic)

1:250 000
Wight (Solid geology)
Wight (Seabed sediments)
Wight (Gravity)
Wight (Aeromagnetic)

* Out of print

CONTENTS

FIGURES

PLATES

TABLES

NOTES

The word 'district' used in this memoir means the area included in 1:50 000-scale Geological Sheet 315 (Southampton). Figures in square brackets are National Grid references; all places within the Southampton district lie within 100-km square SU. The grid letters are omitted for localities within the district. Numbers preceded by A refer to photographs in the Survey's collections. The authorship of fossil species is given in the index of fossils.

SU22		SU32		SU42		SU52
SW *RAE* 1977-78	SE *RAE* 1978	SW *RAE* 1979-80	SE *RAE* 1978-79	SW *RAE* 1979-80	SE *MTH* 1979	SW *RCS* 1979
NW *RAE* 1977	NE *RAE* 1975-77	NW *RAE* 1975	NE *RAE, ECF* 1975, 1979-80	NW *RAE, ECF, MTH* 1979-80	NE *MTH* 1979	NW *RCS* 1980
SU21		SU31		SU41		SU51
SW *RAE* 1977	SE *RAE* 1976	SW *ECF* 1978	SE *ECF, RAE* 1977, 1980	SW *ECF, RAE* 1980	SE *ECF, RCS* 1979-80	SW *ECF* 1979
NW *ECF* 1975	NE *ECF* 1975	NW *ECF* 1975-76	NE *ECF, RCS* 1976	NW *ECF* 1980	NE *ECF* 1980	NW *ECF* 1978-79
SU20		SU30		SU40		SU50
SW *ECF* 1975	SE *ECF* 1975	SW *ECF* 1976	SE *ECF* 1977	SW *ECF* 1978	SE *ECF* 1978	SW *ECF* 1978

The component 1:10 000-scale National Grid sheets of Geological Sheet 315 are shown on the diagram above together with the dates of survey and the initials of the surveyors. The surveying officers were: R. A. Edwards, E. C. Freshney, M. T. Holder and R. C. Scrivener. Uncoloured dyeline copies of the maps are available for purchase from the British Geological Survey, Keyworth, Nottingham NG12 5GG.

PREFACE

The first geological survey of the Southampton district was on the one-inch scale (1:63 360) by Mr H. W. Bristow in 1854. The results were published on Old Series Sheets 11 and 15 in 1856 and 1858 respectively. The district was surveyed on the six-inch scale (1:10 560) by W. Whitaker and C. Reid between 1889 and 1898 and the results were incorporated in the first colour-printed edition of New Series one-inch Sheet 315, published in 1899. The accompanying explanatory memoir, written principally by Reid with contributions by Whitaker, was issued in 1902.

The present resurvey, on the 1:10 000 scale, was commenced in 1973 and completed in 1980. Most of the southern, central and north-western parts of the district were surveyed by Dr R. A. Edwards and Dr E. C. Freshney; Dr M. T. Holder and Dr R. C. Scrivener surveyed the north-eastern part. The work was carried out under the direction of Mr G. Bisson, District Geologist. It was supported by a consortium funded by the Natural Environment Research Council and the Departments of the Environment, Industry and Energy.

The present work has benefited greatly from contributions made by various specialists. Mr C. King, of Paleoservices Ltd., has identified faunas from the London Clay and the Bracklesham Group—mainly macrofossils and ostracods—and has reported on their stratigraphical significance. Mr J. Cooper of the British Museum (Natural History) has identified macrofossils from the London Clay and Bracklesham and Barton groups. Geological Survey contributors include Mr M. J. Hughes, who was mainly responsible for identifying foraminifera from the London Clay and Bracklesham and Barton groups, Dr R. Harland, who identified dinoflagellate cysts, and Mr R. D. Clark who identified various macrofossils. Dr M. C. Boulter of the North East London Polytechnic studied pollen and spores, partly under contract to the Institute of Geological Sciences. Most of the palaeontological results have been presented in the form of unpublished internal reports; the appropriate parts of these have been incorporated into the memoir.

Mr R. J. Merriman carried out X-ray diffraction studies to determine the clay mineralogy of samples, and Mr A. C. Morton has studied the heavy mineralogy of the sands. Mr I. F. Smith has contributed a map based on seismic sections showing the depth to the base of the Tertiary deposits within the district. Dr J. D. Cornwell carried out geophysical investigations to determine the thickness of the Older River Gravels at several localities.

Four cored boreholes were drilled in 1976–77 and in 1984–85 by the Survey's drilling rig, under the direction of Mr S. P. Thorley, to provide samples and stratigraphical data to supplement the field survey.

The memoir has been written and compiled by Dr Edwards and Dr Freshney and incorporates notes provided by Drs Holder and Scrivener, an account of the Chalk by Dr Scrivener, and results taken from reports by the specialists listed above. Mr R. A. Monkhouse has provided a contribution on the hydrogeology and water supply.

Acknowledgement is made to numerous individuals and organisations for their help and cooperation in allowing ready access to their land for the purpose of drilling boreholes and carrying out other work in connection with the survey. Particular thanks are due to the Garrett family of Copythorne Lodge, Cadnam, for their hospitality during several years of the resurvey. We thank the Forestry Commission for access to the New Forest, and Southampton City Council, Eastleigh District Council, Fareham District Council, New Forest District Council and Hampshire County Council who were most helpful in allowing us to examine borehole samples and records. Permission to reproduce details of boreholes drilled for hydrocarbon exploration by Amoco (UK) Exploration Co. Ltd, Ultramar Exploration Ltd, and Gas Council (Exploration) Ltd, is acknowledged with thanks. Amoco (UK) Exploration Co. Ltd, Ultramar Exploration Ltd, Carless Exploration Ltd, Clyde Petroleum plc, Gas Council (Exploration) Ltd and Shell UK Exploration and Production are also thanked for their permission to use the seismic data on which Figure 41 is based.

This memoir has been edited by Dr R. W. Gallois and Mr W. B. Evans.

G. Innes Lumsden, FRSE
Director

British Geological Survey
Keyworth
Nottingham
NG12 5GG

17 September 1986

CHAPTER 1

Introduction

GEOGRAPHICAL SETTING

The Southampton district has an area of 553 km² included mostly within the county of Hampshire, except for about 25 km² in the north-west which lie in Wiltshire (Figure 1). It is drained mainly by the rivers Test and Itchen which rise on the Chalk; they enter the district from the north and combine to flow into the broad estuary of Southampton Water. The River Hamble enters the estuary in the extreme south-east of the district.

About 150 km² of the western and south-western parts of the district are occupied by the woodland and heathland of the New Forest, which has its origins, probably in the 11th Century, as a Royal Forest set aside for hunting by William the Conqueror. It is probably the largest area of semi-natural vegetation remaining in lowland Britain, and is a very popular tourist and recreation area.

The Southampton district lies in the central part of the Hampshire Basin, a broad downwarp filled with Tertiary (Palaeogene) clays and sands (Figure 2). The Tertiary formations rest on Cretaceous Chalk, the highest part of which crops out in small areas in the north-west and north-east of the district. These solid deposits are overlain by extensive areas of Quaternary deposits, mainly flint gravels.

Flint gravels, which at Pipers Wait [249 165] near Nomansland, form the highest point (129 m above Ordnance Datum (OD)) in the New Forest, give rise to high plateaux, locally called Plains, covered by heather and acid-tolerant grassland. The Plains are probably the dissected remnants of extensive terrace levels of old rivers, and drop in altitude from north to south. Landscapes dominated by heather or ling are widespread on infertile soils developed on the sandy Tertiary formations of the district. The heaths that form on the sandy Tertiary formations in the south of the

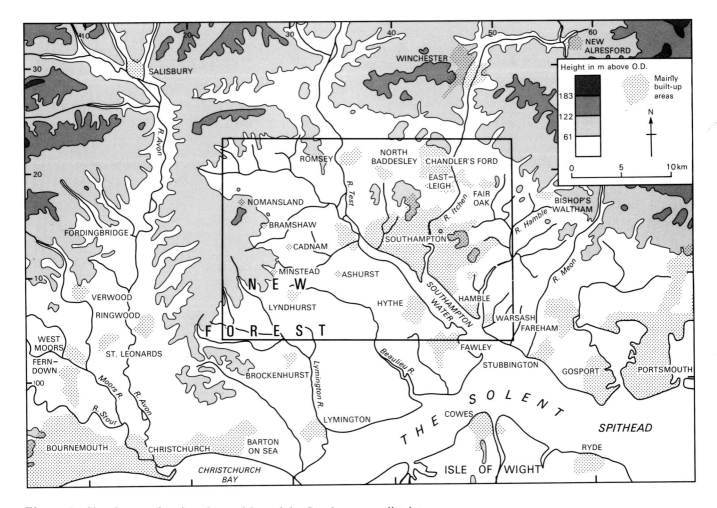

Figure 1   Sketch-map showing the position of the Southampton district

district include valley bogs and wet heaths, some of which contain accumulations of peaty alluvium which have been worked in the historically recent past.

The more clayey Tertiary formations in the New Forest give rise to more fertile soils that are mainly covered by woodland. Pleasant streams, locally called 'gutters' or 'waters', flow through the woodland from the margins of the gravel plateaux. Attractive streamside grasslands, called 'lawns', are fertile and thus of considerable value to the grazier. The woodlands are of two main types: unenclosed broadleaved woodlands consisting mainly of beech and oak with an understorey of holly, and 'Inclosures' of dominantly coniferous woodland, which are fenced off to protect them from grazing animals. Many commoners' grazing rights still exist, which gives rise to the characteristic sight within the Forest of free-ranging cattle, ponies, and pigs.

The main settlement in that part of the Forest which lies within the district is Lyndhurst, the so-called 'capital' of the New Forest. Small settlements include Minstead and Bramshaw. The villages of Nomansland, Cadnam, and Ashurst lie along and just outside the northern boundary of the Forest. The strip of land lying between the New Forest and Southampton Water includes the town of Hythe and the site around Fawley of part of one of the largest petrochemical complexes in Europe.

The largest settlement in the district is the city of Southampton, population about 250 000, which is situated at the head of Southampton Water (Plate 1). It is one of the leading ports in the country and is the centre, with outlying districts, for numerous light industries and services. The towns of Romsey, North Baddesley, Eastleigh, Chandler's Ford, and Fair Oak lie to the north of Southampton. East of the city, built-up areas interspersed with light industry, horticulture, and mixed farming, extend to Hamble and Warsash. That part of the district north of the New Forest is mainly an area of mixed farming with some woodland.

The main extractive industry in the area is gravel working from river terrace deposits. Sand is also dug from a small number of pits sited on the outcrops of the Reading Formation and Whitecliff Sand. Brickmaking ceased in 1974 with the closure of the pits that worked the London Clay at Lower Swanwick near Bursledon.

The public water supply of the district is mainly taken from the rivers Test and Itchen, but important quantities are also pumped from the Upper Chalk at Otterbourne.

GEOLOGICAL HISTORY

The oldest known rocks in the Southampton district, proved in the Marchwood [3991 1118] and Southampton (Western Esplanade) [4156 1202] boreholes, are fluviatile sandstones of probable early Devonian age. No later Devonian or Carboniferous rocks have been proved in the district. After folding and low-grade metamorphism during the Variscan Orogeny, the Devonian rocks were uplifted and eroded during the Triassic. The oldest Triassic rocks in the district are fluviatile sandstones and conglomerates, belonging to the Sherwood Sandstone Group, that were deposited as alluvial fans by flash floods in a hot arid climate. With a decline in the availability of coarser sediments owing to the reduction

in relief, reddish brown silty mudstone and siltstone of the Mercia Mudstone Group were laid down in playa lakes. At times, the lakes dried out and evaporites, mainly anhydrite, were formed. At the end of this period of red-bed deposition a major marine transgression occurred in the late Triassic which ushered in a period of mainly marine sedimentation that lasted until the end of the Cretaceous.

Jurassic sedimentation in the district took place in shallow seas on a broad continental shelf in an equable warm climate. World-wide changes in sea level combined with local tectonic events led to a series of transgressions and regressions. Most of the Jurassic sediments of the Southampton district are marine clays, with subordinate beds of sandstones and shelly and oolitic limestones which were deposited in near-shore environments or on rises that were subject to winnowing currents.

At the end of the Jurassic the sea retreated leaving coastal lagoons in which the marls, limestones, evaporites and fossil soils of the Purbeck Beds were formed. Lagoonal and lacustrine conditions continued into the early Cretaceous when they were replaced by the fluvial environments in which the sands of the Wealden were deposited. Earth movements at that time caused uplift and erosion, and most of the Portland Beds, Purbeck Beds and Wealden sequences were eroded from the Southampton district. Another widespread marine transgression introduced the sands of the Lower Greensand and, subsequently, the marine clays of the Gault. After deposition of the sands of the Upper Greensand, the district and much of north-west Europe was transgressed by the Chalk sea.

Earth movements and subsequent erosion in the late Cretaceous caused much of the Chalk to be removed prior to deposition of the Tertiary sediments. Little folding occurred, and there is generally no obvious angular discordance between the Tertiary and Cretaceous rocks.

The Tertiary sediments of the Hampshire Basin are markedly cyclical and record numerous transgressive–regressive events. The first major marine transgression occurred at the base of the Reading Formation, but the district soon became the site of coastal lagoons and rivers. The next transgression marks the base of the London Clay, which is composed mostly of five cycles of marine sedimentation. During the fifth cycle the sea shallowed and the district lay within an area of dominantly intertidal to subtidal sedimentation, in which the Wittering Formation was deposited. Glauconitic sands of the Earnley Sand were deposited in a shelf sea during the next transgression; the overlying Marsh Farm Formation marks the retreat of the sea from the district, which again became the site of predominantly intertidal sedimentation. The Selsey Sand marks another marine transgression over most of the district, and glauconitic silty sands were deposited in a shallow shelf sea. Further deepening of the water led to a decrease in grain size and deposition of the Barton Clay. The sea then gradually shallowed as the shoreline prograded, giving rise to the clayey silty sands of the Chama Sand, probably deposited on the lower shoreface, and the overlying well-sorted Becton Sand which was probably deposited in environments ranging from middle or upper shoreface to beach, with some possible wind-blown sand. At the top of the Becton Sand a palaeosol with a rootlet bed indicates subaerial conditions; the succeeding shelly clays of the lower Headon Formation were deposited in freshwater

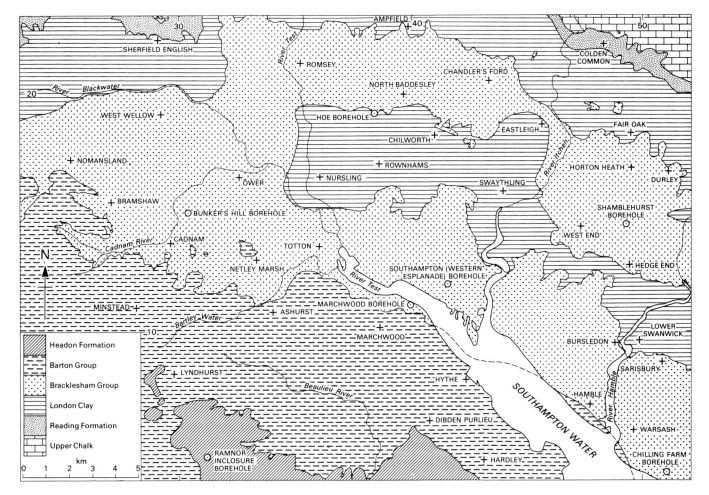

Figure 2   Sketch-map showing the generalised solid geology of the Southampton district, and the locations of selected boreholes

lagoons. The Lyndhurst Member marks a marine to brackish-water transgression which regresses to freshwater lagoonal clays in the upper Headon Formation.

The Alpine Earth Movements caused uplift and gentle folding of the Tertiary and earlier sequences.

During the Quaternary glaciations the district lay south of the ice sheets, but there is ample evidence in the form of cryoturbation features and solifluction deposits, to show that it experienced a periglacial climate and that the ice sheets were at times not far distant. The Quaternary history of the district is difficult to unravel owing to the difficulty of dating the deposits.

PREVIOUS RESEARCH

Owing to poor exposure, the district does not figure prominently in geological literature. It is, however, commonly referred to in works dealing with the Hampshire Basin as a whole. Prestwich laid the foundations of the stratigraphy in a series of papers (1847; 1850; 1854). Fisher (1862) produced the definitive work on the Bracklesham Beds, which included references to the Selsey Sand in the New Forest. Keeping

and Tawney (1881) described the palaeontology of inland exposures of the Headon Beds, which had earlier been defined, together with the Osborne, Bembridge, and Hamstead beds, from the Isle of Wight by Forbes (1853). The first edition of this memoir, by Reid with contributions by Whitaker, was published in 1902. Whitaker's (1910) description of the water supply of Hampshire incorporates details of many wells and boreholes in the present district.

In 1933 Burton described the stratigraphy of the Barton Group in the cliff sections at Barton on Sea, using a lettering scheme which is still employed today; mention is made also of localities within the Southampton district. Shore and Elwes (1889) described the stratigraphy and palaeontology of the Quaternary and Tertiary strata exposed during construction of docks in Southampton; Anderson (1933) and Wrigley (1934) described the rich faunas of the Earnley Sand exposed during later dock excavations. Curry and King (1965) described the stratigraphy and palaeontology of the London Clay in exposures at Lower Swanwick. The Eocene succession in the Fawley Transmission Tunnel was described by Curry and others (1968); Gilkes (1968, 1978) described the clay mineralogy of Tertiary successions in the Hampshire Basin. Stinton (1970) gave an account of New Forest fossil localities. Eaton (1976), Costa and Downie (1976) and Bujak and others (1980) erected zonal schemes for various parts of the Palaeogene on the basis of dinoflagellate cysts.

Curry and others (1977; 1978), King and King (1977) and King (1981) have described and discussed the stratigraphy and palaeontology of the Palaeogene of the Hampshire Basin, including sequences in the Southampton district. A sedimentological study of the Hampshire Basin Tertiary was made by Plint (1983). Collinson and others (1981) and Morton (1982) have described pollen and spores, and heavy-mineral assemblages respectively from the Palaeogene in boreholes in the district.

The Quaternary sediments of the buried channel of Southampton Water were described by Everard (1954) and Hodson and West (1972).

CHAPTER 2

Concealed formations

The proved concealed formations that underlie the Southampton district range from Devonian to Cretaceous in age. The uppermost part of the Chalk crops out in the north-west and north-east of the district. Information concerning the older parts of the Chalk and the underlying formations has been obtained from boreholes drilled for geothermal energy at Marchwood [3991 1118] and Western Esplanade [4156 1202], Southampton. The generalised sequence penetrated in these boreholes is shown in Figure 3; the sequences proved in deep boreholes in adjacent districts at Portsdown [SU 6394 0738] and Fordingbridge [SU 1876 1181] are shown for comparison.

?DEVONIAN

The oldest rocks proved in the Marchwood and Western Esplanade boreholes consist of hard, pale greyish green and reddish brown fine- to very fine-grained sandstone with some reddish brown to purplish brown siltstone and mudstone. A total of 890 m of these lithologies was proved in the Marchwood Borehole between 2609 and 1719 m depths, and 31 m in the Western Esplanade Borehole, between 1823 and 1792 m depths. These sequences contain fining-upwards cycles that Whittaker (1980) has suggested to be of fluviatile origin; he likened them to cycles in the Old Red Sandstone. Similar lithologies have been proved in deep boreholes elsewhere in the region, notably at Arreton [SZ 5320 8580] in the Isle of Wight, and at Wytch Farm [SY 9804 8526] and Cranborne [SU 0341 0907], Dorset. At Arreton, $^{40}Ar/^{39}Ar$ age-dating indicates that the shales and sandstones were deposited between 380 ± 2 million years (Ma) and 390 ± 4 Ma ago, and were affected by metamorphism 340 ± 8 Ma ago (Gas Council (Exploration) Ltd, Well-Completion Report, Arreton No.2, 1974). At Wytch Farm, K-Ar dating of greenish grey phyllites suggests two periods of metamor-

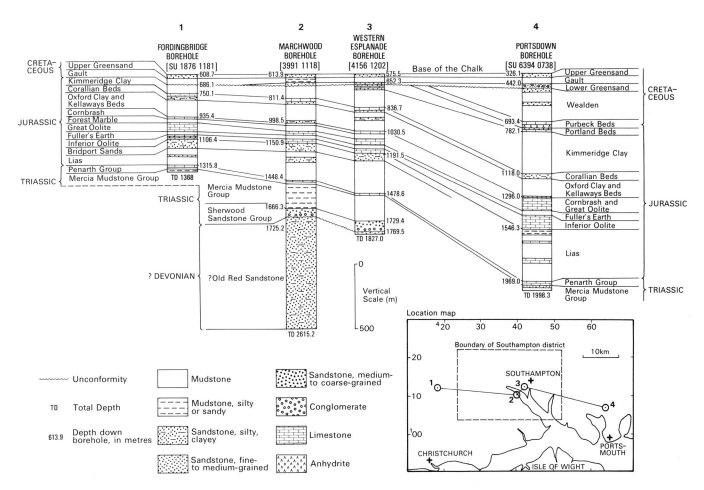

Figure 3 Correlation of the pre-Chalk sequences proved in the Fordingbridge, Marchwood, Western Esplanade and Portsdown boreholes

phism that occurred at 357 ± 5 Ma and 337 ± 5 Ma (Colter and Havard, 1981). At Cranborne, greenish grey mudstone and siltstone contain a poorly preserved fauna indicative of a mid or late Devonian age (Butler, in BP Petroleum Development Ltd, Well-Completion Report, Cranborne No.1, 1972).

Dips in the presumed Devonian sediments of the Southampton district range between horizontal and 45°, with cleavage dips ranging from horizontal to vertical. The structural style of these basement rocks is probably similar to that which affects the Devonian and Carboniferous rocks of parts of the Variscan fold belt of Devon and Cornwall. No Carboniferous sediment has been recorded in the district.

TRIASSIC

The Triassic sequences proved in the Marchwood and Western Esplanade boreholes are thin in comparison with those proved in adjacent districts. The Triassic strata rest with marked unconformity on the ?Devonian rocks. The following succession was proved between 1792 and 1505 m depths in the Western Esplanade Borehole:

		Thickness m	Depth m
PENARTH GROUP			
Langport Member	Limestone, pale grey to white, with some clay partings	10	1515
Cotham Member	Mudstone, grey and greenish grey	4	1519
Westbury Formation	Mudstone, grey to black, pyritic, with thin clayey limestone beds	6	1525
MERCIA MUDSTONE GROUP			
Blue Anchor Formation	Mudstone, grey to greyish green, silty; and siltstone, clayey	20	1545
Variegated Marl	Mudstone, greyish green; and siltstone, reddish brown, micaceous, clayey, with traces of anhydrite	13	1558
Upper Red Marl	Mudstone, reddish brown, slightly calcareous; and siltstone, clayey, with pale green reduction spots. Anhydrite throughout	40	1598
Anhydritic Siltstone	Mudstone, reddish brown; and siltstone, clayey; anhydrite abundant at some levels	28	1626

		Thickness m	Depth m
Saliferous Marl (equivalent)	Mudstone, reddish brown, silty, with some very fine-grained sandstone. Anhydrite common	45	1671
Lower Red Marl	Mudstone, reddish brown, and siltstone	17	1688
'Waterstones' (equivalent)	Siltstone, reddish brown, clayey, with thin very fine-grained sandstone interbeds	37	1725
SHERWOOD SANDSTONE GROUP			
Otter Sandstone	Sandstone, reddish brown, fine- to medium-grained, with siltstone and pebble interbeds	38	1763
Budleigh Salterton Pebble Beds	Conglomerate, green to reddish brown	29	1792

The Sherwood Sandstone forms a single fining-upward sequence within which there are thinner fining-upwards cycles.

JURASSIC

The distribution of the Jurassic formations of the district was markedly affected by early Cretaceous earth movements, and an angular unconformity occurs at the base of the Lower Greensand. This unconformity cuts progressively down westwards. In most of the district west of Southampton Water, the Lower Greensand rests on Kimmeridge Clay. Elsewhere in the district, for example near Lyndhurst, seismic sections show that the Lower Greensand rests on the Oxford Clay. The extent of this pre-Aptian erosion was controlled by early Cretaceous movements on fault-blocks that are bounded by west-trending faults. The pre-Aptian strata in each block are usually tilted to the north, and thus the amount of Jurassic strata preserved tends to increase northward in each block. East of Southampton Water, Portland Beds were proved in the Western Esplanade Borehole, and Purbeck Beds and Wealden Beds were penetrated in the Portsdown Borehole (Falcon and Kent, 1960).

A total of 757 m of Jurassic was proved in the Marchwood Borehole (between 1442 and 685 m depth, and 857 m in the Western Esplanade Borehole (between 1505 and 648 m depth). The following sequence was proved in the Western Esplanade Borehole:

		Thickness m	Depth m
Portland Beds	Sandstone and limestone, grey, silty and sandy	49	697

		Thickness m	Depth m
Kimmeridge Clay	Mudstone, brown to grey, calcareous, with some thin sandy limestones	135	832
Corallian Beds	Limestone, grey, oolitic and rubbly, with clay partings; interbedded sandstone, clayey siltstone and silty mudstone	42	874
Oxford Clay	Mudstone, grey, calcareous, silty; and siltstone, greyish brown, calcareous, thinly laminated	134	1008
Kellaways Rock	Sandstone and siltstone, white, calcareous	7	1015
Kellaways Clay	Mudstone, greyish brown, silty	11	1026
Cornbrash	Limestone, pale grey to white	15	1041
Forest Marble	Mudstone, pale grey, calcareous, with thin sandy and shelly limestone interbeds; limestone, buff to white	46	1087
Great Oolite Limestone	Limestone, oolitic; and limestone, sandy	37	1124
Fuller's Earth	Mudstone, grey, calcareous, silty, with carbonaceous streaks; limestone, thin, sandy and clayey, in the middle part	29	1153
Inferior Oolite	Limestone, shelly, oolitic and sandy	34	1187
UPPER LIAS Bridport Sands	Sandstone, greyish green, very fine-grained, micaceous, with layers of calcareous-cemented doggers; becoming siltier and clayier with depth	70	1257
Upper Lias Clay	Mudstone, grey, calcareous, silty; and siltstone, grey, calcareous, clayey	33	1290

		Thickness m	Depth m
MIDDLE LIAS Marlstone Rock Bed	Limestone, grey to cream	3	1293
Silts and Clays	Mudstone, grey, calcareous, silty; and siltstone, grey, calcareous, clayey	50	1343
LOWER LIAS Green Ammonite Beds	Siltstone, grey, micaceous; and mudstone, silty	12	1355
Belemnite Marl	Siltstone, grey, calcareous, clayey; and mudstone, silty	18	1373
Black Ven Marl and Shales-with-Beef?	Siltstone, grey, calcareous; and mudstone, silty	8	1381
Blue Lias	Mudstone, grey; and limestone, pale grey, clayey, interbedded	124	1505

The Jurassic sequence beneath the district differs from that at outcrop in Dorset, particularly in its greater development of limestones in the Middle Jurassic. The Great Oolite Limestone, absent at outcrop in Dorset, is about 39 m thick in the Marchwood Borehole and thickens south-eastwards to 104 m in the Portsdown Borehole. Similarly, the Inferior Oolite limestones are much thicker in the Southampton district and the Portsdown Borehole than in south Dorset. The Lias also shows local thickness variations; it ranges from 210 m thick in the Fordingbridge Borehole to 255 m thick in the Western Esplanade Borehole and 424 m thick in the Portsdown Borehole. The Bridport Sands, at the top of the Lias, are fine-grained silty sandstones with calcareous doggers at all three localities.

CRETACEOUS

The full thickness of the Cretaceous was penetrated in the Marchwood and Western Esplanade boreholes. The higher part of the Chalk has been entered by numerous shallow water boreholes; details are given in Chapter 3.

The following sequence was proved between 648 and 178 m in the Western Esplanade Borehole:

		Thickness m	Depth m
Upper Chalk	Limestone, soft white, micritic, with flints	258	436
Middle Chalk	Limestone, soft, white, micritic	54	490
Lower Chalk	Limestone, soft, grey, micritic, silty; basal 2 m sandstone, calcareous, glauconitic	81	571

		Thickness m	Depth m
Upper Greensand	Sandstone and siltstone, greyish green, glauconitic	30	601
Gault	Mudstone, grey, silty	40	641
Lower Greensand	Sandstone, greyish green, glauconitic	7	648

The Gault, Upper Greensand and Chalk show little variation in lithology or thickness beneath the district. In contrast, the Lower Greensand shows considerable variation. It is absent to the west of the district at Fordingbridge, 8.2 m thick at Marchwood, and 28 m thick to the east of the present district in the Portsdown Borehole.

CHAPTER 3

Cretaceous: Chalk

About 6.5 km^2 of Upper Chalk crops out in the north-east of the district near Colden Common. Three smaller outcrops are present in the north-west of the district between Newton and Sherfield English. Exposures are rare; many of the former chalk-pits, which were worked for agricultural or building lime, are now overgrown or backfilled.

The Upper Chalk of the district typically consists of white or greyish white, microcrystalline limestone with lines of nodular flints at many levels. In places, flints are scattered throughout the chalk. At outcrop the chalk varies from soft and friable to firm and blocky, with rare, thin, indurated layers of porcellanous texture. Weathered sections are commonly rubbly, and the chalk may be stained yellowish brown or reddish brown, the latter being particularly pronounced at localities close to the junction with the overlying Reading Formation. Macrofossils are rare and usually consist of echinoderm or bivalve debris. Brydone (1912) attributed the three small outcrops of Chalk in the north-west of the district to the zone of *Belemnitella mucronata*. The outcrop near Colden Common has yielded faunas indicative of the zones of *Gonioteuthis quadrata* and *Offaster pilula* (Brydone, 1912). In addition, White (1912) recorded *Belemnitella mucronata* from a locality in this outcrop near Hensting, and this may indicate that the *mucronata* Zone is also present.

A few boreholes in the Southampton district have penetrated the full thickness of the Upper Chalk. A borehole [4173 1456] at Southampton Common is quoted by Reid (1902) as having proved 248 m of Upper Chalk beneath 139 m of younger strata, but there is uncertainty about the identification of the boundaries of the Upper Chalk. The Western Esplanade Borehole proved 258 m of Upper Chalk beneath 183 m of Tertiary deposits. Neither borehole yielded information about the age of the highest Chalk. However, the Marchwood Borehole, which proved 257 m of Upper Chalk, yielded foraminifera that Bigg (1980) identified as indicative of the upper part of the *quadrata* Zone from an horizon 15 m below the top of the Chalk. The *mucronata* Zone is either absent or is represented only in the highest few metres of the Chalk. The basal Tertiary unconformity appears, therefore, to lie at a similar stratigraphical level in the Chalk both at outcrop and in the borehole.

DETAILS

There are few exposures in the small Chalk outcrops in the north-west of the district. A large disused pit [295 231] near Manor Farm, Sherfield English, contains small exposures of blocky white chalk. Another disused pit [3030 2345] in the Chalk inlier 650 m north of Birchwood House Farm contains poor exposures of white chalk overlain by the Basement Bed of the Reading Formation (Reid, 1902, p.5).

A section exposed in a disused chalk-pit [4806 2280] north of Colden Common consists of 5.0 m of white to yellow, hard blocky chalk with layers of nodular flints. Hard blocky white chalk with flints is also exposed in a disused pit [4981 2229] which is only 250 m from the contact with the Reading Formation. In this locality the chalk is characterised by large fissures and pipes filled with Clay-with-flints.

An old quarry [5121 2274] near Whaddon Farm shows 0.3 m of clayey loam resting on 5.5 m of firm white chalk with a few layers of irregular flint nodules. Brydone (1912) recorded numerous *Offaster pilula* at this locality, but none were collected during the present survey. A pit [5029 2194] near Marwell Hall, now partially filled with refuse, shows up to 1.2 m of brown sandy clay piped into 4.7 m of firm white chalk with layers of fusiform flint nodules and some thin bands of porcellanous chalk.

The Upper Chalk is a major aquifer in the district and has been exploited by boreholes at numerous localities. A borehole [5146 2161] near Marwell House proved Upper Chalk to a depth of 91.4 m. Within the outcrop of the Reading Formation, a borehole [5126 2042] proved 21.3 m of Upper Chalk. A water borehole [4474 2153] at Brambridge Lodge penetrated 28.3 m of chalk with flints beneath Tertiary deposits. A borehole [5192 1995] at Stroudwood Farm penetrated 29.3 m of Upper Chalk; another [5024 1894] at Fairoak Park proved 48.5 m of Upper Chalk, and one [4792 2031] at Stoke Park Farm penetrated 14.6 m of very soft chalk with flints. A water-supply borehole [4501 1901] at Eastleigh proved 70 m of Upper Chalk described as 'chalk and flints', with a 1.5 m-thick 'hard band' in the middle of the sequence.

Middle Chalk has only been proved in the deep Southampton Common, Western Esplanade and Marchwood boreholes. Reid (1902) quotes two alternative interpretations for the Southampton Common Borehole, the more probable of which includes 13 m of Middle Chalk. The full thickness of the Middle Chalk was penetrated in both the Western Esplanade and Marchwood boreholes, where 54 m and 50 m respectively were attributed to the formation on the basis of the geophysical logs. Thicknesses of 81 m and 78 m were attributed to the Lower Chalk in the same two boreholes.

CHAPTER 4

Palaeogene: Introduction

The Palaeogene deposits of the Southampton district crop out in the central part of the Hampshire Basin, which contains up to 700 m of Palaeogene strata; much of the sequence is well exposed in the famous coastal sections on the Isle of Wight and in Hampshire. The Palaeogene formations which underlie most of the district total around 400 m in thickness; they consist almost exclusively of siliciclastic rocks ranging from clays to pebble beds, and have been divided during the present survey into formations and members on the basis of their dominant lithological characters (Figure 4).

The sequence consists of a number of sedimentary cycles each of which commenced with a marine transgression, the transgressive surface commonly being marked by a thin bed of flint pebbles. These pebbly deposits are overlain by less marine sediments which were deposited as the coastline advanced into the former marine areas. Each cycle probably lasted between 1 and 2 million years. The relationships between sedimentary cycles (called divisions by some authors), transgressive horizons, and the lithological units into which the Tertiary sequence has been divided are shown in Figure 5.

The structure of the district is simple and is dominated by a low southward dip. As a result, the older Palaeogene formations crop out in the north and the younger formations in the south. This general outcrop pattern is complicated by the presence of an anticlinal structure north and east of Southampton which creates an inlier of London Clay (Figure 2).

The Palaeogene of the Southampton district is poorly exposed; boreholes were, therefore, drilled at Ramnor Inclosure [3114 0475], Bunker's Hill [3038 1498], Shamblehurst [4927 1456], and Chilling Farm [5098 0443] to provide stratigraphical reference sections within the district.

The positions of the Palaeocene/Eocene and Eocene/Oligocene series boundaries within the Palaeogene System have been the subject of much discussion in the past. The general practice followed in this memoir has been to take the base of the Eocene at the base of the London Clay, the Reading Formation thus being assigned to the Palaeocene. Curry and others (1978) have placed the base of the Oligocene within the Bembridge Beds of the Isle of Wight, and this classification is followed in the present work. The youngest Palaeogene formation in the present district, the Headon Formation, was included in the Oligocene on the 1899 edition of the one-inch geological map; it falls within the Eocene in the new classification. In view of the general disagreement about their definition (Curry and others, 1978), stage-names have not been used for the Palaeogene in this memoir.

The stratigraphy shown on the present map differs considerably from that of the 1899 edition (Figure 4). Most of these changes have arisen from the recognition of transgressive–regressive cycles within the Palaeogene of the Hampshire Basin. The cycles were used to define informal divisions in the London Clay (King, 1981) and Bracklesham Group (Curry and others, 1977) (Figure 5). Much of the modern nomenclature derives from Curry and others (1978), in which the bases of the formations within the former Bracklesham Beds are defined as coincident with the bases of divisions. In practice, the present work has shown that these horizons are not everywhere coincident with mappable lithological changes. For example, we have included their Huntingbridge Formation within the Barton Clay because it is lithologically similar to the latter. Four separately mappable sands have been recognised in the upper part of the London Clay. One of these, the Whitecliff Sand, represents the bulk of the Bagshot Sands of older classifications.

PALAEONTOLOGY

Attempts have been made to produce a biostratigraphical framework for the Palaeogene sediments of the Hampshire Basin, using foraminifera, molluscs, dinoflagellate cysts, pollen and spores. The Reading Formation is generally unfossiliferous except for oysters and sharks' teeth in its basal bed. The argillaceous parts of the London Clay are fossiliferous, with molluscs common at some levels, but no fossil has been recorded from the Portsmouth, Whitecliff or Durley sands. Macrofossils are rare in the Wittering and Marsh Farm formations, although dinoflagellate cysts, pollen and spores are common. The Earnley and Selsey sands, however, contain abundant macrofaunas where they have not been decalcified. The Barton Group is commonly decalcified at surface and few fossils are preserved, but where unweathered it is very fossiliferous at some levels. The Headon Formation is very shelly at some levels; the Lyndhurst Member contains a fauna of thick-shelled marine bivalves; the remainder of the formation is dominated by fresh- to brackish-water molluscs.

In the Bracklesham Group, the Barton Group and the Headon Formation, many local names have been used to describe units that contain characteristic faunal assemblages that can be correlated across the Hampshire basin. None of these units has been formally defined. Many of them vary in lithology and so they are not 'beds' in the lithostratigraphical sense, although the term has commonly been applied to them, but are effectively recognised by their fossil content. They do not constitute biozones, since their fossil assemblages are largely made up of long-ranging species. However, since the characteristic faunas are to some degree controlled by conditions of sedimentation, some of the units are also identifiable lithologically. Specific instances of faunal units, such as the Cardita Bed for example, are described under the appropriate formational heading.

Benthonic foraminifera are common, particularly in the London Clay, but their distribution is largely environmentally controlled and they are of limited value for stratigraphical use. Planktonic foraminifera are more useful for correlation. In the London Clay of most of the Hampshire Basin, Wright

(1972b) recognised an influx of several species of planktonic foraminifera which he called the 'Planktonic Datum'. Species of the large foraminifer *Nummulites* are among the most stratigraphically useful fossils in the Bracklesham Group and Barton Clay. Flood occurrences of *Nummulites planulatus* and *N.* cf. *aquitanicus* form marker bands in the Wittering Formation in the Isle of Wight. *Nummulites laevigatus*, a large coin-shaped nummulitid, is abundant near the top of the Earnley Sand in the Southampton district, and provides a correlation with the Eocene of the Paris Basin. The Selsey Sand and the lowest Barton Clay contain a complex sequence of nummulitid faunas including *N. variolarius* and *N.* cf.

prestwichianus. *Nummulites prestwichianus* and *N. rectus* occur in the Barton Clay.

Approximately 350 species of mollusc have been described from the London Clay, and approximately 500 each from the Bracklesham Group and Barton Group. Many of the locally-named units mentioned above are based largely on their molluscan assemblages. Although the molluscan assemblages are facies-controlled, some species have sufficiently short ranges to be useful for correlation. King (1981) noted that '*Corbula*' *pseudopisum*, *Astarte subrugata*, '*Pecten*' *duplicatus*, *Turritella* gr. *imbricataria*, '*Dentalium*' *constrictum* and *Venericor* aff. *planicosta* were useful for correlation in the London Clay.

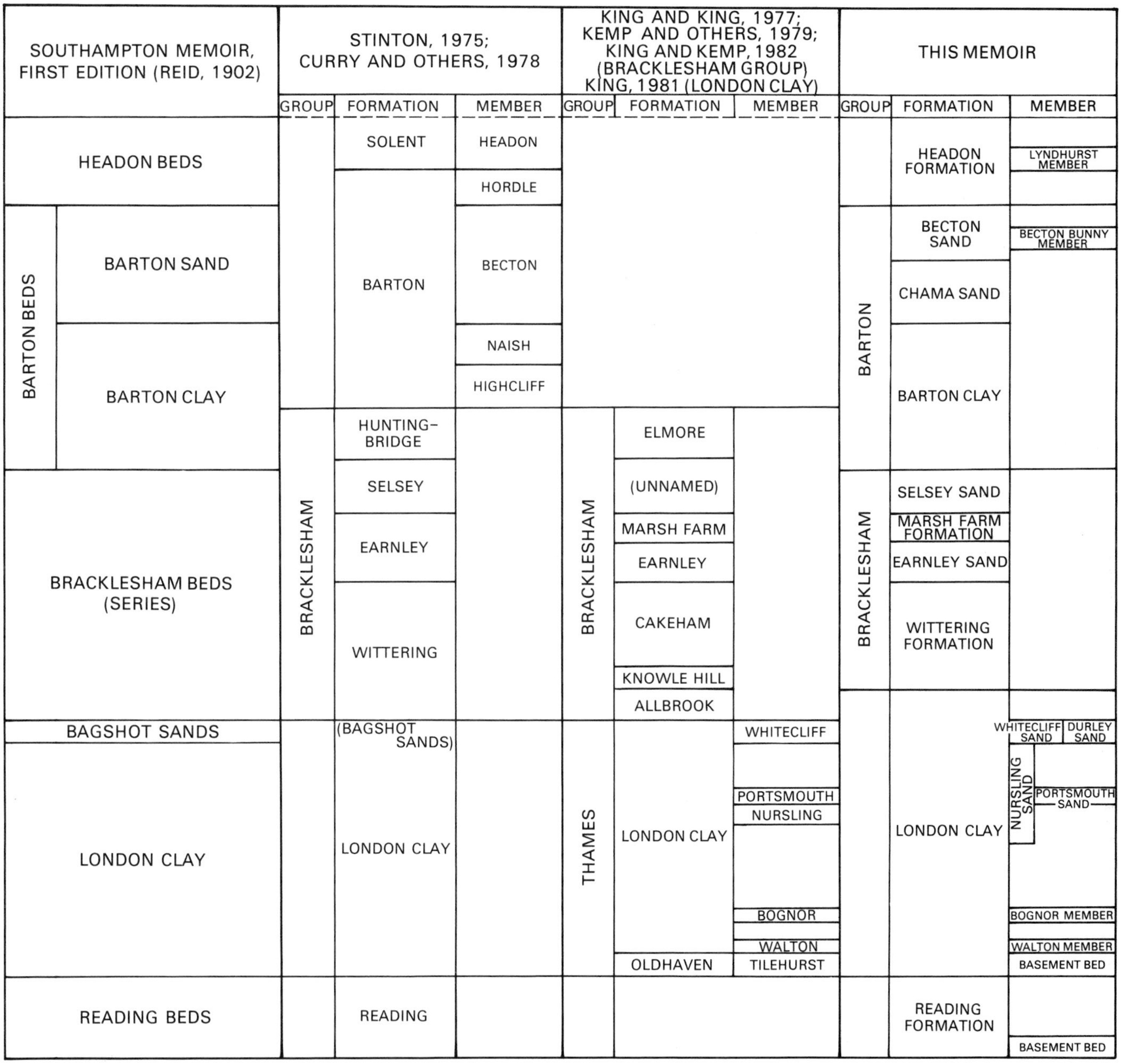

Figure 4 Previous nomenclatures for the Palaeogene of the Hampshire Basin compared with the scheme adopted in this memoir

Costa and Downie (1976) erected eight zones for the Tertiary of north-west Europe based on assemblages of species of the dinoflagellate genus *Wetzeliella*. Independently, Eaton (1976) correlated the Bracklesham Group on the east and west coasts of the Isle of Wight also using dinoflagellate cysts; Bujak and others (1980) added dinoflagellate zones for the Barton Group.

The dinoflagellate cyst assemblages of large numbers of samples from outcrops and boreholes were identified during the present work. The results confirm the sequence of assemblage zones reported by Bujak and others, and Costa and Downie.

However, dinoflagellates appear to have rather less value for detailed correlation in rapidly fluctuating marginal marine environments such as those represented in the Bracklesham Group than has previously been realised. Comparison of selected lithostratigraphical sequences with the dinoflagellate assemblages (Figure 6), suggests that the assemblages are probably controlled by fluctuating salinities. The dinoflagellate assemblages from the London Clay of the Hampshire Basin show a disparity between the boundaries of the assemblage zones and correlations based on what are thought to be chronostratigraphical boundaries between divisions (Figure 7). The Barton Clay has a well developed dinoflagellate flora which has recently been studied by Bujak and others (1980) as part of a

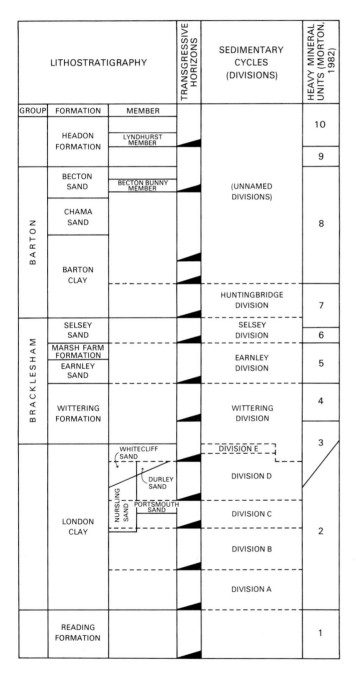

Figure 5 Sedimentary cycles (divisions) and transgressive horizons in the Hampshire Basin Palaeogene, and their relationship to lithological units and heavy-mineral units

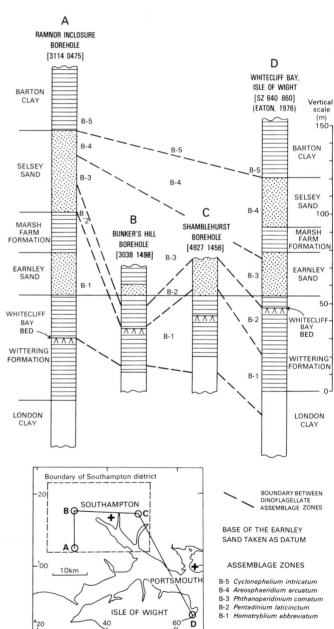

Figure 6 Relationship between selected dinoflagellate zones of Bujak and others (1980) and Palaeogene formations of the Hampshire Basin

larger study of Eocene dinoflagellate floras. Because of the more marine nature of the Barton Clay compared to the Bracklesham Group, the dinoflagellate floras have proved more reliable for correlation purposes.

Hubbard and Boulter (1983), using the statistical method of 'principal components analysis', have identified 20 pollen associations in the Palaeogene sequences proved in Geological Survey boreholes in the Hampshire Basin. Each of these associations falls within one of three groups indicative of deciduous forest, fern and conifer forest, or paratropical rain forest (tropical rain forest with a significant temperate forest element). These three groups have been used to divide the Eocene into six climatic phases. The recognition of these phases has enabled broad correlations to be made in the more argillaceous formations within the district. Comparison of individual palynological events, such as the local abundance of a particular genus, has also proved to be stratigraphically useful at some levels.

PETROGRAPHY

During the resurvey about 500 sand samples from the Tertiary formations of the district were sieved to determine their grain-size distributions. Various scales have been devised to divide the particle sizes into grades; that used in this memoir is the phi (ϕ) scale, introduced by Krumbein (1934) as a logarithmic transformation of the Wentworth grade scale (Wentworth, 1922). The relationship between the two scales is shown below:

ϕ Value	Particle diameter	Wentworth grade	Geotechnical classification
	(mm)		
		Cobbles	
−6	64		
		Pebbles	Gravel
−2	4		
		Granules	
−1	2		
		Very coarse	
0	1		
		Coarse	
1	0.5		
		Medium	Sand
2	0.25		
		Fine	
3	0.125		
		Very fine	
4	0.0625		
		Silt	
8	0.0039		Fines
		Clay	

The statistical parameters of mean size, sorting, and skewness were calculated from the grain-size curves using the formulae of Folk and Ward (1957). Comparison of these parameters formation by formation has revealed vertical and horizontal variations within individual formations; and it has also assisted in the interpretation of the conditions of deposition. Sorting is a measure of the degree of scatter of a grain-size distribution; the lower the sorting value, the better sorted the sample. The following classification (Folk, 1968) is used in this memoir: under 0.35 ϕ very well sorted; 0.35 to 0.50 ϕ well sorted; 0.50 to 0.71 ϕ moderately well sorted; 0.71 to 1.00 ϕ moderately sorted; 1.00 to 2.00 ϕ poorly sorted; 2.00 to 4.00 ϕ very poorly sorted; over 4.00 ϕ extremely poorly sorted. Skewness provides a measure of the degree of asymmetry of a grain-size distribution. Samples with a relative preponderance of finer grains have positive skewness values; those dominated by coarser grains have negative skewness values.

In a study of the heavy-mineral contents of the Palaeogene sands in the Bunker's Hill, Ramnor Inclosure, Shamblehurst and Christchurch [SZ 2002 9301] boreholes, Morton (1982) recognised three heavy-mineral associations. These are believed to have been derived from a Scottish source, an Armorican source and a Cornubian source.

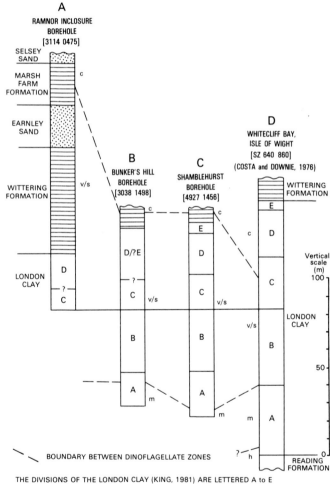

THE DIVISIONS OF THE LONDON CLAY (KING, 1981) ARE LETTERED A to E
BOUNDARY BETWEEN DIVISIONS B AND C OF THE LONDON CLAY TAKEN AS DATUM
? DENOTES UNCERTAINTY

c = *Wetzeliella (Wetzeliella) coleothrypta* Zone
v/s = *W. (W.) varielongituda/W. (W.) similis* Zone
m = *W. (W.) meckelfeldensis* Zone
h = *W. (W.) hyperacantha* Zone

Figure 7 Relationship between the *Wetzeliella* dinoflagellate zones and divisional and formational boundaries in the London Clay and Bracklesham Group

The London Clay and Barton Group are characterised by Scottish-derived heavy minerals, and the Reading Formation, Bracklesham Group and the lower Headon Formation mainly by Armorican-derived minerals. The Wittering Formation, Earnley Sand, upper Selsey Sand and lower Barton Group are dominated by Cornubian assemblages. Cornubian-derived minerals become dominant in the western part of the Hampshire Basin at all stratigraphical levels.

By comparing the relative proportions of each association at different stratigraphical levels, Morton defined 10 heavy-mineral-assemblage units in the Palaeogene of the Southampton district (Figure 5). The most abrupt changes in the heavy-mineral assemblages occur at transgressions. For example, the base of the London Clay marks an upward change from predominantly Armorican-derived to Scottish-derived minerals; the base of the transgressive Barton Clay is also marked by an influx of Scottish-derived minerals. The regressive parts of the Palaeogene sequence, such as the upward passage from the London Clay into the Bracklesham Group, are less well marked mineralogically.

The heavy-mineral assemblages enable broad correlations to be made between the fully marine sequences of the eastern part of the Hampshire Basin and the more continental deposits of the western part. More detailed local correlations have been made within the Southampton district by comparing the mineral assemblages in samples from shallow boreholes and outcrops with the standard sequence proved in the deeper cored boreholes.

CLIMATE

Recent studies of Tertiary floras have contested the view of Reid and Chandler (1926, 1933) that most of the land areas of southern England were covered by tropical rain forest during the Tertiary. Daley (1972) has suggested greater variations in temperature, humidity and lower mean temperatures than had hitherto been supposed. He postulated the presence of a frost-free temperate climate that allowed tropical floras to co-exist with temperate floras. Differences in soil-moisture content controlled the local distribution of the vegetation types with the result that tropical forests grew in moist conditions near rivers and temperate floras grew on drier ground.

Hubbard and Boulter (1983) have demonstrated a change from fern and coniferous forest in the youngest London Clay to paratropical rain forest in the Wittering Formation on the basis of pollen and spore assemblages. Fern and coniferous forest returned in earliest Barton Group times and was then replaced by angiosperm forests. They have suggested that these vegetational changes indicate mean annual air temperatures of around 15°C in the London Clay (with a short lived peak at 21°C), 22°C in the Wittering Formation, and about 15°C in the higher part of the Bracklesham Group. A steady fall in mean temperature, to as low as 10° to 12°C, occurred in the Barton Group. The earliest Headon Formation was marked by a short (c.0.3 Ma) warm interlude with a mean annual temperature of 20°C before a return to a cooler climate.

The formation of kaolinite in the Palaeogene of the Southampton district appears to be climatically influenced. Low kaolinite levels in the Bracklesham Group and the Barton Group correlate with low mean temperatures deduced from the floral data. A high concentration of kaolinite in the Whitecliff Bay Bed (see p.39) probably indicates warm humid conditions.

CHAPTER 5

Palaeogene: Reading Formation

The Reading Formation has two main areas of outcrop in the district. In the north-west, near Sherfield English, the strike is approximately E–W. In the north-east where it is 0.5 to 1.0 km wide, the outcrop strikes ESE–WNW and runs from just south of Otterbourne, through Colden Common to the district boundary.

Natural exposures are rare, but the sandy and pebbly parts of the formation are exposed in disused and operating pits and in road cuttings. The clayey parts of the sequence are nowhere exposed. The Reading Formation was fully cored in the Bunker's Hill and Shamblehurst boreholes.

The formation is lithologically variable and consists of clays, clay-breccias, fine- medium- and coarse-grained cross-bedded sands, pebble beds, and a basal bed composed of glauconitic sand and clay with flint pebbles. This last-named bed rests unconformably on the Upper Chalk. The sands, thicker clays, and flint-pebble beds can be readily mapped and are shown on the published geological map: the basal bed is too thin to be shown separately on the map. Marked lateral and vertical variations in lithology occur in the formation and have often been commented on in the past (e.g. Reid, 1902; White, 1912; Hawkins, 1946). Thus, the formation may pass from sand to clay in a distance of a few hundred metres. In contrast, the basal bed, although thin, is laterally persistent throughout the district and most of the Hampshire Basin. An example of lateral facies variation in the Reading Formation in the north-west of the district, between Newton and The Frenches, is shown in Figure 8.

The full thickness of the formation in the district, taken mainly from drillers' records of water boreholes, ranges from 14.7 to 32.4 m, the average of 24 measurements being 26.8 m. No regional pattern of thickness variation is apparent (Figure 9). The thinnest sequence was recorded in the north-west near Landford Lodge and the thickest recorded in a borehole at Stoke Park Farm in the north-east.

The basal bed of the Reading Formation is a thin bed of greenish grey and greyish green, glauconitic clayey sand and clay with angular to subrounded flint pebbles; it locally contains oysters and sharks' teeth. It rests on an uneven and bored surface of Upper Chalk. This bed, the 'Bottom Bed' of some authors, is referred to here as the Reading Formation Basement Bed. Its thickness varies in the district between 0.1 and 2.1 m, the average of 18 measurements being 1.0 m. In the north-eastern outcrop it is apparently 0.2 to 0.6 m thick and contains dark green- or red-coated flints.

The predominant lithology of the formation above the Basement Bed in the district is red-mottled clay. It is the commonest lithology at outcrop in the north-east of the district and, as far as is possible to deduce, from the available boreholes, in most of the subcrop (Figure 9). Sands are predominant at outcrop in the north-west of the district, although, even there, mottled clays locally form the entire thickness of the formation (Figure 8). In the north-east of the district between Otterbourne and Colden Common, the up-

per half of the formation consists of sand, and the lower of clay. East of Colden Common, the formation consists of clay with lenses of sand (Figure 9). In the Sherfield English and The Frenches areas the sands contain lenticular beds of rounded flint pebbles which occur in the middle to upper part of the formation (Figure 8). In The Frenches area the London Clay rests on one of these pebble beds.

In detail the red-mottled clays include silty clays, sandy clays and clay-breccias; the colour-mottling is in shades of red, reddish brown, greyish red-purple, olive-brown, greenish grey and grey. The red colours are caused by ferric iron minerals, the unoxidised clays being predominantly grey. Buurman (1980) has shown that lithologically similar strata in the Reading Formation sequence at Alum Bay, Isle of Wight, contain fossil soil profiles. He suggested that the mottling was formed in gley soils, in which alternating reduction and oxidation in the zone of water-table fluctuation caused the segregation of iron and manganese minerals. He also identified small tubular burrows, which he called striotubules, throughout most of the Reading Formation at Alum Bay. Similar burrows, 2 to 3 mm in diameter, occur throughout much of the Reading Formation clays in the Bunker's Hill and Shamblehurst boreholes. The nature of the burrowing animal is uncertain.

A feature of the mottled clay sequences in the district, not previously recorded from the Reading Formation, is the presence of clay-breccia at several levels. The breccias consist typically of angular clasts of clay, rarely >3mm in diameter, set in a clay matrix. The brecciation probably resulted from subaerial exposure and desiccation shortly after deposition.

Scattered, small coalescent white calcareous nodules (typically 92% calcite) occur in silty and sandy clays in the

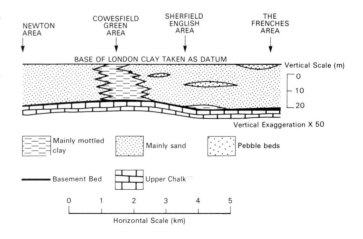

Figure 8 Lithological variation in the Reading Formation at outcrop in the north-west of the Southampton district

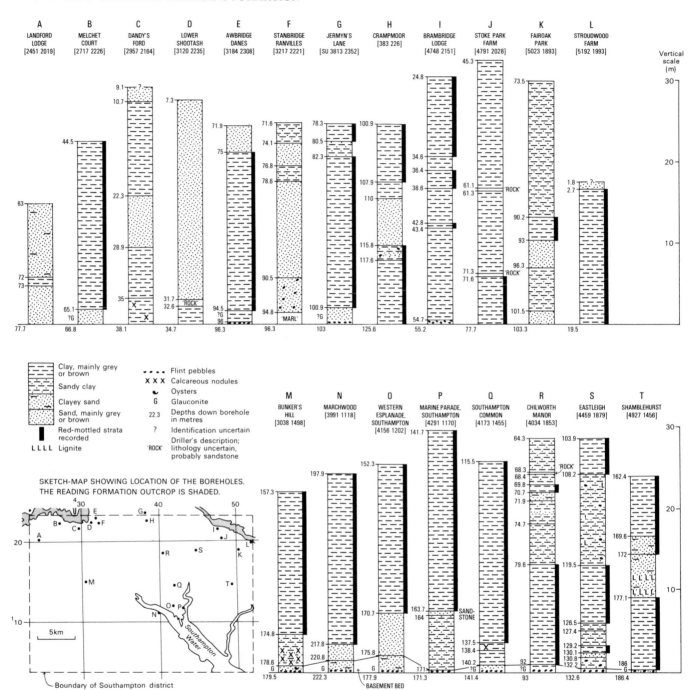

Figure 9   Borehole sections through the Reading Formation of the Southampton district

All boreholes reach the Upper Chalk, which is taken as the datum. Most strata details are based on drillers'
records, except for the Bunker's Hill (M) and Shamblehurst (T) boreholes which are based on examination
of core samples, and the Marchwood (N) and Western Esplanade (D) boreholes which are based on
examination of cuttings samples and geophysical logs

lower part of the formation in the Bunker's Hill and
Southampton Common boreholes. Similar concretions in
ancient continental red beds have been compared with
caliche soils forming in modern semi-arid regions.

The clay mineralogy of the Reading Formation was in-
vestigated by X-ray diffraction analysis of core samples from
the Bunker's Hill and Shamblehurst boreholes. Samples
from the Basement Bed in both boreholes are rich in smectite

(up to 65% of the $< 2\,\mu$m fractions), accompanied by illite
and traces of kaolinite. Similar concentrations of smectite
were reported from the basal 2 m of the Reading Formation
at Studland Bay by Gilkes (1968), who suggested that the
mineral was derived as an insoluble residue from the Chalk.
It now seems more likely that the smectite is of volcanic
origin and related to contemporaneous ash bands in the
southern North Sea and in the London Basin (Knox and

Harland, 1979). In the Bunker's Hill Borehole, an unusual clay assemblage occurs 3 m above the smectite-rich clay. It consists of halloysite (c.60%) with random mixed-layer chlorite- vermiculite and chlorite-smectite. This assemblage is thought to have formed by *in situ* subaerial weathering of the underlying volcanigenic clay. The remainder of the Reading Formation possesses a fairly consistent illite-dominated (c.50%) mineralogy in which illite > smectite ≃ kaolinite. Minor amounts of chlorite and vermiculite are also present; the latter is present at most levels in the Reading Formation in the Bunker's Hill Borehole.

At outcrop the Reading Formation sands are mainly yellowish brown to greyish orange, medium-grained, and commonly contain sand-sized pale brown to very pale orange, angular flint chips which give them a distinctive speckled appearance. In the larger exposures, the sands can be seen to form erosionally-based lenses of variable lateral extent. Silty clays, silts and fine-grained sands occur as rare lenses and pods; some sand beds contain gravel-sized clay clasts. The sands are commonly cross-bedded, with trough cross-bedding the most abundant type; beds of parallel-laminated sand are present at some localities.

Pebbles and cobbles of flint occur as lenses up to 3 m thick, either in a closely packed sand matrix or, less commonly, interbedded with the sands. The pebbles rarely exceed 50 mm in diameter, but can attain 150 mm at some localities. Pebbles coarser than 16 mm from a bed in a sand-pit [282 227] near Sherfield English were rounded to very well rounded, while those finer than 16 mm were subrounded to well rounded. The pebbles are commonly somewhat discoidal, and imbricate arrangement of the clasts is present at some localities. The surfaces of pebbles usually bear abundant crescent-shaped percussion cracks ('chatter marks').

Grain-size analyses of 22 sand samples showed that most (17) have a mean size between approximately 1ϕ and 2ϕ, (medium-grained sand), with a range of mean sizes from 0.99ϕ to 3.17ϕ. Sorting has a wide range, from 0.27ϕ to 1.02ϕ (very well sorted to poorly sorted). The range of skewness is 0.00 to + 0.71 (symmetrical to strongly positively skewed). Grading analyses of sands from around Sherfield English are given in Table 2 (p.88).

No fauna has been recorded from the Reading Formation above the Basement Bed. A leaf bed was reported from the upper part of the formation at Colden Common (White, 1912, p.48), but was not relocated during the present survey. Chandler (1961, p.20) noted two leaves from Colden Common in Winchester City Museum, one of which she referred to *Cinnamonum*. A sample from the Bunker's Hill Borehole yielded a sparse assemblage, including *Apectodinium parvum*, indicative of the *hyperacantha* Zone. Possible glauconite in the sample suggests marine influence.

CONDITIONS OF DEPOSITION

The fauna and abundant glauconite content of the Basement Bed indicate that it was deposited by a sea that transgressed across a wave-cut platform in lithified Upper Chalk. The succeeding mottled clays, a widespread facies that extends from the Hampshire Basin into the London Basin and Paris Basin, contain abundant evidence of subaerial exposure and

soil formation in a fairly hot, semi-arid climate. The presence of glauconite at several levels may indicate periodic marine influences. Ellison (1983) suggested that mottled clays of the Reading Beds in the western London Basin were deposited in brackish-water lagoons, and a similar depositional environment is likely for the lithologically similar clays of the Southampton district. Streams flowing into the lagoons deposited sands and pebble beds which show features characteristic of braided-river deposits, and can be interpreted as channel-lag gravels and channel-bar and braid-bar sands. The sands contain a few silt and clay lenses, probably deposited in abandoned channels. The grain-size distributions of the sands show positive skewness, a feature characteristic of many river sands. Cross-plots of sorting and skewness for 22 Reading Formation sand samples from the district show that all but six lie within the fluvial field of Friedman (1967, figure 15). The high degree of rounding of many of the flint pebbles suggests that they have been derived from older Tertiary beach deposits.

DETAILS

Newton – Sherfield English – The Frenches

At outcrop between the western margin of the district at Newton, and near Cowesfield Gate [271 232], the formation consists of up to 20 m of yellowish brown, fine- to medium-grained sand with rare clay beds. Sand was worked in a now-infilled sand-pit [2335 2313], south of which are small exposures [2332 2303] of up to 2.0 m of yellowish brown to pale orange brown, fine- to medium-grained sand with flint chips, with a few 5 cm-thick bands of grey clay in the central part. The extension of the sand-dominant facies southwards into the subcrop is demonstrated by a borehole [2451 2019] at Landford Lodge (Figure 9). However, red-mottled clays at outcrop [SU 260 237 to SU 263 237], just north of the district boundary near Cowesfield Green, locally form the entire thickness of the formation. Red and grey mottled clays were augered in shallow, long-disused brick-pits [2617 2318 to SU 2620 2350] at Cowesfield Green. The subcrop extension of the red-mottled clays was proved in a borehole [2717 2226] at Melchet Court which also penetrated a 1.7 m-thick Basement Bed of green sand (Figure 9).

From near Cowesfield Gate to The Frenches [310 227], the formation is dominantly sand with lenticular pebble beds which commonly form small hill-cappings. Both sands and pebble beds have been worked fairly extensively, the pebble beds generally in many small, now disused, shallow pits, [e.g. 2787 2290; 2830 2303; 2889 2280; 2920 2322; 2996 2261; 2997 2245; and 3069 2267].

Readily accessible sections [2764 2298] in cuttings beside the A27 road show yellowish brown, cross-bedded, medium-grained sands.

About 1 km NW of Sherfield English, Reading Formation sand and pebble beds have been worked in three pits [2796 2293; 2820 2276 and 2840 2280]. The eastern face [2825 2278 to 2821 2270] of the most recently worked of these pits shows 1.0 to 3.0 m of well-rounded flint pebbles, with an irregular base, on up to 3.0 m of pale yellowish brown to greyish orange, cross-bedded, medium- to coarse-grained sand and pebbly sand, containing lenticular beds of well-rounded flints. Minor lenses of very pale yellowish brown silty clay, and clay clasts, occur within the sand. Grading analyses of sands from around Sherfield English are given in Table 2 (p.88).

A disused gravel-pit [2920 2321] at Berryfield Copse, Sherfield English, contains 2 m of somewhat discoidal, well-rounded flint pebbles in a matrix of brown, medium-grained sand. The pebbles show imbricate structure. In the subcrop SE of Sherfield English, the formation is dominantly clay. A central intercalation of sand was proved in a borehole [2957 2164] at Dandy's Ford (Figure 9).

A sand-pit [302 226 to 3305 224] near Birchwood House Farm shows sandy and pebbly Reading Formation very close to the junction with the London Clay. A section [302 226] in the north bay of the pit shows:

	Thickness m
Gravel of well-rounded flints with sand interbeds	2.0–3.0
Sand, yellowish brown and greyish orange, medium-grained	2.0–3.0
Clay, grey	0.3
Sand, grey to yellowish brown and orange brown, laminated, with clay clasts	2.0

The sequence, dominantly sand with 3 m of clay at the base, proved in a borehole [3120 2235] near Lower Shootash (Figure 9) is comparable to that at outcrop around the small inlier of Chalk [304 230], north of Birchwood House Farm. Whitaker (*in* Reid, 1902, p.5) recorded the following section in a chalk-pit [3030 2315], now classified as follows: Reading Formation, mottled clay 1.5 m; Basement Bed, glauconitic clayey sand with green- coated flints and an oyster at the base 0.4 m; Upper Chalk, the top 0.3 m or so with irregular holes filled with green sand.

Two boreholes, one at Awbridge Danes [3184 2308], the other at Stanbridge Ranvilles Farm [3217 2221], are only 1 km apart, but demonstrate the typical variability of the Reading Foundation. That at Awbridge Danes penetrated mainly mottled clay, but that at Stanbridge Ranvilles proved mainly sand (Figure 9).

The Basement Bed was 2.1 m thick and recorded as 'green sand and stone' in a borehole [3813 2352] at Jermyns Lane, the remainder of the formation being dominantly mottled clay (Figure 9). Another borehole [3830 2260] near Crampmoor, proved a central intercalation of sand in mottled clay; no Basement Bed was recorded (Figure 9).

Otterbourne – Colden Common

Between Otterbourne and Colden Common, the formation consists of a lower clay member and an upper sand member which lenses out east of Colden Common [483 218]. A pit [4810 2185] on a rise above Vear Lane displays 3.0 m of orange brown and buff, slightly clayey sand, apparently near the top of the formation. In contrast, a borehole [4748 2151] at Brambridge Lodge, 700 m farther SW (Figure 9), showed the formation to be entirely clay, the Basement Bed being represented by 0.2 m of 'red flints'. The formation was also entirely clay, except for two rock bands, in a borehole [4791 2028] (Figure 9) at Stoke Park Farm. This and the Brambridge Lodge Borehole [4748 2151] were recorded as penetrating black (?carbonaceous) clays 15 to 16 m below the top of the formation; this lithology was not recorded at outcrop in the numerous brick-pits (mostly now infilled) excavated in the formation around Colden Common.

The formation is dominantly mottled clay at outcrop in the Marwell to Lower Upton area, thinning eastwards from around 25 m in the Marwell area to 17.7 m in a borehole [5192 1993] (Figure 9) at Stroudwood Farm. A borehole at Fair Oak [5023 1893] (Figure 9) showed the formation to be 29.8 m thick and sandier in the subcrop than at outcrop around Stroudwood.

Copythorne: Bunker's Hill Borehole

The full thickness of the Reading Formation was cored between 179.5 and 157.3 m depth in the Bunker's Hill Borehole (Figure 9; Appendix 1). The Basement Bed, 0.9 m thick, consists of greyish green, glauconitic, clayey to very clayey, fine- to medium- grained sand, with scattered oysters and unabraded flints and chalk fragments in the basal 0.17 m. The 3.8 m of the formation overlying the Basement Bed consist of clays with about 40% sand content. Possible caliche concretions occur in sandy and silty clays in the lower part of this bed. The topmost 17.5 m of the formation consist of grey, smooth to very silty clays and clay-breccias, with red, reddish brown and greyish red mottles.

Marchwood – Southampton City

Boreholes at Marchwood [3991 1118] (Figure 9) and beneath Southampton City [4156 1202; 4291 1170] (Figure 9) penetrated broadly similar Reading Formation sequences that consist of up to 7 m of sand or sandy clay overlain by mottled clays. A Basement Bed of glauconitic sand and flint pebbles is present in all three boreholes. In the Southampton Common Well [4173 1455] (Figure 9) the formation is 25.9 m thick and entirely mottled clay, except for a 1.2 m-thick Basement Bed of green sand with flint and chalk pebbles. The driller's description 'plastic clay with chalk' in the lower part of the sequence may indicate a development of caliche comparable to that in the Bunker's Hill Borehole.

Chilworth – Eastleigh

Water boreholes at Chilworth Manor [4034 1853] and Eastleigh [4459 1879] (Figure 9) penetrated broadly similar sequences, in which the lowermost 12 to 13 m is mainly mottled clay. The upper part of the formation is more variable and consists of sandy clays and sands, with pebbles and lignite traces present at Eastleigh. A nearby borehole [4501 1901] includes layers of sandstone, ironstone and conglomerate, indicating local cementation of the sands and pebble beds.

Hedge End: Shamblehurst Borehole

A total of 24 m of Reading Formation was cored between 186.4 and 162.4 m depth in the Shamblehurst Borehole [4927 1456] (Figure 9; Appendix 1). The Basement Bed is 0.34 m thick and consists of a pebble bed, 0.16 m thick, of angular to subrounded flints in a greyish green, glauconitic sand matrix, sandwiched between two bands, each 0.08 m thick, of greyish green and light olive-brown, extremely clayey glauconitic sand. The lower band contains scattered angular flints. The top 0.36 m of the Chalk contains irregular cavities filled with greyish green clayey sand and chalk fragments. Above the Basement Bed are 9.0 m of vividly colour-mottled clays which are red, reddish brown and greenish grey; the proportion of greenish grey and greyish green coloration increases in the basal 0.7 m. Overlying the mottled clays are unmottled sands 5.1 m thick, overlain by 2.4 m of red and reddish brown mottled, extremely clayey, fine- to very fine-grained sand. The topmost 7.2 m of the formation are red, reddish brown and light olive-brown and grey mottled, burrowed and brecciated clay.

CHAPTER 6

Palaeogene: London Clay

The main outcrop of the London Clay in the Southampton district is generally 4 to 6 km wide and extends in an arc along the northern edge of the district between Hamptworth and Durley. The formation also crops out in an anticlinal inlier between Nursling and Lower Swanwick (Figure 10) along the extension of the Portsdown Anticline. The thickness of the London Clay varies from 30 m or less in the west of the Hampshire basin to over 140 m in the east; thicknesses in the Southampton district lie within the range 53 to 114 m (Figure 11).

The base of the formation is taken at a sedimentary break and sharp upward lithological change from red-mottled clay or clean, yellowish brown, medium-grained sand of the Reading Formation to olive-grey, glauconitic, sandy clayey silt, sandy silt or very silty fine-grained sand of the London Clay. Olive-grey to greenish grey bioturbated silty and sandy clays, clayey silts, sandy clayey silts, sandy silts, and silty sands, comprise over 90% of the formation by volume.

Material coarser than 0.25 mm (fine-grained sand) is virtually absent in these lithologies; mica is common, glauconite occurs sparingly but widely, and lignitic debris occurs in the silts. Claystone nodules, commonly septarian, occur at various levels, mostly in the silty clays. Molluscan shellbanks occur within some of the silty sands and are locally cemented to form shelly calcareous sandstones. Pebble beds made up of grey to black, well-rounded flint pebbles up to 100 mm across set in a matrix of glauconitic, fine- to coarse-grained quartz sand, silt and clay, occur in units mostly <1 m thick. Lenticular beds of fine- to medium-grained, cross-bedded sand up to 10 m thick, occur at two horizons. Interlaminated and interbedded clay and sands occur rarely at some localities.

King (1981) recognised that the London Clay of the London area consists of five coarsening-upward sedimentary cycles, the base of each usually marked by a transgressive

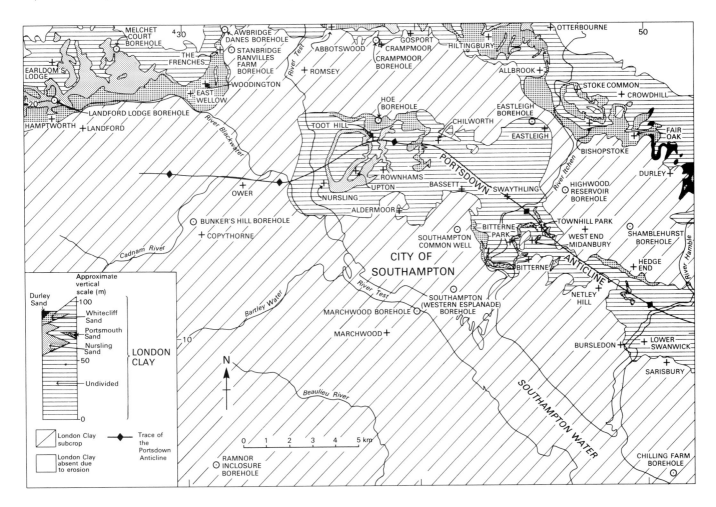

Figure 10 Distribution of the London Clay and its constituent members in the Southampton district, showing localities and boreholes referred to in the text

Figure 11 Thickness and distribution of the London Clay in the central part of the Hampshire Basin

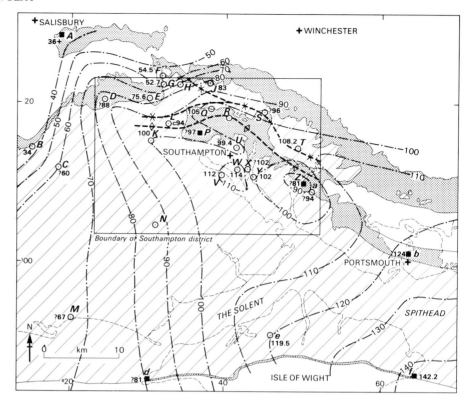

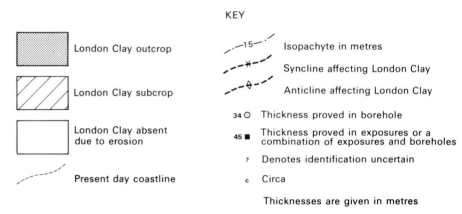

KEY

▨	London Clay outcrop
▧	London Clay subcrop
☐	London Clay absent due to erosion
⌇	Present day coastline

—15—	Isopachyte in metres
—✳—	Syncline affecting London Clay
—◇—	Anticline affecting London Clay
34 ○	Thickness proved in borehole
45 ■	Thickness proved in exposures or a combination of exposures and boreholes
?	Denotes identification uncertain
c	Circa

Thicknesses are given in metres

Key to localities

A Clarendon Hill railway cutting and Alderbury bypass [SU 185 283] (King, 1981, p.88)

B Fordingbridge Gasworks Borehole [SU 1445 1412] (King, 1981, p.90)

C Fordingbridge Borehole [SU 1876 1181]

D Landford Lodge Borehole [2451 2019]

E Manor Farm Borehole [3040 2036], East Wellow

F Awbridge Danes Borehole [3184 2308]

G Stanbridge Ranvilles Farm Borehole [3217 2221]

H Roke Manor Borehole [3419 2223]

J Crampmoor Borehole [c.383 226]

K Bunker's Hill Borehole [3038 1498]

L Wigley Borehole [3268 1743]

M Christchurch Borehole [SZ 200 930]

N Ramnor Inclosure Borehole [3114 0475]

P Nursling [360 170] temporary sections and boreholes (King, 1981, p.85)

Q Hoe Borehole [3845 1915]

R Chilworth Borehole [4034 1853] (King, 1981, p.84)

S Eastleigh Borehole [4501 1901]

T Shamblehurst Borehole [4927 1456]

U Southampton Common Well [4175 1455] (King, 1981, p.83)

V Marchwood Borehole [3991 1118]

W Southampton (Western Esplanade) Borehole [4156 1202]

X Northam Borehole [4336 1268]

Y Woolston Borehole [4363 1084]

Z Lower Swanwick [500 100] brickpit sections and boreholes (King, 1981, p.80)

a Sarisbury Borehole [512 098]

b Portsmouth [SU 636 012], temporary sections and boreholes (King, 1981, p.78)

d Alum Bay cliff section [SZ 305 855], Isle of Wight (King, 1981, p.91)

e Sandhills Borehole [SZ 4570 9085], Isle of Wight

f Whitecliff Bay cliff section [SZ 640 860], Isle of Wight (King, 1981, p.75)

flint pebble bed. He called these cycles divisions, and lettered them A to E in upward sequence. The divisions recognised in the London area can be identified in the Southampton district by means of lithological and faunal correlations. These indicate that the topmost London Clay of the district, included in the Wittering Division by Curry and others (1977), correlates with Division D2 and part of Division E of the London area, the base of Division E correlating with a glauconite-rich level in the middle part of the former Wittering Division (Figure 5). The idealized cycle begins with a pebble bed or glauconite-rich horizon; this is succeeded by silty clays that coarsen upward into silts and silty sands, and ends with lenticular bodies of fine- to medium-grained sand that are channelled into the underlying strata. In a few areas the youngest beds in some cycles consist of interbedded or interlaminated sand and clay. The main facies variations in the London Clay of the Hampshire Basin and their relationships to the sedimentary cycles are shown in Figure 12.

The coarsening-upward profiles of King's five cycles are superimposed on a coarsening-upward trend in the London Clay as a whole, with the result that sands are more common in divisions C, D and E. These divisions contain in their highest parts lenticular units of fine- to coarse-grained, cross-bedded sand—called here the Portsmouth Sand (Portsmouth Member of King, 1981) and Whitecliff Sand (Whitecliff Member of King, 1981). In the north-western and northern parts of the district, much of divisions C and D consist of silty,

ty, very fine-grained sand and sandy silt that is lithologically distinctive from the Portsmouth and Whitecliff sands and is here called the Nursling Sand. It is partly equivalent to the Nursling Member of King (1981). Around Durley clayey fine-grained sand, called here the Durley Sand, is thought to be laterally equivalent to the Whitecliff Sand. All four named sands were included partly or wholly in the 'Bagshot Sands' on the 1899 Geological Survey map.

Selected sections in the London Clay and their correlation are shown in Figure 13.

The London Clay contains a diverse fauna that includes foraminifera, sponge spicules, solitary corals, annelids, bryozoa, brachiopods, gastropods, bivalves, ostracods, cirripedes, insects, crinoids, asteroids, echinoids, and holothurian spicules. The flora includes coccoliths, diatoms, dinoflagellates, discoasters, plant macrofossils, spores and pollen. Fish, reptiles and birds have also been recorded.

In the clays and silts, the macrofauna consists mainly of scattered bivalves and gastropods. A more diverse molluscan fauna occurs in the silty sands and sandy silts and includes algal-browsing gastropods. Some of the molluscan species can be used for correlation (King, 1981).

Although facies-controlled, the ostracod assemblages are useful for correlation, and Keen's (1977, 1978) ostracod zonation was largely confirmed by King (1981, figure 45). Benthonic foraminifera are common throughout the London Clay, but their vertical and lateral distribution is largely

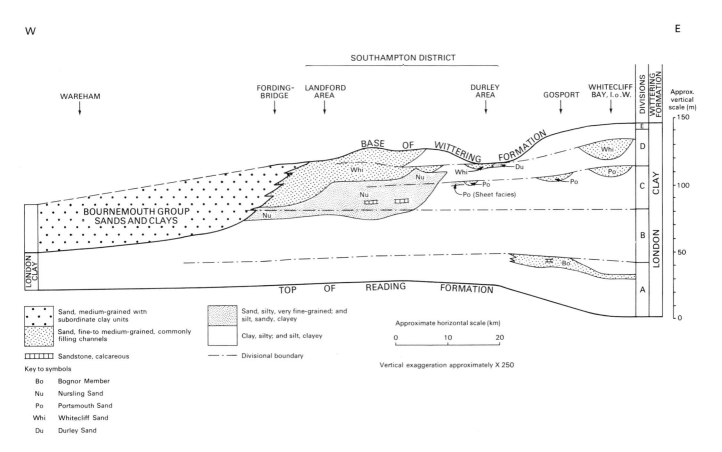

Figure 12   Major lithological variations in the London Clay of the Hampshire Basin and their relationship to sedimentary cycles (divisions)

environmentally controlled (Murray and Wright, 1974), and they are of limited use for correlation. Planktonic foraminifera first become common in the London Clay about 2 m above the base of Division B, at an horizon referred to as the 'Planktonic Datum' by Wright (1972b). Elsewhere in the formation, they generally form <10% of the foraminiferal fauna, and are rare or absent in the silts and sands.

The terrestrial flora of the London Clay is represented almost entirely by fossil fruits and seeds. Most are dicotyledons, with a few conifers and palms (Chandler, 1961). The only macrofloral locality of significance in the district is in the Nursling Sand at Nursling [362 170] (Chandler, 1961, pp.325–337). The results of studies on the Palaeogene flora

from the Hampshire Basin and their palaeoclimatological interpretation are discussed in Chapter 4.

A zonation based on the stratigraphical distribution of species of the dinoflagellate genus *Wetzeliella* in the London Clay sequences at Studland Bay, Dorset, and Alum and Whitecliff bays in the Isle of Wight has been applied to the formation throughout the Hampshire Basin by Costa and Downie (1976). The zones are, in ascending order, those of *Wetzeliella* (*Wetzeliella*) *hyperacantha*, *W.* (*W.*) *meckelfeldensis*, *W.* (*W.*) *similis*, *W.* (*W.*) *varielongituda* and *W.* (*W.*) *coleothrypta*. The sequence of *Wetzeliella* zones has been confirmed for samples from cored boreholes and exposures in the Southampton district, with the exception that the *similis* and

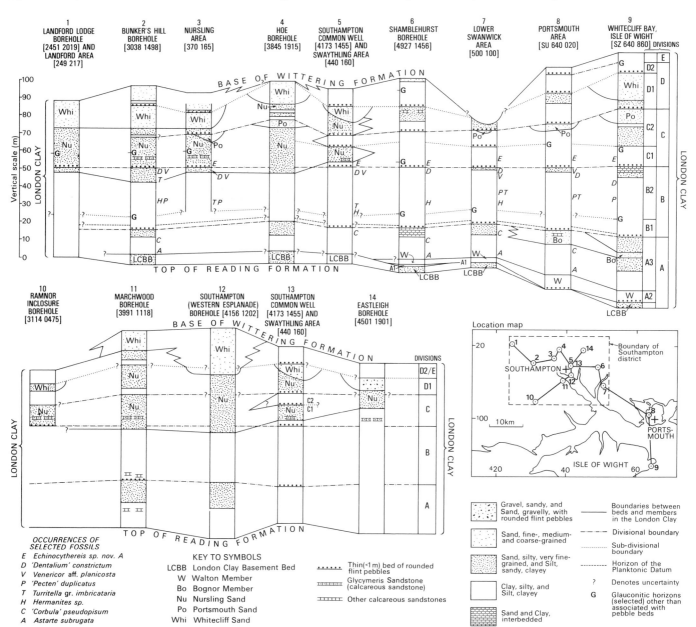

Figure 13 Sections in the London Clay of the Southampton district, compared with those at Portsmouth and at Whitecliff Bay, Isle of Wight

Columns 3, 5, 7, 9 and 13 are mainly after King (1981); column 8 is after King (1981) and King and Kemp (1980). Base of Division C taken as datum. Boundaries between the two main lithologies of the London Clay (silty sand/sandy clayey silt, and silty clay/clayey silt) are commonly gradational and have been much simplified

varielongituda Zones could not be differentiated; they are referred to as the *similis/varielongituda* Zone in the present account. However, the bases of the zones occur within different divisional units in different areas (Figure 7). King (1981, p.32) considered the divisional boundaries to be essentially synchronous; if so, the dinoflagellate zones are likely to be diachronous. The dinoflagellate assemblages were probably partly controlled by environmental factors.

The clay fractions ($<2\mu$m) of samples from the London Clay in the Bunker's Hill and Shamblehurst boreholes commonly consist of clay-mineral assemblages in which illite > smectite > kaolinite. Kaolinite is much less abundant in the London Clay than in the Reading Formation. At the base of the London Clay, a significant increase in smectite content is accompanied by a decrease in kaolinite. A gradational upward increase in the proportion of smectite in divisions A and B culminates, near the top of Division B, in approximately equal contents of smectite and illite (c.40% each), with kaolinite forming the remainder. The bases of divisions C and D in the Shamblehurst Borehole both coincide with a marked increase in smectite content. In divisions D and E in the Shamblehurst Borehole, the clay-mineral assemblage is smectite-dominated with smectite c.50%, illite c.35% and kaolinite 10 to 15%. In contrast, the presumed equivalent of Division D in the Bunker's Hill Borehole contains illite c.45%, kaolinite c.25% and vermiculite up to 20%, and smectite c.10%. The analyses from these two boreholes are in agreement with Gilkes's (1968) observation that smectite is more plentiful in the London Clay in the eastern part of the Hampshire Basin and is replaced westwards by kaolinite. Chlorite is commonly present in minor amounts throughout the London Clay; it forms up to 10% of the clay fractions in Division C in the Shamblehurst Borehole.

The regional differences in the clay mineralogy of the London Clay may reflect differences in the source rocks. In the east, particularly in divisions D and E, smectite may have been derived from a source of volcanic rocks that lay to the east. In the western part of the basin, the presence of vermiculite and high kaolinite contents in the upper part of the London Clay may indicate the proximity to source areas undergoing terrestrial weathering.

Most of the sand-grade heavy minerals in the London Clay of the district were derived from the Scottish Highlands (Assemblage 2 of Morton, 1982). Garnet (20% to 30%) and the epidote group (20% to 50%) are the major components, with tourmaline present in moderate amounts and zircon, staurolite, kyanite, chloritoid minerals, glaucophane, hornblende, sphene and tremolite in minor amounts. The base of Morton's Assemblage 2 coincides with the base of the London Clay and is likely to be a synchronous surface. However, the base of Assemblage 3, characterised by the appearance of a zircon-dominated assemblage derived from Armorica, is diachronous (Morton, 1982, pp.470–471) with respect to the divisional boundaries. In the Bunker's Hill Borehole and in the Isle of Wight the base of Assemblage 3 lies at the base of the Whitecliff Sand or its presumed equivalent. In the Shamblehurst Borehole, the base of the assemblage lies at the base of the Wittering Formation.

STRATIGRAPHY

Division A

The thickness of Division A in the Hampshire Basin varies from around 10 m in the north to over 45 m in the Isle of Wight. In the Southampton district, the greatest proved thickness is 29.5 m beneath Southampton, although over 30 m may be present in the south-eastern corner of the district (Figure 14). The distribution of thicknesses suggests that they may have been influenced by the growth of the Portsdown Anticline and its westward continuation.

The basal bed of Division A is laterally persistent (Figure 13) and consists of intensely bioturbated, highly glauconitic, extremely clayey, silty, fine-grained sand and sandy silt, with a few thin clay bands. This is referred to here as the London Clay Basement Bed, a name first used by Prestwich (1850). It rests with a marked sedimentological break on the Reading Formation, and at some localities in the Hampshire Basin contains quartz grit, flint pebbles and pebbles of Reading Formation clay at its base. Its thickness decreases from around 6 m in the west of the district to around 3 m in the south-east. The Basement Bed is commonly shelly and contains the serpulid *Ditrupa*, the gastropods *Aporrhais triangulata*, *Sigatica obovata*, *Siphonalia subnodosa*, and the bivalves *Dosiniopsis bellovacina*, *Glycymeris plumstediensis*, *Nemocardium plumstedianum*, and *Pitar obliquus* (King, 1981). The upper limit of the Basement Bed is poorly defined within the district, and is transitional in the Shamblehurst and Bunker's Hill boreholes. Elsewhere in the Hampshire Basin a pebble bed or glauconitic layer occurs at the base of the overlying strata.

The beds of Division A above the Basement Bed have been divided into three, lettered A1 to A3, by King (1981). Within the district, Division A1 is known only from Lower Swanwick [505 097], where it consists of less than 1 m of shelly clay with the bivalve *Astarte* cf. *tenera* and the ostracod *Cytheridea unispinae* (King, 1981, p.82), and from the Shamblehurst Borehole, where it consists of 1.4 m of very silty clay with *Astarte*. Division A2, consisting typically of clayey silt and silty clay, with partings and laminae of very fine-grained sand and silt, and beds of bioturbated sandy silt (the Walton Member of King) is up to 3 m thick. It crops out only in the eastern half of the district, being overstepped by Division A3 in the west. The strata are locally shelly, but commonly decalcified; the bivalve *Arctica* was recorded in the Shamblehurst Borehole. Pyritised diatoms, mainly species of *Coscinodiscus* and *Triceratium*, and disseminated carbonaceous debris are common. A sparse calcareous microfauna includes the foraminifer *Nonion laeve* and polymorphinids. Division A3 comprises the bulk of Division A in the Hampshire Basin. It is a coarsening-upward sequence that commences with silty clays which pass up locally into fine- to medium-grained sands with calcareous concretions. These sands, the Bognor Member of King (1981), may be present in the extreme south-east of the district. Fine- to very fine-grained silty sands with irregular clay flasers and partings occur at the top of Division A3 in the Shamblehurst Borehole. Division A3 contains a distinctive mollusc assemblage which includes *Astarte subrugata*, *Arctica planata*, '*Glycymeris*' *wrigleyi* in the lower part of the subdivision, and '*Corbula*' *pseudopisum* and abundant *Ditrupa* in the upper.

A Division A. Numbers at individual localities are (in descending order) thickness of Division A; thickness of the Bognor Member; and thickness of the Walton Member

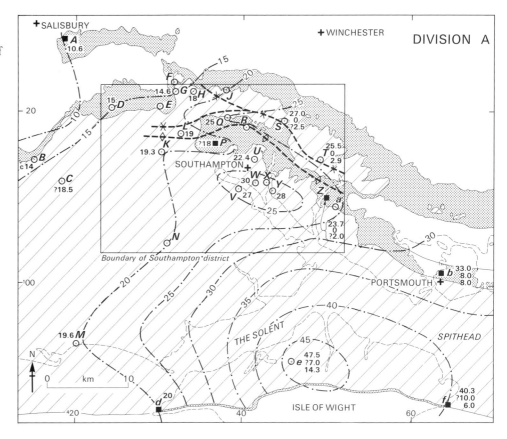

B Division B. Numbers at individual localities are the thickness of Division B

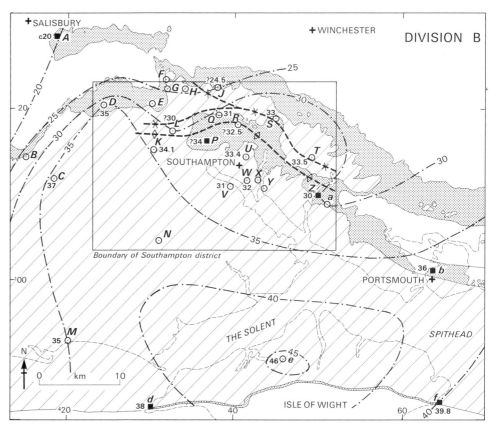

Figure 14 Isopachyte maps for divisions of the London Clay in the central part of the Hampshire Basin. See Figure 11 for key to localities and boreholes

C   Division C. Numbers at individual localities are the thickness of Division C

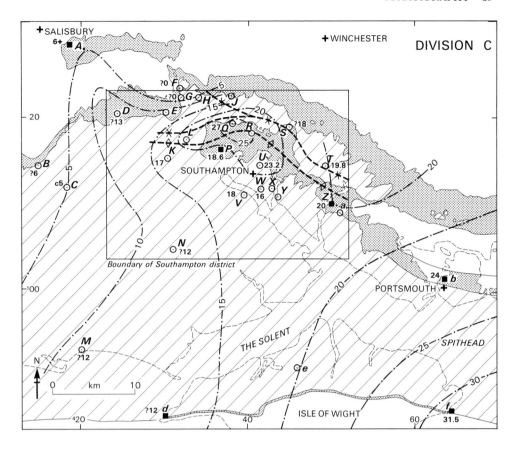

D   Division D1. Numbers at individual localities are the thickness of Division D1

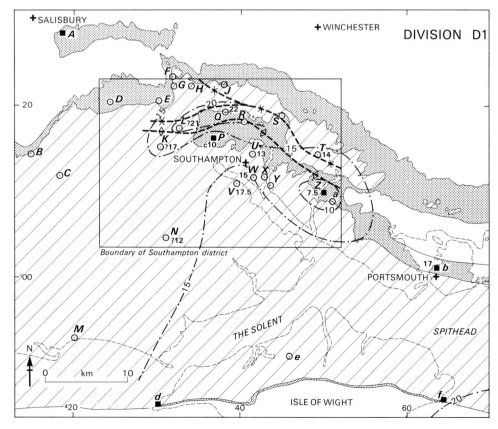

Division B

The base of Division B is marked nearly everywhere by a pebble bed, above which a coarsening-upward sequence of silty clays with occasional claystones passes up into sandy clays. Within the Hampshire Basin, Division B thins westward from around 45 m at Selsey to less than 20 m in Dorset. Within the district, the range of thickness is 25 to 35 m; there is no evidence of structurally-influenced thickness variations (Figure 14).

King (1981) recognised two divisions, B1 and B2, the junction between them being marked by a glauconitic horizon in the Southampton district and eastern Hampshire Basin, and by a pebble bed in the western Hampshire Basin. Division B1 is generally 7 to 8 m thick in the Southampton district.

The Division B sediments are commonly shelly and contain a diverse gastropod fauna and a less diverse bivalve fauna. Species of *Turritella* are locally abundant and *Crassostrea multicostata* and *Venericor* are common. The ostracod *Hermanites sp. nov.* occurs in the lower part of Division B2; the scaphopod '*Dentalium*' *constrictum* occurs widely in the upper part of Division B2 and is apparently restricted to that level. *Turritella* gr. *imbricataria* and *Venericor* aff. *planicosta* have been widely recorded in Division B2; '*Pecten*' *duplicatus* is a useful marker fossil in the same subdivision. An horizon about 2 m above the base of Division B, the 'Planktonic Datum' of Wright (1972b), marks the influx of planktonic foraminifera throughout the Hampshire and London basins.

Division C

The base of Division C is defined by a pebble bed at most localities. East of a line from Otterbourne to Southampton, the division consists dominantly of sandy silty clay and sandy clayey silt; west of that line, Division C and part of Division D are occupied by very fine-grained sand and sandy silt, called the Nursling Sand. Channel-fills of fine- to coarse-grained sand, the Portsmouth Sand, occur at the top of Division C in the eastern part of the Hampshire Basin. In the Bitterne area, the Portsmouth Sand has a sheet-like form and may represent the culmination of a coarsening-upward cycle.

Division C ranges from 30 m thick in the eastern part of the Hampshire Basin to 10 m or less in the west; it is mostly 10 to 25 m thick in the present district (Figure 14). King (1981) recognised two divisions, C1 and C2, in the eastern part of the Hampshire Basin, the junction between them marked by a glauconitic horizon or by a pebble bed. He suggested that Division C2 thinned westwards from Southampton and was absent west of Nursling.

In unweathered sections at Nursling and in the Bunker's Hill Borehole, Division C contains a diverse and abundant mollusc assemblage (King, 1981). The brachiopod *Terebratula* cf. *hantonensis* and sharks' teeth are present in the basal pebble bed at Nursling; there, the overlying silts contain *Pinna* and *Turritella*, and the ostracod *Echinocythereis sp. nov.* which forms a useful faunal marker at the base of Division C.

PORTSMOUTH SAND

The Portsmouth Sand is up to 10 m thick in the present district; it crops out mainly around Bitterne and near Nursling, Hedge End, and Swanwick (Figure 10). It lies in the top part of Division C and is overlain by the basal pebble bed of Division D.

The member consists of two sand types which differ in their geometries and in grain-size parameters. Around Bitterne, the sands have a sheet-like form, are fine grained, and moderately well sorted to well sorted, with negatively skewed to strongly positively skewed grain-size distributions. A plot of mean size against sorting (Figure 15) shows that the Nursling Sand and sheet-type Portsmouth Sand occupy separate fields. The sheet sands appear to be the culmination of the coarsening-upward cycle that produced Nursling Sand in the west of the district.

At Nursling, near Hedge End and at Swanwick, the Portsmouth Sand occupies channels cut into the underlying London Clay. Samples of the channel sands are generally coarser (fine- to medium-grained) than the sheet-like sands. They are well sorted to only moderately sorted, and have more consistently symmetrical skewness values than the sheet sands. Pebble beds occur in the channel sands in the Bursledon area. King (1981) reported cross-bedding in them at Swanwick, and bidirectional cross-bedding and *Ophiomorpha* burrows are present at Whitecliff Bay, Isle of Wight. The Portsmouth Sand is generally decalcified, and no fauna has been recorded.

NURSLING SAND

The Nursling Sand has an extensive outcrop in the north and north-west of the district between Hamptworth and East Wellow, where it gives rise to a feature on the underlying clay. Where unweathered, it consists of bioturbated, olive-grey, silty, very fine-grained sand and clayey sandy silt with a few bands and thicker beds of olive-grey sandy and silty clay. Fine-grained glauconite is generally scattered throughout. A glauconite-rich horizon in the Bunker's Hill Borehole forms a lithological marker band that can also be recognised in a road cutting [2495 2168] at Earldoms Lodge (Figure 16).

In the western outcrops, the Nursling Sand is up to 30 m thick and occupies the topmost few metres of Division B, the whole of Division C, and probably part of Division D, this correlation being based on the local extension of the basal pebble beds of the latter two divisions into the Nursling Sand. Near Gosport, Ampfield, however, using the same criterion, the base of the Nursling Sand lies some 15 m above the base of Division C and the sand may be wholly or partly within Division D. Thus although the thickness of the Nursling Sand varies from about 10 m near Eastleigh to possibly 44 m in the Marchwood Borehole, these thicknesses do not represent the same stratigraphical interval.

Glycymeris-rich shelly sands, locally cemented to form tabular calcareous sandstones, called the '*Glycymeris* sandstones' by King (1981), occur at one or more levels below the glauconite-rich horizon; they are generally less than 1 m thick. The sandstones at Nursling contain *Callista proxima*,

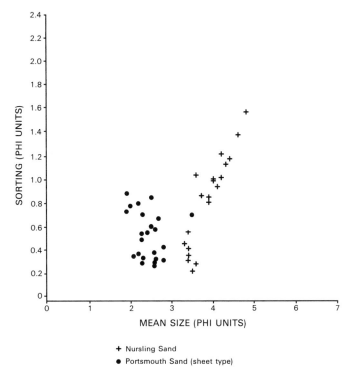

Figure 15 Scatter-plot of mean size against sorting for Nursling Sand and sheet-type Portsmouth Sand

'*Corbula' globosa, Glycymeris spissus, G. brevirostris, Lutetia umbonata, Sigatica hantoniensis, Tibia sublucida* and *Turritella spp.* The foraminifera *Asterigerina spp.* and the ostracods *Leguminocythereis spp.* are common elements of the microfauna.

Division D1

The base of Division D1 is marked by a pebble bed over most of the district. This is overlain by a sequence that coarsens up from sandy clayey silt to sandy silt. West of a line from Southampton to Otterbourne much of the division is occupied by the Nursling Sand. The Whitecliff Sand and its presumed lateral equivalent the Durley Sand occur at the top of the division. Division D1 varies in thickness in the district from 7.5 m at Lower Swanwick to 22.5 m in the Hoe Borehole [3845 1915]; the greatest thicknesses are in an approximately west-trending belt between Ower and Eastleigh (Figure 14). These thickness variations are probably related to structural control along the extension of the Portsdown Anticline during sedimentation.

The strata are commonly decalcified at outcrop but King (1981) recorded an horizon rich in the oyster *Crassostrea multicostata*, with *Musculus* and *Calyptraea*, in boreholes near Swaythling [440 160]. The fauna recorded from the Shamblehurst Borehole includes the gastropods *Athleta elevatus*, *Cantharus morrisii*, *Muricopsis sp. nov.*, and *Turritella* gr. *imbricataria*; the bivalves *Callista proxima*, *Caryocorbula sp.*, *Crassostrea multicostata*, *Parvilucina sp.*, *Phacoides squamulus*, *Pitar (Calpitaria) sulcatarius*, and *Venericor* aff. *planicosta*; and the ostracods *Echinocythereis reticulatissima*, *Leguminocythereis sp.*, *Pterygocythereis cornuta* and *Oertliella aculeata*.

WHITECLIFF SAND

The Whitecliff Sand consists at outcrop mostly of clean, fine- to medium-grained sand, commonly cross-bedded and locally pebbly, that weathers to yellowish brown. It has a continuous outcrop between Hamptworth and East Wellow, and more discontinuous outcrops east of the River Test, notably between Abbotswood (Romsey) and Otterbourne, between Toothill and Chilworth, and between Eastleigh and Fair Oak. Because of its value as building sand, it has been worked at several localities, particularly at East Wellow, Hoe, and between Bishopstoke and Fair Oak. East of the River Test, most of what is now called the Whitecliff Sand was shown as Bagshot Sands on the 1899 geological map.

The Whitecliff Sand occurs at the top of Division D1 as lenticular bodies that are channelled into the underlying strata; its outcrop is therefore discontinuous in some areas (Figure 10). In the area west of The Frenches, the outcrops shown on the published map may include parts of the Portsmouth Sand and sand in the basal part of Division E because the sedimentary breaks that define the junction of divisions C and D and divisions D and E could not be recognised in that area.

In the Bunker's Hill Borehole, the Whitecliff Sand consists of about 21 m of greenish grey, slightly clayey, silty, fine- to very fine-grained sand, sparsely glauconitic and with scattered lignitic material and a few clay bands.

At outcrop in the Toothill and Chilworth areas, the sands are mainly cross-bedded, clean, fine to medium grained and well sorted to very well sorted. Samples from Abbotswood, near Romsey, are fine to very fine grained and moderately well sorted; samples from near Gosport (Ampfield) are very well sorted to well sorted and slightly coarser. Pebble beds occur in the Whitecliff Sand between Abbotswood and Stoke Common, near Bishopstoke. Up to 6 m of cross-bedded sand with abundant black, rounded, flint pebbles occur near Stoke Common (Plate 2); farther east, at Fair Oak, the Whitecliff Sand consists of at least 6.7 m of well sorted, fine- to medium-grained sand with bimodal ('herringbone') cross-bedding (Plate 3). There is no marked trend in the variation of mean grain size in the Whitecliff Sand in the district; maximum values (1.57ϕ; medium-grained sand) occur in the west around Hamptworth and minimum values (3.68ϕ; very fine-grained sand) occur in samples from motorway cuttings between West End and Hedge End.

DURLEY SAND

The Durley Sand is present only around Durley (Figure 10) where it comprises up to 8 m of buff, clayey, fine-grained sand. Exposures are few, but it has been possible to demonstrate a lateral passage from Durley Sand into clean, medium-grained Whitecliff Sand over a distance of 15 m.

No fauna has been recorded from the Whitecliff Sand or Durley Sand, both of which are normally decalcified. Steavenson (1957) recorded a log bored by molluscs within the Whitecliff Sand at Woodington, East Wellow.

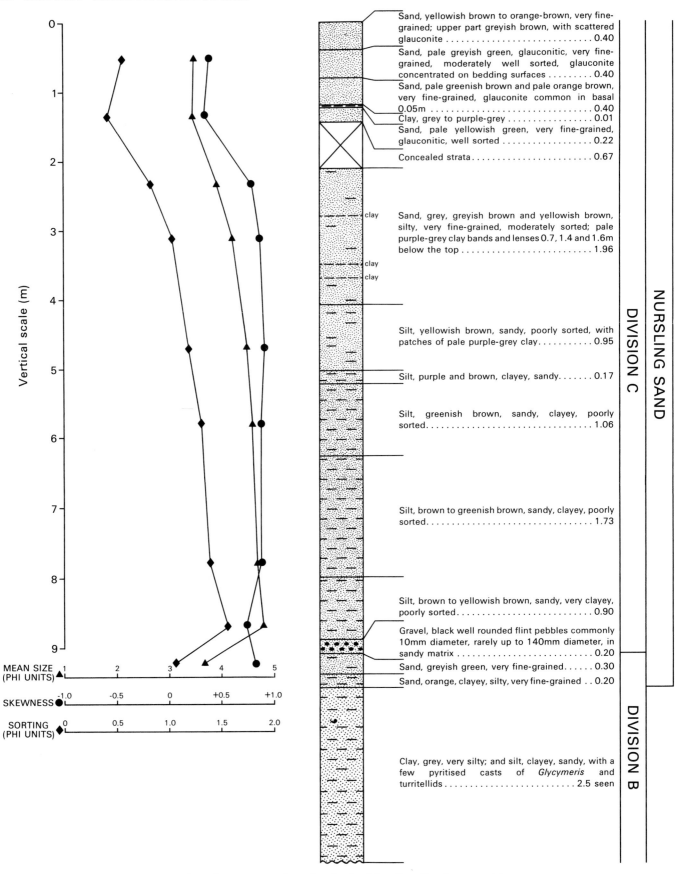

Figure 16 Variations in mean size, skewness, and sorting in the Nursling Sand exposed in a road cutting [2495 2168] near Earldoms Lodge, Landford

Plate 2   Normal faulting of flint pebble bands in the Whitecliff Sand at Breach Farm Sand-pit [4651 2032], near Stoke Common. (A14270)

Divisions D2 and E

In the north-eastern part of the district around Allbrook, and in the Shamblehurst Borehole in the subcrop, Division D1 of the London Clay is overlain by clays that were called the Allbrook Formation by King and Kemp (1982), who regarded them as the basal beds of the Bracklesham Group, part of their Wittering Division. Because these clays are lithologically indistinguishable from the London Clay of the district they are shown as such on the geological map. They probably correlate with Division D2 and the lower part of Division E of the London area. The base of Division D2 is taken at a pebble bed which rests on an erosion surface. Where unweathered, the divisions consist of olive grey, very silty clay with some sandy clayey silt and silty very fine-grained sand. The base of Division E is marked by a glauconite-rich horizon in both the Shamblehurst Borehole (Figure 13) and the Allbrook Brick-pit (Figure 17). Elsewhere in the Hampshire Basin, this horizon is represented by a pebble bed, for example near Portsmouth (Figure 13).

The thickness of these clays varies between 7 and 16 m in the district, and may have been influenced by tectonic activity related to the Portsdown Anticline. Few sections have

yielded fossils but the gastropods *Teinostoma sp. Turritella hybrida* and *T.* gr. *imbricataria*, the bivalves '*Corbula*' *globosa*, *Garum sp.*, *Lentipecten corneus*, *Pitar* (*Calpitaria*) *sulcatarius* and the ostracod *Oertliella aculeata* have been recorded from the Shamblehurst Borehole.

CONDITIONS OF DEPOSITION

Each division of the London Clay is a coarsening-upward sequence that commences with intensely bioturbated clays which contain a marine fauna indicative of deposition on an open-marine shelf. King (1981) considered that small-scale scour structures, sand layers, and shell concentrates within the clays were probably caused by periodic storm-generated surges. The clays pass up into silts that were probably deposited close offshore. The Whitecliff Sand and the channel facies of the Portsmouth Sand contain bidirectional cross-bedding and were probably deposited in distributary channels that were subjected to tidal influence. Bimodal cross-bedding in the Whitecliff Sand at Whitecliff Bay, Isle of Wight, dips approximately north and south. Few cross-bedding measurements have been made in the Southampton

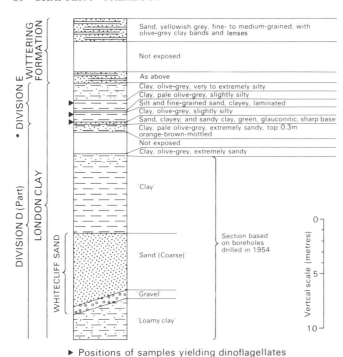

Figure 17 Composite section in London Clay and Wittering Formation at Allbrook Brick-pit [453 216]. That part of the section proved in boreholes was provided by Mr C. King (personal communication, 1983). Driller's descriptions are given within quotation marks

district; those in the Whitecliff Sand near Fair Oak [4975 1839] dip ESE and WNW (Plate 3).

The sheet facies of the Portsmouth Sand in the district is made up of well-sorted sands that have symmetrical grain-size distributions and contain cross-bedding and *Ophiomorpha*, a trace fossil common in nearshore marine sands. Taken together, these features suggest deposition in relatively shallow water above wave base. The tendency towards symmetrical grain-size distributions in some of the fine-grained sands indicates strong winnowing action, possibly in a shoreface environment (the zone commencing at mean low tide level and terminating at the fairweather wave base). A 40 cm-high cliff-like feature of sand at West End [4591 1476] with >30°-dipping, cross-bedded sand banked against its face suggests the possibility of aeolian deposition. Some of the well-sorted, positively-skewed sands contain grains with frosted surfaces that may also indicate the presence of wind-blown sand.

The distribution of facies within the London Clay (Figure 12) suggests that its shoreline lay a little west of its present outcrop in the Hampshire Basin during the early part of each cycle. The shoreline prograded eastward in the later part of each cycle. Nearshore marine sands in the upper parts of divisions C and D in the Southampton district probably coalesce and become more fluvial farther west in the Ringwood and Bournemouth districts.

Comparison of the isopachyte maps (Figure 14) for the London Clay divisions with the structural map of the district (Chapter 10) suggests that the thicknesses were locally controlled by intra-Eocene movements along the westerly continuation of the Portsdown Anticline. Some structurally-related control of the distribution of facies also occurred; for example, the sheet facies of the Portsmouth Sand was restricted to the area close to the axis of the Portsdown Anticline. Similarly, Division D2 and Division E clays are restricted in the north-east of the district to an area lying along the northern flank of the Portsdown Anticline, but are absent close to the anticlinal axis.

Plate 3 'Herringbone' cross-bedding in the Whitecliff Sand at Stubbington Farm Sand-pit [4975 1839], near Fair Oak. The bi-directional cross-bedding indicates the probable influence of tidal currents (A 14265)

DETAILS

Hamptworth – Landford – East Wellow – Awbridge Danes

Near Hamptworth Farm, a small disused 4 m-deep sand-pit [2341 1986] in Whitecliff Sand contains yellowish brown, cross-bedded, moderately well sorted, medium-grained sand; foresets in one bed dip 22° at 312°.

Cuttings [2495 2168] for the A36 road near Earldoms Lodge revealed about 12 m of strata belonging to divisions B and C (Figure 16). Most of the section is decalcified and oxidised Nursling Sand which coarsens upward; there is a flint pebble bed near the base.

A water borehole [2451 2019] 180 m west of Landford Lodge (Figure 13), penetrated London Clay to 77.7 m depth. Division A, recorded as 'clay', is 15 m thick. Division B, a coarsening-upward sequence of clays and 'clays with hard rock layers' (probably claystones), is 35 m thick. A 1.5 m-thick pebble bed at 14.6 m depth, recorded as 'coarse gravel' by the driller, occurs at the base of Division C. The overlying Nursling Sand consists of silty sands and sandy silts. In a nearby piston-sampler borehole [2442 2016], a glauconitic level at 8.7 m depth is probably close to the junction between divisions B and C. The overlying Nursling Sand is olive-grey, decalcified, clayey, silty, fine-grained sand and sandy silt. Sandy clay of Division B at 13.05 m depth contained common small pyritised diatoms, the seed *Scirpus lakensis*, foraminifera including common *Anomalinoides nobilis*, *Cibicidoides alleni* and *Nonion sp.*, molluscs including common *Turritella* cf. *imbricataria*, *Nuculana sp.*, and the problematical microfossil *Pseudarcella trapeziformis*.

North of Landford, cuttings [2566 2017] for the A36 road revealed 3 m of white and yellowish brown, cross-bedded, well sorted, fine- to medium-grained sands belonging to the Whitecliff Sand. Whitecliff Sand was formerly worked in pits [308 207 to 310 201] between East Wellow and Woodington. A section [3091 2071] shows 3.5 m of yellowish brown and grey, moderately well sorted, well sorted and very well sorted, fine- to medium-grained sand with some reddish brown colour-banding, and two thin beds of well rounded flints. Steavenson (1957) recorded a nearby locality [c.311 204] where pale buff, cross-bedded sands with wisps and partings of clay contained a ?coniferous tree trunk 6 m × 0.3 m, extensively bored by molluscs.

A water borehole [2717 2226] at Melchet Court penetrated London Clay to 44.5 m depth. Division A, 13.7 m thick, was recorded as 'pale brownish clay', the lower 5.5 m being sandy. An 0.3 m-thick bed of rounded flint pebbles at 30.8 to 30.5 m depth is probably the basal pebble bed of Division B. The overlying 26.8 m of strata, probably mainly within Division B, were recorded as 'pale brown clay'. Nursling Sand, recorded as 'ferruginous yellow-brown sand', was penetrated in the top 4 m of the borehole. The position of the boundary between divisions B and C is uncertain.

Thin London Clay sequences (52.7 m and 54.5 m thick respectively) were recorded in boreholes at Stanbridge Ranvilles Farm [3217 2221] and at Awbridge Danes [3184 2308]. In the first of these, a bed of 'sand, clay and pebbles' (at 71.6 to 70.7 m depth) at the base of the London Clay is overlain by 14.6 m of Division A strata, recorded as 'sandy clay', 'brown clay', and 'grey clay'. A bed of 'grey clay with pebbles' at 57.0 to 55.5 m depth is the basal bed of Division B. 'Grey clay' between 55.5 and 25.9 m depth probably lies mainly within Division B, and is overlain by 'dark grey sandy clay' between 25.9 and 18.9 m depth. This last is overlain by the Wittering Formation.

Romsey to Fair Oak

A borehole [3551 2305] north of Romsey penetrated 2.3 m of grey, finely sandy clayey silt (probably Nursling Sand) resting on 0.6 m of hard, grey, shelly 'limestone' (possibly the Glycymeris Sandstone). A borehole [3546 2285] farther south penetrated 2.15 m of dense, grey, fine- to medium-grained sand (? Whitecliff Sand) resting on 8 m of alternating beds of grey, silty, fine-grained sand and grey, sandy, clayey silt with thin shell-rich bands and a few greyish brown clay bands.

Lakeside exposures [3837 2300] at Crampmoor show the following section:

	Thickness m
Division D2	
Clay, extremely sandy; and sand, orange, yellowish brown and grey, soft, extremely clayey, fine-grained	1.7
Division D1	
WHITECLIFF SAND	
Pebble beds: rounded and discoidal flint pebbles up to 60 mm across in a matrix of orange-brown-stained pale grey extremely sandy clay	1.2
Sand, pale yellowish brown, clean, medium-grained	1.0

The Crampmoor Borehole [c.383 226], about 350 m NNW of Crampmoor Farm, penetrated London Clay between 100.9 and 18.0 m depth. Divisions A and B, together totalling 43 m, were recorded as 'blue clay'. The basal Division C pebble bed is at 57.9 to 56.4 m depth and is overlain between 56.4 and 40.2 m by 'sandy to very sandy blue clay'. 'Dark sand with bands of clay' at 40.2 to 35.7 m is probably that mapped at outcrop as Nursling Sand. Whitecliff Sand, the top 6.1 m pebbly, was proved between 35.7 and 21.6 m depth. 'Very sandy blue clay' at 21.6 to 18.0 m depth is probably in Division D2.

A gas-pipeline trench [SU 3922 2338] near Ampfield, sited about 15 m below the Nursling Sand, revealed sandy clay with *Tibia sublucida*, *Turritella* gr. *imbricataria*, *Lutetia* cf. *umbonata*, and *Pitar sp.* This fauna is indicative of an horizon within Division C. Near Gosport, Ampfield, Division D2 clay with a shell-bed containing abundant *Venericor sp.* and less common *Turritella* gr. *imbricataria*, was revealed in spoil from a gas-pipeline trench [3946 2276]. A similar shell-bed was recorded by King (1981, p.109) in the Division D2 clays at a locality [4280 1810] near Chilworth. The shell-bed was also reported from a depth of c.1.5 m in a gas-pipeline trench [400 223] beside Pound Lane, about 1 km south of Gosport.

West of Hiltingbury, Whitecliff Sand pebble beds overlie fine- to medium-grained sand, but in and east of Hiltingbury they directly overlie Nursling Sand or undifferentiated London Clay. For example, excavations [4538 2251] for a reservoir on Otterbourne Hill Common (Whitaker, in Reid, 1902, fig. 8) proved c.4.6 m of pebble beds with local orange-brown sandy patches at their base, resting on 'brown and grey loam'. However, the pebble beds overlie 1 m of clean, medium-grained sand in a road cutting [4553 2220] 300 m SSE of the Otterbourne Hill reservoir.

Division D2 and E clays were formerly worked in Allbrook Brickpit [453 216]. The lithological sequence proved in the faces and shallow boreholes is summarised in Figure 17. The clays total 14 m thick, but most of Division D2, 10.4 m thick, is now concealed beneath water. A 0.18 m bed of greenish black, extremely glauconitic, sandy clay and clayey sand marks a sedimentary break at the base of Division E, and rests on an irregular surface of orange-brown ferruginously stained clay. Samples from this sand and the overlying clay (Figure 17) yielded the dinoflagellates *Dracodinium solidum* and *D. varielongitudum*, indicative of the *similis/ varielongituda* Zone. Boreholes sunk below the level of the floor of the pit penetrated Whitecliff Sand.

Whitecliff Sand, comprising 6 m of yellow to white coarse-grained sand with abundant black, rounded flint pebbles (Plate 2), was exposed (1980) in a large pit [4652 2933] near Breach Farm, Stoke Common, beneath 3 m of drift. Alternating 5 to 50 cm-thick beds of coarse-grained sand and gravel in the upper part of the pit are block-faulted on a small scale. The faults, 2 to 5 m apart, dip 65° to 70° NNW or SSE; throws range from 1 cm to 1 m. The individual pebble beds vary in thickness; they become less common with depth in the section and, towards the base of the pit, only sporadic pebbles are present. The lowest bed is reported to rest on clay. The sand is cross-bedded throughout; foreset measurements indicate deposition by currents that moved towards the WSW. Small lignite fragments occur scattered throughout the sand, and dendritic manganese growths occur at some levels.

Fossils collected during the previous survey of the district from sandy clays with fossiliferous septaria in the now-infilled Crowd Hill Brick-yard [4890 1987] are listed in Reid (1902, p.10). Specimens at Winchester Museum examined by Mr C. King (written communication, November 1980) indicated that the strata belong to Division B2.

Whitecliff Sand, comprising 6.7 m of white to orange, cross-bedded, fine- to medium-grained sand, is exposed in a disused sand-pit [4976 1840] at Fair Oak. The bases of units of trough and foreset cross-bedding in the lower part of the pit are marked by 2 to 5 mm-thick layers of pale grey, slightly sandy clay. Units of structureless sand up to 0.4 m thick are also present and commonly contain randomly oriented clay flakes. Open, vertical joints with iron-stained faces and N–S orientations occur about 1.5 m apart in the sand. 'Herringbone' cross-bedding in the upper 5 m of the sand (Plate 3) indicates that currents were probably tidal, and moved to and from the WNW. In the SE corner of the pit, diapiric contortions of the sand layers, up to 1.5 m in amplitude and with eroded tops, probably formed by dewatering shortly after deposition. Along the south wall of the pit, a channel within the sand contains angular blocks, mainly 0.1 to 0.2 m across but with some up to 1.0 m across, of grey to pale brown, very sandy clay and clayey sand with pale grey sand pockets.

Ramnor Inclosure Borehole

London Clay was penetrated between 341.07 and 311.0 m depth in the Ramnor Inclosure Borehole. A generalised graphic log and correlation with other sections is shown in Figure 13; a detailed log is given in Appendix 1. Lithological boundaries in the uncored part of the borehole (327 to 311 m) have been picked from geophysical logs. An interval, 322 to 318 m, of low gamma-ray counts probably represents the Whitecliff Sand, and high counts between 318 and 311 m are interpreted as Division D2 and possibly Division E clays: In the cored part of the borehole, the basal Division C pebble bed was proved at the bottom of the borehole (341.07 m). The overlying beds consist of olive-grey, bioturbated, clayey sand and sandy silty clay. The Glycymeris Sandstone, calcareous silty sandstone packed with Glycymeris, is present at 338.93 to 338.19 m. The fauna recorded between 341 and 331 m is indicative of Division C and includes the serpulid Ditrupa sp., the brachiopod Lingula tenuis, the gastropods Eocantharus sp., Euspira sp., Eutriofusus sp., Pollia sp., a naticid, Tibia sublucida, and Turritella sp., and the bivalves Bucardiomya sp., Calpitaria sp., Glycymeris brevirostris, Lentipecten corneum, Nucula sp., Panopea intermedia, and Pitar (Calpitaria) sp.. Division D1 is probably represented in the clays between 331 m and the base of the Whitecliff Sand at 322 m.

Copythorne – Nursling – Rownhams

The full London Clay sequence was cored between 157.34 and 58.00 m in the Bunker's Hill Borehole, Copythorne. The generalised graphic log is shown in Figure 13; an abbreviated lithological log is given in Appendix 1. At the base of Division A (157.34 to 137.97 m), the Basement Bed (157.34 to 151.31 m) rests sharply on Reading Formation mottled clay; the Basement Bed consists of olive-grey glauconitic clayey silty very fine-grained sand with a few clay bands and scattered fossils. The remainder of Division A is

olive-grey silty clay, grading above about 142 m into olive-grey clayey silty very fine-grained sand and silt. The base of Division B (137.97 to 103.85 m) is marked by a bed of flint pebbles; that part of the division below c.112 m consists of olive-grey silty clay with scattered fossils and sporadic claystones. Strata between 112 m and 81 m depth are mainly olive-grey, silty, very fine-grained sand, sandy silt and silt, and have been classified as Nursling Sand. These beds can be correlated with strata elsewhere in the district that lie in the uppermost part of Division B, Division C and Division D. There is no good evidence for the position of the Division C/D boundary in the borehole. The Glycymeris Sandstone is present at 97.7 m to 97.3 m; a glauconitic level at c.96 m correlates with a similar level at outcrop at Nursling.

The beds between 81 m and 58 m are fine- to very fine-grained sand, and their correlation is uncertain. A pebble bed at 69 m probably separates Whitecliff Sand (sensu King, 1981) from sands that lie within Division D2 and possibly Division E, but for practical purposes both sands are classified as Whitecliff Sand in this memoir. Whitecliff Sand at outcrop in the north-west of the district probably also includes unbroken sequences of Division D1 sands together with sands in Division D2 and Division E. The sands below 69 m depth in the Bunker's Hill Borehole are generally better sorted (10 out of 14 samples are moderately sorted to well sorted) than the overlying sands which are generally moderately sorted to moderately well sorted.

The London Clay sequence in the Nursling area, summarised by King (1981) from exposures in Lee gravel-pits [360 175] and sections in CEGB trial boreholes [360 169], is shown in Figure 13. Division B, of which about 25 m were penetrated in boreholes, consists predominantly of silty and sandy clay. The fauna includes Arctica, large Pinna and Turritella gr. imbricataria in the lower part, and abundant T. gr. imbricataria in the upper. The base of the Nursling Sand is taken 4.5 m below the top of Division B, just beneath a thin (c.1.5 m) silty sand unit containing Ditrupa sp. and Venericor aff. planicosta. The topmost bed of Division B consists of 3 m of shelly, sandy clayey silt with abundant Turritella aff. circumdata, Crassostrea multicostata and rare 'Dentalium' constrictum. The basal Division C pebble bed contains abraded sharks' teeth and common Terebratula cf. hantonensis. Most of Division C consists of Nursling Sand. Above the basal pebble bed are 4m of sandy clayey silt with Pinna sp., Turritella sp. and Echinocythereis sp., succeeded by about 13 m of bioturbated silty sand with a diverse molluscan assemblage, including abundant Callista proxima, 'Corbula' globosa, Glycymeris spissus, G. brevirostris, Lutetia umbonata, Sigatica hantoniensis, Tibia sublucida, and Turritella spp.. The microfauna includes common Asterigerina sp., and Leguminocythereis spp. About 2 to 3 m above the base of Division C, the Glycymeris Sandstone consists of tabular blocks <1m thick of grey calcareous sandstone or sandy limestone, packed with Glycymeris sp. About 9 m above the base of Division C, a glauconite-rich horizon is comparable with that at 96 m depth in the Bunker's Hill Borehole and at outcrops in the Earldoms Lodge road cutting (Figure 16). At the top of, and within, Division C, up to 4 m of fine- to medium-grained sand of the Portsmouth Sand channels into the Nursling Sand. The base of Division D1 is marked by a pebble bed, overlain by about 3 m of silty sand, succeeded by fine- to medium-grained Whitecliff Sand, upon which rests the basal Division D2 pebble bed.

Nursling Sand was extensively exposed in cuttings [369 164 to 376 168] for the M27 motorway near Upton, Nursling. Mr C. King recorded the following section [3733 1669], which is decalcified except for the basal 1.0 m and the Glycymeris Sandstone:

	Thickness m
DIVISION D (basal pebble bed)	
Sand, loose, clayey, fine-grained, poorly sorted, with black rounded flints concentrated in the basal 0.1m	0.37

DIVISION C

Portsmouth Sand

	Thickness m
Sand, fine- to medium-grained, with a few rounded flint pebbles	0.10
Ironstone	0.08

Nursling Sand

	Thickness m
Silt, massive, 'shaly', clayey, yellow in the upper part, bluish grey below. Intensely 'streaky' on a small scale with abundant very small burrows; the top is coarser grained and with small sand-filled burrows; one pebble noted at the base	2.88
Silt, sandy, to sand, very silty, with many small very fine-grained sand lenses, streaks, and burrows; pyrite nodules common at the top; long vertical clay-lined burrows present	0.90
Sand, loose, yellow, bioturbated, very fine-grained, even-bedded in parts and with thin clay lenses. At the top, a locally developed 0 to 0.35m-thick unit of clay layers separated by sands	1.94
Clay	0.10
Sand, very silty, very fine-grained, bioturbated	0.36
Sand, loose, even-bedded, very fine-grained	0.44
Sand, silty, very fine-grained, bioturbated becoming clayey, with thin clay bands in the lower part	3.40
Variable unit of clayey sand, clay bands and even-bedded very fine-grained sand. At the base a glauconite-rich level associated with a clay band	0.90
Sand, silty, very fine-grained, with clay layers	0.74
Sand, silty, very fine-grained, bioturbated, with (at the top) large shelly calcareous sandstone concretions packed with *Glycymeris* (the *Glycymeris* Sandstone). *Lingula* common near the top. At 1 m above the base lenses packed with small *Glycymeris, Tibia,* and *Callista*. At the base, *Turritella* common, together with *Panope* and *Tibia*, in very silty sand	seen to 2.56

The Hoe Borehole [3845 1915], drilled for hydrocarbon exploration, penetrated c.105 m of London Clay between 111 and 6 m depth. No core sample was taken from this interval and the lithological sequence and its classification is based on a study of rock cuttings and the geophysical logs. The sequence is summarised in Figure 13. Division A is 25 m thick, the lowest 8 m being clayey sandy silt possibly representing the London Clay Basement Bed. About 11 m of clay occupy the middle part of the division, with clayey sandy silt, 6 m thick, at the top. Division B, 31 m thick, is mainly clay; the topmost 3 m are probably silty sand and belong with the Nursling Sand. Division C, 27 m thick, is occupied mainly by Nursling Sand, with lower gamma-ray counts at the top indicating the presence of about 5 m of Portsmouth Sand. The overlying clay, 8 m thick, probably lies within Division D. It is overlain by 14 m of strata that give low gamma-ray counts and are interpreted as Whitecliff Sand.

Hoe Lane sand-pit [3812 1886], now partly infilled, exposed the following section dipping 7° north:

	Thickness m
Topsoil with scattered flints	0.30

WHITECLIFF SAND

Sand, pale yellowish brown, grey and buff, cross-bedded, clean, fine- to medium-grained, well sorted, with some thin partings of grey clay and ferruginous concretions	2.00
Clay, rippled base, planar top	0.03
Sand, pale buff, clean, fine- to medium-grained, well sorted, with small discoidal clay clasts and some ferruginous concretions. Laterally impersistent 10 mm-thick clay band at base	0.20
Sand, yellowish brown, cross-bedded, clean, medium-grained, moderately well sorted	2.50

Cuttings [3843 1757] for the M27 motorway at Rownhams Lane revealed the following section, recorded by Mr C. King, in oxidised and decalcified, unfossiliferous silty sand and sandy silt of the Nursling Sand:

	Thickness m
Drift deposits	1.00

NURSLING SAND

Sand, even-bedded, silty, with silt laminae showing steep dips; packed pebbles at base	0.50
Silt, sandy, to silty sand, partly clayey; scattered pebbles common near base mark base of Division D	0.80
Silt, yellow, clayey, becoming bluish grey clayey silt below. The lower junction is sharp and burrowed	2.75
Silt, sandy, bioturbated, with sandy streaks and patches, and long vertical burrows; diffuse lower junction	0.70
Clay and sand layers with a clay layer at base	0.30
Sand, bioturbated, silty, with a few clay bands; a thicker clay band 6.41 m below the top; 7.33 m below the top is a glauconite-rich level (probably corresponding to that at Nursling,) associated with a clay band	8.75

Aldermoor – Southampton – Marchwood

A site-investigation borehole [3980 1529] near Southampton General Hospital, Aldermoor, penetrated the following London Clay sequence (driller's log):

	Thickness m	Depth m
Clay, soft, brown	0.90	0.90
Clay, bluish grey	0.93	1.83
Silt, dark grey, sandy	11.88	13.71
Clay, grey, silty, sandy	2.75	16.46
Clay, stiff, blue, laminated, silty	6.70	23.16
Limestone	0.31	23.47
Silt, stiff, dark grey, sandy	3.05	26.52
Limestone	0.15	26.67
Silt, stiff, dark grey, sandy	7.17	33.84
Silt, very stiff, dark grey, with gravel and shells	3.95	33.79

The borehole started at a level a little below the base of the Whitecliff Sand. The *Glycymeris* Sandstone of the Nursling area may be represented by one or both of the 'limestones'; the 'gravel' in the basal bed is probably the basal pebble bed of Division C.

Details of the strata penetrated in the Southampton Common Well [4173 1455] are given in Whitaker (1910, pp.127–128). Division A (115.5 to 93.1 m depth) consists of sandy clay with some claystones, the top 4 m being sandier. The base of Division B is marked by a pebble bed and is overlain by 33.4 m of shelly clay and sandy clay with some claystone. The base of Division C is marked by an 0.15 m-thick pebble bed at 59.7 m. 'Stone with shells' at 54.7 to 52.9 m depth is interpreted here as the *Glycymeris* Sandstone.

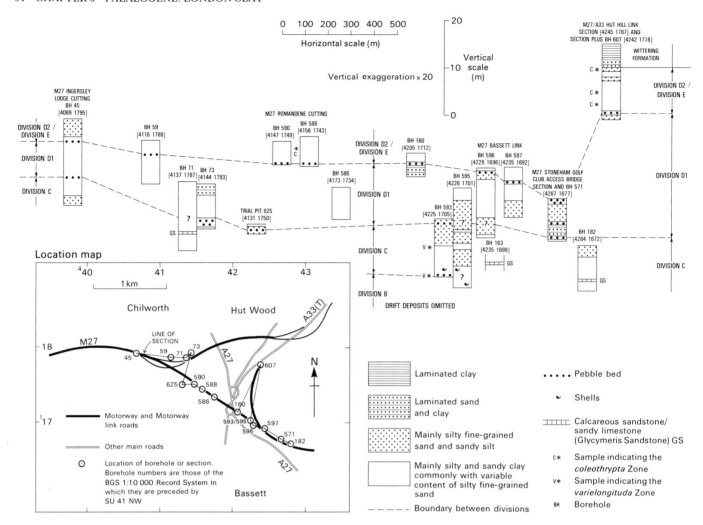

Figure 18 Sections through the London Clay of the Chilworth-Bassett area, based on site-investigation borehole data and sections measured in cuttings for the M27 Motorway link roads

This is overlain by 12 m of shelly 'dead sand' (probably clayey, silty, fine-grained sand), included here in the Nursling Sand, that is capped by a pebble bed at 42.7 m. This pebble bed probably separates divisions C1 and C2; it is overlain by sandy shelly clay between 42.7 and 36.5 m depth. The basal Division D pebble bed at 36.5 m is overlain by 13 m of probably predominantly silty sand and sandy silt of the Nursling Sand. The stratigraphical significance of pebble beds recorded at 27.7, 26.2, 25.6, and 23.5 m is uncertain; the highest is considered to be the basal Division D2 pebble bed, and is overlain by 7.4 m of sandy clay. The graphic section shown in Figure 13 is a composite based on King's (1981) analysis of the well, together with data from numerous M27 trial boreholes at Swaythling [440 160].

The London Clay sequence proved between 198 and c.86 m depth in the Marchwood Borehole [3991 1118], compiled from cutting samples and geophysical logs, is summarised graphically in Figure 13. Division A is mainly sandy and silty clay containing, at 191 to 185 m, a bed of calcareous shelly silty sandstone, above which the clays become silter and sandier. The base of Division B is marked by a pebble bed (173 to 170 m); this is overlain, at 170 to 167 m, by another bed of calcareous shelly silty sandstone. The remainder of the division is mainly silty sandy clay; the base of the

Nursling Sand—silty sand and sandy clayey silt—is about 2 m beneath the top of the division. Most of divisions C, D and possibly part of Division E are occupied by Nursling Sand. The Glycymeris Sandstone is developed in Division C at 140 to 139 m. Sand at the top of the London Clay, at 98 to c.86 m, is classified as Whitecliff Sand; it probably lies partly within Division D2 and partly within Division E.

The Southampton (Western Esplanade) Borehole [4156 1202] penetrated London Clay between 152.4 and 38.8 m depth. The graphic log, summarised from cutting samples and geophysical logs, is shown in Figure 13. None of the calcareous sandstone beds present in the Marchwood Borehole was recorded; neither were any pebble beds noted, but divisional boundaries can be determined from the geophysical logs. Division A, 30 m thick, consists of a lower part of clay, and an upper, coarsening-upward sequence, 13 m thick, that culminates in silty sand. The base of Division B is marked by a sharp decrease in grain size, and much of the division consists of a gradually coarsening-upward sequence of silty and sandy clay, with the base of the Nursling Sand present 3m below the top of the division. Nursling Sand probably occupies most of divisions C and D. Whitecliff Sand, present between 62.8 and 38.8 m, probably consists of sand developed within divisions D and E.

Chilworth – Bassett – Eastleigh

In the Chilworth to Bassett area, M27 motorway cuttings and boreholes proved strata ranging from the uppermost part of Division B to Division E (Figure 18). The basal Division C pebble bed, penetrated at 19.9 m in a borehole [4225 1705] near Bassett, yielded *Panope sp.*, *Pinna sp.*, and *Euspira sp.* The foraminiferal assemblage was dominated by *Anomalinoides nobilis* and *Cibicidoides proprius;* the dinoflagellates include *Dracodinium varielongitudum*, indicative of the *similis/varielongituda* Zone. Division C in the area comprises mainly very silty and clayey fine-grained sand and silty sandy clay; the Glycymeris Sandstone was penetrated in several boreholes [e.g. 4137 1787; 4235 1698 and 4284 1672]). The base of Division D is marked by a persistent pebble bed; the overlying beds, generally c.15 m thick, comprise mainly very sandy and silty clays, locally very silty clayey fine-grained sand. Whitecliff Sand is present only in the western end of the Ingersley Lodge cutting of the M27 motorway [4013 1803 to 4053 1798]. A pebble bed is widely developed at the base of Division D2 which comprises around 12 m of silty clay with some silty, fine-grained sand towards the top. A borehole [4242 1778] at Hut Hill yielded the dinoflagellates *Kisselovia coleothrypta* and *Dracodinium condylos*, indicative of the *coleothrypta* Zone. The contact between the London Clay and the Wittering Formation was exposed in cuttings [4245 1787] for the A33/M27 link road at Hut Hill east of Chilworth. The following section is a composite based on the cutting and that proved in the borehole cited above; the beds dip north at about 1°:

	Thickness m
Wittering Formation	
Sand, yellowish brown, orange-brown and grey-weathered, with clay bands; and laminated clay with partings of fine-grained sand	2.5
London Clay	
DIVISION E	
Clay, yellowish brown and orange brown, stiff, silty	1.3
Clay, dark grey, very silty, with a few pockets of pale grey and orange, silty fine-grained sand. The basal 1.1 m is dark grey, very silty, finely sandy clay with lenses of dark grey and orange, silty fine-grained sand	5.7
Clay, orange-brown, extremely silty, finely sandy, with well rounded flint pebbles in the bottom 0.6 m	2.1
DIVISION D	
Sand, brown, clayey, very silty, fine-grained, with some pockets of grey, silty, fine-grained sand	1.8

A water borehole [4501 1901] in Eastleigh penetrated 94.2 m of London Clay beneath 6.4 m of drift. The sequence, interpreted from the driller's log and a BGS gamma-ray log, is shown graphically in Figure 13. Division A (100.6 to 73.1 m) is recorded as 'dark blue clay with occasional claystones'. Division B, recorded mainly as 'green sandy clay' and 'dark grey sandy clay', forms a coarsening-upward sequence between 73.1 and 40.5 m. Strata between 40.5 and 30 m, recorded as 'brown sandy clay', probably belong to Division C; a bed of 'stone and shells' (probably the Glycymeris Sandstone) is present between 37.2 and 36.9 m. Above 30 m depth is Nursling Sand, recorded as 'grey sand', probably lying partly within Division C and partly within Division D. Pebbly sand between 20.6 and 14.0 m is interpreted as Whitecliff Sand and is comparable to that at outcrop near Breach Farm, Stoke Common, 2 km NE of the Eastleigh Borehole. 'Blue sandy clay' between 14.0 and 6.4 m is interpreted as from within Division E.

Highwood Reservoir Borehole – Shamblehurst Borehole – Bitterne area – Netley Hill – Swanwick – Chilling

A cored borehole [4647 1612] at Highwood Reservoir penetrated the topmost 6 m of the London Clay, from 40.0 to 34.0 m depth; the strata belong to divisions D2 and E. The sequence consisted of 4 m of olive-grey, bioturbated, very sandy clay and extremely clayey, fine-grained sand with irregular pods of sand, overlain by 2 m of dark greenish grey, finely micaceous, clayey, silty fine-grained sand. Finely laminated clay with very fine-grained sand partings was present between 37.56 and 37.50 m. Shells, including turritellids, were present between 40.0 and 38.4 m. Samples from 38.05 and 37.08 m yielded dinoflagellates of 'London Clay' aspect and are indicative of the *coleothrypta* Zone. Samples from 40 m contain *Kisselovia clathrata* and may belong with the *similis/varielongituda* Zone. Foraminiferal assemblages from samples at 40.00 and 38.05 m are dominated by *Cibicidoides alleni* and *Pulsiphonina prima*.

The fully cored Shamblehurst Borehole [4927 1456], near Hedge End, proved 108.2 m of London Clay between depths of 162.36 and 54.16 m. The lithological sequence and occurrence of selected fossils are summarised in Figure 13, and an abbreviated log is given in Appendix 1. The Basement Bed (162.36 to 158.38 m) consists of glauconitic sandy clayey silt and sandy silt with a few thin clay bands. The remainder of Division A (158.38 to 136.90 m) is mainly very silty clay; the topmost 4.75 m consists of sand with clay flasers and partings. The base of Division B at 136.90 m is marked by a sharp reduction in grain size and a scatter of flint pebbles; the division (136.90 to 103.40 m) is mainly silty to very silty clay. The B1/B2 boundary at 129.86 m is marked by a bed of clay with disseminated glauconite and scattered angular flint grains (129.86 to 129.72 m). The base of Division C at 103.40 is defined by a pebble bed, succeeded (at 103.40 to 83.45 m) by very clayey sandy silt transitional to sandy silty clay. The Portsmouth Sand is absent. Division D1 (83.45 to 69.60 m) has a basal pebble bed, and is predominantly very clayey sandy silt. The topmost 9 m are mainly sandy silt that contains (between 71.34 and 71.13 m) a bed of glauconitic shelly limestone with oysters. The Whitecliff Sand is absent. The basal Division D2 pebble bed is succeeded by a sequence (69.60 to 60.85 m) which is predominantly very clayey sandy silt. A glauconitic level at 60.85 to 60.51 m marks the base of Division E, which consists of very clayey sandy silt and very silty clay with 1.95 m of silty sand at the top.

Near Bitterne Park, a wooded bank [4439 1455] at the SE end of school playing fields, shows the following section:

	Thickness m
DIVISION D	
Sand, yellow- and orange-stained, brownish grey, micaceous, very clayey, silty, fine-grained; and extremely clayey fine-grained sand with ferruginous veins	5.0
Pebbles, well rounded, flint, in a clayey sand matrix	0.1
DIVISION C	
Portsmouth Sand	
Sand, buff and grey, clean, fine-grained	2.1

A sand-pit [4591 1476] near Townhill Park shows 0.2 m of greyish brown silt and extremely silty clay (Division D), resting on a discontinuous bed, up to 0.2 m thick, of well rounded, ferruginously-cemented flint gravel. This overlies at least 4 m of Portsmouth Sand which consists of yellow and buff, clean, fine-grained sand with some clay layers. Some of the sand beds show evidence of contemporaneous erosion; cross-bedding indicates currents that flowed from around 040°.

A piston-sampler borehole [4568 1400] in Midanbury penetrated the following strata belonging to Division D:

	Thickness m	Depth m
Clay, yellow- and orange-brown-weathered, grey, and silty sand passing down into extremely sandy clay	3.60	3.60
Clay, olive-grey, micaceous, very sandy, with bioturbated sandy pods and patches, passing down into extremely sandy clay at 10.6 m and into silty clay at the base	12.43	8.83

Samples from 12.93 and 8.81 m yielded dinoflagellates indicative of the *reticulata* Zone of Bujak and others (1980).

Several boreholes sunk for the M27 motorway site investigation at Netley Hill proved Portsmouth Sand 14 to 15 m below the top of the London Clay. One borehole [47995 1265] penetrated 12.26 m of greyish brown to grey sands and silty clays of Division D resting on 4.5 m of Portsmouth Sand, consisting of very dense, dark grey, silty fine-grained sand with a few layers of dark grey sandy clay. A sample from 0.08 m below the top of the Portsmouth Sand yielded dinoflagellates characteristic of the *reticulata* Zone. Another borehole [4846 1114] in the same area penetrated gravelly Portsmouth Sand. The sequence is as follows:

	Thickness m	Depth m
Drift deposits, gravel wash	2.13	2.13
DIVISION D (part)		
Clay, stiff, brown and grey, silty, with partings of brown sand	1.68	3.81
Clay, very stiff, dark grey, silty, with pockets of grey fine-grained sand	2.59	6.40
DIVISION C		
Portsmouth Sand		
Sand, dark grey, fine-grained and medium-grained, with some carbonaceous clay layers; rounded gravel and cobbles in the top 4.57 m	8.69	15.09
Clay, very stiff, fissured, dark grey, silty	1.67	16.76

The stratigraphy and palaeontology of the London Clay sequence at Lower Swanwick Brick-pit [500 100] were studied by Elwes (1888), Wrigley (1949), Curry and King (1965), Wright (1972a), and James (1974). The discovery of *Rhabdopleura* at Swanwick Brick-pit by Thomas and Davis (1949) was the first fossil record of the subphylum Hemichorda. King (1981) has provided a composite section from which Figure 13, column 7 is partly drawn, based on pit sections and borehole cores. Most of the exposures are now degraded, but the highest part of the formation is still visible in the '1955 pit' [504 097] of Curry and King (1965), where 4.5 m of London Clay are present beneath 8.0 m of Wittering Formation. The London Clay consists of grey, micaceous, slightly clayey, fine-grained sand that passes down by increase in clay content to olive-grey extremely sandy clay with a basal layer of flints. Laminated clays that overlie the London Clay were considered by Curry and King (1965) to be part of the London Clay. They are included in the Wittering Formation in this account.

The '1957 pit' [509 100] of Curry and King (1965) is now flooded, and the only sections visible are in olive-grey and brownish olive-grey, silty sandy clays with some layers of scattered claystone concretions (Division B2). No exposure of Portsmouth Sand is now visible in the Swanwick pits, but two nearby site-investigation boreholes [5048 0941 and 5047 0937] for the M27 motorway proved sands which, by comparison with the level in the Swanwick pit, were probably Portsmouth Sand. The first of these proved 3.66 m of brown, fine- and medium-grained sand with some flint gravel. This sequence becomes thinner and rapidly finer-grained in the direction of the second borehole, where it consists of 1.83 m of fine-grained sand. The distribution of the Portsmouth Sand in the boreholes and in disused claypits suggests that it may occupy a N–S-trending channel.

Chilling

The Chilling Farm Borehole [5098 0443] cored the topmost 36.41 m of the London Clay between the bottom of the borehole at 122 m depth and 85.59 m. An abbreviated lithological log is given in Appendix 1.

The lowest strata penetrated belong to Division C, consisting of olive-grey silty to extremely silty clay with scattered shelly fossils (122.0 to 111.6 m), overlain by Portsmouth Sand (111.60 to 107.45 m), consisting of olive-grey fine- to medium-grained sand, sparsely to moderately glauconitic, locally cross-laminated, and with rare shell fragments. The basal Division D pebble bed (107.45 to 107.25 m) is succeeded by olive-grey clayey to very clayey silt and clayey silty very fine-grained sand, finely micaceous, and with scattered shells. The basal Division D2 pebble bed (94.05 to 93.75 m) is succeeded by olive-grey silty clay with scattered shell fragments below 87.5 m.

CHAPTER 7

Palaeogene: Bracklesham Group

The Bracklesham Group, as defined in this memoir, corresponds approximately to the Bagshot Sands and Bracklesham Beds of the earlier memoir (Reid, 1902)—that is the strata lying between the London Clay and the Barton Clay. It has proved possible during the resurvey to map four formations which together comprise the Bracklesham Group. These are, in ascending order, the Wittering Formation, Earnley Sand, Marsh Farm Formation and Selsey Sand. East of the River Test, the lower boundary of the Bracklesham Beds shown on the 1899 map differs from that of the Bracklesham Group on the revised map, because Reid's Bracklesham Beds locally included strata that are now grouped with the London Clay. West of the River Test, much of the Bracklesham Beds outcrop of the 1899 map corresponds to the outcrop of the Selsey Sand; the Wittering

Formation, Earnley Sand and Marsh Farm Formation were included in the Bagshot Sands.

At Barton on Sea, Gardner and others (1888) placed the boundary between the Bracklesham Beds and the overlying Barton Clay at the level of the earliest occurrence of the foraminifer *Nummulites prestwichianus* (formerly *N. elegans*). This definition has been followed by most subsequent workers including Curry and others (1978). It is, however, unmappable because it does not coincide with a marked lithological change. In the present work, the lithological change that marks the junction of the Selsey Sand and Barton Clay occurs at a variable distance below the incoming of *N. prestwichianus*, with the result that some clays included in the Bracklesham Beds on the 1899 map are now included in the Barton Clay.

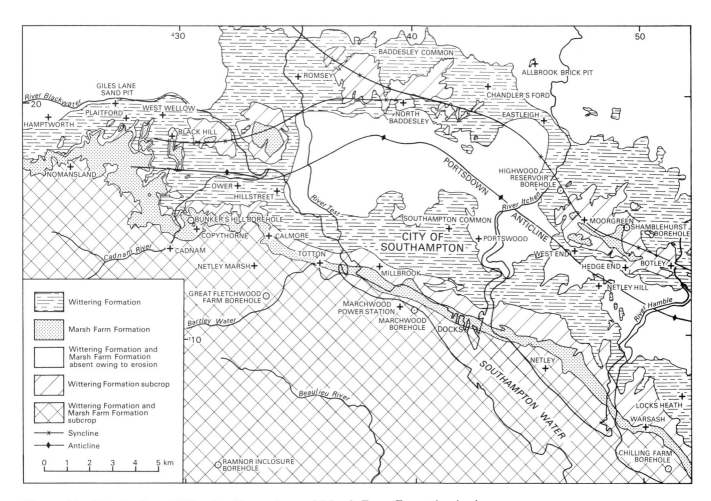

Figure 19 Distribution of Wittering Formation and Marsh Farm Formation in the Southampton district, showing also the main localities and boreholes referred to in the text

WITTERING FORMATION

The Wittering Formation crops out in a curved belt that crosses the district from Hamptworth in the west to Botley and Locks Heath in the east (Figure 19). An anticline and syncline cause the outcrop to broaden considerably between West Wellow and Ower. East of the River Test, the outcrop bifurcates around the Portsdown Anticline; the northern branch occupies a syncline between Romsey and Botley.

The base of Wittering Formation is taken at the base of thinly bedded to laminated clays or sands that rest on a variety of London Clay lithologies. In some areas the Wittering Formation overlies clays of Division D or E of the London Clay; elsewhere it rests on the Whitecliff Sand.

The clays were widely worked in the past in small brick-pits, but all are now disused or infilled, and exposures are rare. The full thickness of the formation was cored in boreholes at Bunker's Hill, Shamblehurst, Highwood Reservoir, near West End and in the Chilling Farm Borehole. Thicknesses in the district range between 23 and 57 m, the average being around 38 m; no systematic thickness variation is apparent.

There are three main lithologies. The first and most widespread is clay-dominated; it consists of olive-grey to brownish grey clay with partings, thin beds and lenses of pale grey or greyish green, very fine-grained sand or silt. Typical examples are shown in Plate 4. The second comprises wavy- to lenticular-bedded sand interbedded with clay in approximately equal proportions. The third consists of fine- to medium-grained, sparsely glauconitic sand that weathers yellowish brown, and includes laminae and flasers of grey silty clay and thicker intercalations of laminated clay. Other lithologies, present only locally or as thin beds, include bioturbated clays, and seatearth clays penetrated by carbonaceous rootlets; glauconitic sand occurs in the north-east of the district.

The three main lithologies interfinger both laterally and vertically, and their relationships are so complex that it is impossible to produce a generalised vertical section for the formation of the district. Representative sections are shown in Figure 20. The lower part of the formation tends to be sand-dominated in the south; even there, closely spaced sections show the sequence to be laterally variable over very short distances (Figure 21).

a

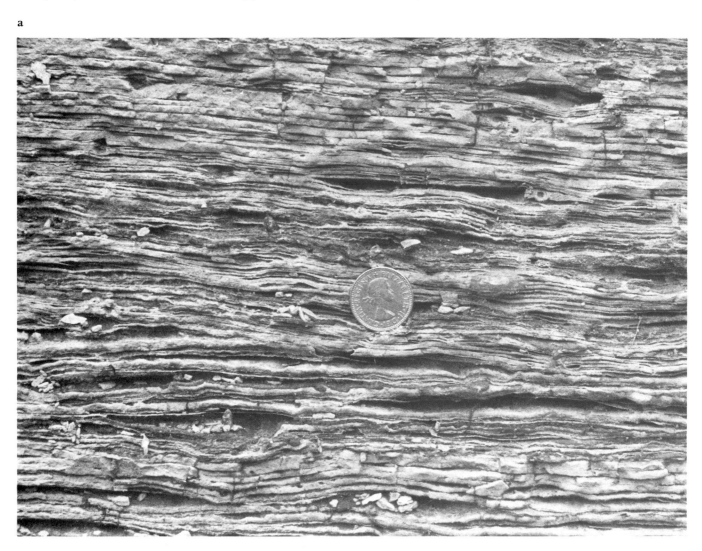

Plate 4 Selected bedding types in Wittering Formation at Giles Lane Sand-pit [2735 2002], Plaitford.
(a) Clay finely interlaminated with silty or very fine-grained sand.
(b) Clay with thin beds and lenses of fine- to very fine-grained sand. The coin is 28 mm in diameter

The glauconitic fine-grained sands that are present in the north-east of the district pass within a short distance westwards into clays with glauconitic sand interbeds, and are not separately mappable. The glauconitic sands were penetrated in the Shamblehurst Borehole (p.43) and in a borehole on Baddesley Common (p.41)

A distinctive bed, the Whitecliff Bay Bed, consisting of black to brown carbonaceous clay or lignite that rests on a kaolinitic seatearth clay penetrated by rootlets, forms a widespread marker band in the upper part of Wittering Formation throughout the Hampshire Basin. It is mostly less than 4 m thick; it has been recognised in most modern cored boreholes that have penetrated this stratigraphical level in the district (Figure 20).

Carbonaceous material is common in some sand beds and partings in the Wittering Formation, and nodular pyrite occurs sporadically. Vertical and horizontal sand-filled burrows occur sparsely throughout the formation, but apart from these, the sediments are only weakly bioturbated. Between 1 and 5% of glauconite is generally present in the sands. The formation contains abundant lamination, lenticular-, wavy- and flaser-bedding; thinly to thickly interlayered sand and clay beds are very common. These sedimentary features are widespread in, but not exclusive to, sediments deposited in tidally influenced environments. Markedly rhythmic lamination is present at some localities. For example, laminated clays between 51.03 and 45.20 m depth in the Bunker's Hill Borehole contain an average of 465 regularly spaced partings of very fine-grained sand per metre. This lamination may indicate deposition in intertidal environments in which the clays were deposited from suspension.

The only macrofossils from the Wittering Formation of the district found during the resurvey were vertebrate scales and teeth from near the top of the formation at West Wellow. A sample from the same locality contained numerous examples of *Pediastrum*, a colonial alga. Kemp (1984b) recorded abundant vertebrate remains, dominantly the teeth of sharks and rays, a turtle carapace, and *Lepidosteus* scales, also from near the top of the formation, from near West End (p.45).

b

The formation contains an abundant microflora of dinoflagellates, pollen and spores. The dinoflagellates are mainly indicative of the *abbreviatum* Zone, but at some localities the *laticinctum* and *comatum* zones are also represented (Figure 6). At several levels the formation contains dinoflagellates attributable to the *Wetzeliella (Apectodinium) homomorpha* plexus (Harland, 1979) which is thought to characterise nearshore brackish-water environments. *Inaperturopollenites*, a pollen thought to be related to the modern Taxodiaceae (redwoods and swamp cypresses), is very abundant throughout the Wittering Formation, except for one thin band which lies 2.5 and 5 m respectively below the Whitecliff Bay Bed in the Ramnor Inclosure and Shamblehurst boreholes and 12 m below the bed in the Bunker's Hill Borehole (Figure 20). Hubbard and Boulter (1983) established a zonation for the Tertiary of the Hampshire Basin based on pollen and spores. The base of their 'Zone b' lies close to the base of the Wittering Formation in the Ramnor Inclosure, Bunker's Hill and Shamblehurst boreholes.

The clay mineralogies of the $<2\,\mu$m fractions of samples from the Wittering Formation in these three cored boreholes have been determined. At Bunker's Hill the clay fraction commonly consists of illite c.50%, kaolinite 25%, and smectite and vermiculite 25%. Vermiculite forms up to 15% of the total in that part of the formation below the Whitecliff Bay Bed. The smectite-dominated assemblage of the London Clay extends 3 to 4 m up into the Wittering Formation in the Shamblehurst Borehole, and then passes upward into an illite-dominated assemblage in which the illite concentration is appreciably higher than at Bunker's Hill, and smectite is more abundant than kaolinite. The Ramnor Inclosure mineralogies are broadly similar to those at Shamblehurst, except that kaolinite is more abundant than smectite. In all three boreholes, kaolinite is most plentiful in the Whitecliff Bay Bed, and is indicative of subaerial weathering. Chlorite ($<5\%$) and discrete vermiculite are present in minor amounts throughout the formation.

The heavy-mineral assemblages of the Wittering Formation belong to Unit 4 and, in part, to Units 3 and 5 of Morton (1982). The base of Unit 3 in the Shamblehurst and Highwood boreholes is coincident with the base of the Wittering Formation, but in the Bunker's Hill Borehole and at Whitecliff Bay, Isle of Wight, it extends down into the London Clay, to approximately the base of the Whitecliff Sand. The base of Unit 4 is taken at the influx of heavy minerals of Cornubian provenance into the district; it lies 10 to 15 m below the Whitecliff Bay Bed throughout most of the district (Figure 20).

Grain-size analyses of sands from all lithologies in the formation have shown that mean size is greatest in the north-west around Plaitford, where medium-grained sands are present. Mean grain-size decreases steadily south-eastwards so that, around Sarisbury, the sands are fine- to very fine-grained. The grain-size distributions of sands show a tendency to become less symmetrical and more positively skewed from north-west to south-east. Sorting values also vary systematically across the district. The sands around Plaitford are mainly very well sorted, but sands in the south-east tend to be only moderately well sorted.

Conditions of deposition

The bulk of the Wittering Formation was deposited close to a coastline, probably mainly on intertidal mud and sand flats, and in the subtidal zone. Rapid transitions between sand-dominated and clay-dominated facies can be caused by relatively small changes in current velocities in such environments (Terwindt, 1971). Some of the sands were deposited in tidally influenced distributary channels. Temporary emergence of the district led to the formation of supratidal marshes that extended over at least 1000 km^2 of the Hampshire Basin. These gave rise to the Whitecliff Bay Bed. Deposition in freshwater is locally indicated at the top of the formation in the north-west of the district by the colonial freshwater alga *Pediastrum*, and near West End by a vertebrate assemblage interpreted by Kemp (1984b) as being derived from marine and freshwater environments.

Details

Plaitford – West Wellow – Copythorne – Hillstreet

A composite section in the Plaitford area, where the formation is around 28 m thick, is shown graphically in Figure 20. Most of the lower 11 m is exposed in a disused sand-pit [273 201] beside Giles Lane (Plate 5); the base of the formation is not visible, but it appears from the field evidence to rest on Whitecliff Sand. A generalised section is:

	Thickness m
Clay, greyish brown, laminated and lenticular-bedded, with lenses of medium-grained sand rarely thicker than 60 mm (Plate 4)	6.5
Clay and sand, wavy- to lenticular-bedded, in approximately subequal proportions, with lenses up to 120 mm thick of cross-bedded medium-grained sand	1.5
Sand, pale yellowish brown and greyish orange, medium-grained, cross-bedded, with subordinate beds of thin-bedded clay and sand, and laminated clay	3.0

Sands from the lower 3.75 m of the section are medium grained, with a restricted mean size range (1.35 to 1.56ϕ). Six out of eight samples are very well sorted (0.19 to 0.27ϕ), and two are moderately well sorted. Skewness values have a wide range (-0.35 to $+0.47$) and show an upward trend from strongly negatively skewed at the base of the section to strongly positively skewed 3.75 m above the base. Measurement of cross-bedding foresets indicates transport of sand from the south.

The Whitecliff Bay Bed which comprises 0.1 m of black extremely carbonaceous clay and lignite, was temporarily exposed beneath 2.5 m of drift deposits in a pit [2747 1941] beside the A36 trunk road at Plaitford.

In West Wellow, an excavation [2875 1941] about 8 m below the top of the formation, revealed grey laminated clay containing the *homomorpha* plexus of dinoflagellates. Another excavation [2872 1930], about 5 m below the top of the formation, revealed laminated clay and sand with scattered fish scales and teeth and numerous examples of the alga *Pediastrum*.

The full thickness of the Wittering Formation was cored in the Bunker's Hill Borehole [3038 1498], Copythorne, between 58.00 and 16.45 m depth. The sequence is broadly divisible into two lithological units (Figure 20 and Appendix 1). The lower 22.11 m is dominantly clay, laminated and lenticular-bedded at some levels.

Carbonaceous clays and associated rootlets, the Whitecliff Bay Bed, occur 20.5 to 19.6 m above the base of the formation. The topmost 19.44 m consists of beds of olive-grey to greenish grey, sparsely glauconitic, fine-grained sand and clayey sand (about 60%), commonly with scattered lignitic debris and bands of olive-grey sandy clay; and olive-grey sandy clay (about 40%) with laminae, thin beds and lenses of glauconitic, fine-grained sand and grey, very fine-grained sand. No macrofauna was recorded; the microflora consists dominantly of pollen and spores, and dinoflagellates, the latter indicating the presence of the *abbreviatum*, *laticinctum* and part of the *comatum* zones.

In motorway cuttings [342 164] just north of Hillstreet, the lower 12 m of the Wittering Formation consists of interbedded clay and sand, and sand with clay bands containing an 0.9 to 2.0 m thick bed of cross-bedded, clean, medium-grained sand with a few flint pebbles. At the base of the formation a bed containing black flint pebbles was penetrated in a borehole [3422 1644].

Near Wade Hill Farm, one of the few natural exposures [3420 1638] in the formation showed 2 m of well laminated and interbedded, greyish brown clay and pale grey silt, and fine-grained sand; thicker beds of very well sorted (0.28φ) fine-grained sand occur near the top of the section.

Romsey – Chandler's Ford – Eastleigh – Shamblehurst Borehole.

A piston-sampler borehole [3431 2056] on Green Hill, west of Romsey, penetrated 7.65 m of brown clay with fine-grained sand partings, greyish green extremely clayey fine-grained sand, and greyish green clay, on 0.4 m of brown slightly silty carbonaceous and lignitic clay (the Whitecliff Bay Bed). Samples yielded dinoflagellates indicative of a possible *abbreviatum* or younger zone, on the presence of the index species and *Kisselovia tenuivirgula*. Sand from 3.3 m depth contained heavy minerals of Unit 4. A nearby borehole [3451 2051] penetrated olive-grey medium-grained sand with Unit 3 heavy minerals at a stratigraphical level about 23 m below the Whitecliff Bay Bed.

Samples from a 12.85 m-deep borehole [4003 2098] near Body Farm, North Baddesley, consist of brownish grey, laminated and lenticular-bedded clay with some beds of sand with clay laminae. Samples from 2.35 m and 4.35 m below the formation top belong to heavy-mineral Unit 4, and those from 9.4 m and 11.4 m below the formation top to Unit 3. Dinoflagellates are mostly indicative of the *coleothrypta* Zone, with some evidence to suggest the presence of the *laticinctum* Zone or a younger zone. These beds overlie a glauconitic sand; 3 m of this bed were penetrated in a second borehole [3976 2122] near Lights Copse, Baddesley Common and contained Unit 3

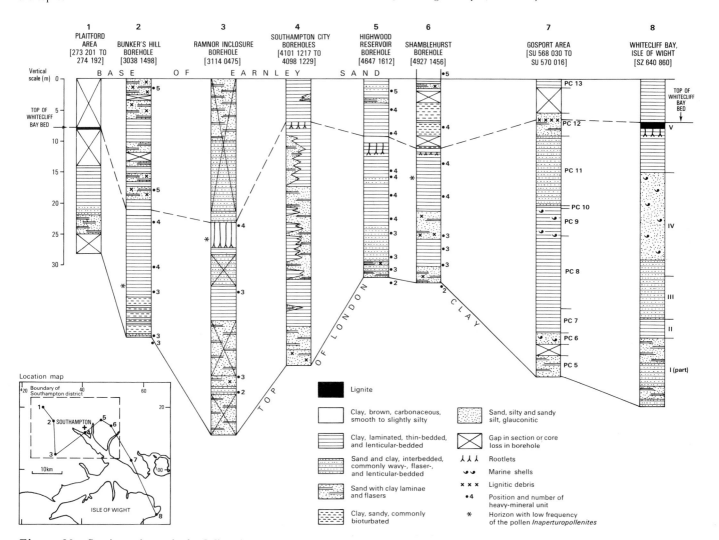

Figure 20 Sections through the Wittering Formation in the Hampshire Basin.

In column 7 the bed numbers are those of King and Kemp (1982), and in column 8 the bed numbers are those of Fisher (1862). Lithologies in poorly sampled parts of the Ramnor Inclosure Borehole are interpreted from geophysical logs

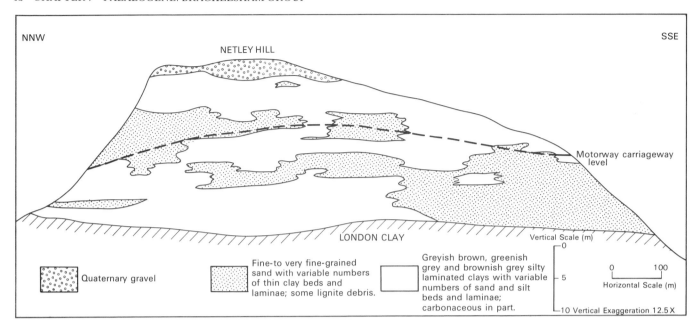

Figure 21 Section in cutting and boreholes for the M27 Motorway at Netley Hill, showing facies variation in the Wittering Formation

Plate 5 Wittering Formation laminated clay, sand with clay laminae, and interbedded sand and clay at Giles Lane Sand-pit [2735 2002], Plaitford. (A14260)

heavy minerals. A third borehole [3898 2178], on the north side of Baddesley Common, penetrated 4 m of grey sandy clay from low in the Wittering Formation, possibly bioturbated, with Unit 3 heavy minerals. Samples were poor in dinoflagellates but an *abbreviatum* or younger zone was indicated by the presence of *Homotryblium abbreviatum* and *Phthanoperidinium echinatum*.

Cuttings for the Chandler's Ford Bypass [4385 1930 to 4363 1895] show exposures of brownish grey laminated clay dipping gently north. An exposure [4378 1913] shows up to 4.5 m of olive-grey to brownish grey, slightly silty to very silty clay with a few partings of very fine-grained sand. The clays are weathered to yellowish brown, orange-brown and grey in the topmost 1.5 m, and are overlain by 2.5 m of drift deposits. A sample yielded dinoflagellates indicative of an *abbreviatum* or younger zone.

Near Ramalley Bridge, Chandler's Ford, the railway cutting [4257 2143] is in brownish grey silty clay with partings of very fine-grained sand, samples of which are visible in spoil heaps west of the cutting. Higher in the formation in that area, sands predominate. A total of 2.4 m of grey and yellowish brown, very well sorted (0.28 to 0.30ϕ), fine- to very fine-grained sand with some thin bands of clay was seen in a trench [4286 2126], 360 m SE of Ramalley Bridge.

The lower 6 m of the Wittering Formation at Allbrook Brick-pit [453 216] comprises yellowish grey to dusky yellow, fine- to medium-grained sand with thin (up to 5 mm) bands of pale olive-grey clay and lenticles of similar clay, some showing wavy bedding. It rests on Division E clays (Figure 17).

A typical sequence in the lower part of the Wittering Formation near Eastleigh was recorded in a borehole [4650 1874], 150 m south of Conegar Lock, in which 12.0 m of grey silty sand with grey clay bands was overlain by 3.0 m of interbedded sandy clay and silty sand and 0.6 m of grey sand. East of Southampton airport, a borehole [4601 1692] penetrated 11 m of stiff grey sandy clay with grey fine-grained sand laminae, overlain by 2 m of green fine-grained sand with shells. No shells were recorded at this stratigraphical level in site-investigation boreholes for a reservoir [464 161] at High Wood, about 900 m SSE. One of these boreholes [4647 1612] was almost continuously cored and proved a 31.8 m thick Wittering Formation sequence resting on London Clay. The sequence is divisible into two parts over the area of the reservoir site. The lower 8 m consists of interbedded clays and glauconitic sands, and glauconitic sands with clay layers and lenticles. The upper part, about 24 m thick, consists dominantly of olive-grey, laminated and lenticular-bedded silty clay, and contains an horizon of carbonaceous clay with associated rootlets, the Whitecliff Bay Bed. The sequence is described in Appendix 1 and is shown graphically, together with the heavy-mineral assemblages, in Figure 20. Samples from 4.05 and 7.13 m depth yielded poor, non-diagnostic dinoflagellate assemblages that suggest the presence of a zone younger than the *similis/varielongituda* Zone. Samples from between 40.0 and 15.0 m depth suggest the presence of the *coleothrypta* Zone; samples from 15.00 m and 18.95 m contained the *homomorpha* plexus. A sample from 24.84 m depth indicated an *abbreviatum* or younger zone.

Kemp (1984b) examined motorway cuttings [4580 1548 to 4611 1535] between Allington Lane and Dummer's Copse, NW of West End, and recorded the following composite section in the topmost 13.5 m of the Wittering Formation:

	Thickness m
Clay, stiff, dark grey, bioturbated, silty, with partings and pockets of grey fine-grained sand and some lignite	1.10
Sand, pale grey, pyritic, with thin grey clay laminae and soft buff clay pellets, erosively channeled, locally divided by 6 mm of stiff clay.	
Contains abundant vertebrate remains dominated by the teeth of sharks and rays including *Eugomphodus spp.*, *'Lamna' sp.*, *Myliobatis spp.*, *Nebrius thielensi*, *Pristis spp.*, turtle carapace and *Lepidosteus* scales (the latter commonly rolled and abraded). Pockets of lignite, plant seeds and pyritic twigs present in the upper part	0.01 – 1.99
Clay, firm to stiff, dark greyish brown, silty, with partings and pockets of fine-grained sand	3.63
Clay, stiff, dark grey, silty, with pockets of grey, very fine-grained sand	1.30
Clay, soft to firm, friable, dark brown, silty, with organic traces	0.50
Clay, firm to stiff, friable, pale bluish grey, silty	0.60
Clay, very stiff and lignitic, bluish brown [?Whitecliff Bay Bed]	0.50
Clay, grey, silty, very stiff, with partings of silty fine-grained sand; contains a 40 mm-thick claystone nodule near the middle	seen 3.40

The section is notable for the occurrence 1.1 m below the top of the formation of a ?channel-bar sand containing an abundant vertebrate fauna, interpreted by Kemp (1984b, p.159) as of mixed marine and freshwater origins. Vertebrate remains, associated with the alga *Pediastrum* have also been recorded from near the top of the formation at West Wellow.

The full thickness (33.2 m) of the Wittering Formation was cored between 54.16 and 20.95 m depth in the Shamblehurst Borehole [4927 1456]. The graphic log and heavy-mineral assemblage units are shown in Figure 20; the detailed lithological log is given in Appendix 1. The basal beds (54.16 to 51.28 m) are glauconitic fine-grained sand with clay bands and lignitic debris, overlain by laminated and lenticular-bedded clays (51.28 to 46.69 m). Above is glauconitic fine-grained sand (46.69 to 42.44 m) overlain by laminated clays (42.4 to 33.20 m). The Whitecliff Bay Bed (33.20 to 32.22 m) consists of yellowish brown, slightly silty clay that rests on olive grey clay penetrated by rootlets. The formation is dominantly bioturbated silty clay and clayey silt above the Whitecliff Bay Bed, with some laminated clays in the topmost 2 m. No macrofauna was recorded. The microflora consists dominantly of pollen and spores, and dinoflagellates; the last named indicate that the formation in the borehole lies entirely within the *abbreviatum* Zone.

Ramnor Inclosure Borehole – Southampton – West End – Netley Hill.

A thick (57 m) Wittering Formation sequence was penetrated between 311.00 and 254.45 m depth in the Ramnor Inclosure Borehole [3114 0475] but core was only recovered from the intervals 282.50 to 275.38 m, 292.27 to 287.49 m and 304.78 to 301.86 m. The graphic log and heavy-mineral assemblage units are shown in Figure 20. The lithologies of the uncored intervals have been interpreted from geophysical logs. The lowermost 18.7 m (311 to 292.3 m) was mostly uncored; geophysical logs indicate that it consists mainly of sand with some clay layers and thicker beds of clay. The overlying cored interval (292.27 to 287.49) consists of olive-grey clay with sand laminae and the overlying bed (287.49 to 282.30 m) is predominantly clayey sand. The Whitecliff Bay Bed (282.3 to 277.5 m) consists of carbonacous clay underlain by about 4 m of seatearth clay penetrated by rootlets (palaeosol). The uncored interval (277.5 to 254.45 m) above the palaeosol forms a coarsening-upwards sequence predominantly of sand with clay beds commoner towards the base. The beds above the palaeosol lie within the *abbreviatum* Zone.

The Marchwood Borehole [3991 1118] penetrated the full thickness, 27 m, of the formation, but no core was taken at this stratigraphical level. The geophysical logs and cuttings indicate that the formation consists predominantly of olive-grey to greyish brown clay, with white to yellow sands in the top 5 m.

The top 15.1 m of the Wittering Formation was penetrated in a borehole [3854 1300] at Millbrook. It consisted of the following strata:

	Thickness m	Depth m
Clay, firm to stiff, grey, laminated; and sand, fine-grained	2.3	8.4
Sand, dense, grey, fine-grained, silty, with some thin clay laminae	3.8	12.2
Clay, stiff, grey, laminated; and sand, fine-grained	1.7	13.9
Sand, dark grey, fine- to medium-grained, silty, with some thin lignite bands and slightly clayey sand	3.7	17.6
Clay, stiff, grey, with partings of fine-grained sand and a few lignite fragments	3.1	20.7
Clay, stiff, black, lignitic (probably the Whitecliff Bay Bed)	0.5	21.2

Boreholes [4101 1217 to 4098 1229] near Southampton city centre illustrated the great lithological variability of the formation; a composite section is shown in Figure 20. In general, the lower part of the sequence consists mainly of sands with thin clay layers, and the upper part mainly of brownish grey and greenish grey laminated clays with some layers of sand. Parts of the section, notably near the middle, consist almost entirely of sand with clay layers. A lenticular bed of sand within laminated clays may have been deposited in a tidal channel. The formation has yielded dinoflagellates that indicate that part of the *abbreviatum*, the whole of the *laticinctum* and part of the *comatum* zones are present.

Much of the older part of central Southampton is built on gravels overlying Wittering Formation. Boreholes [e.g. 4189 1177] have proved up to 12 m of clay with pockets of sand.

Just north of Southampton Common, a borehole [4181 1537] at the University Medical School penetrated c.13 m of soft to stiff laminated clay. A pebble bed at the base of the formation is poorly exposed in a bank [4247 1514] at the University. It consists of about 0.6 m of reddish brown and grey, clayey fine-grained sand with scattered well rounded flint pebbles up to 50 mm across.

In Portswood, a borehole [4261 1354] proved 10.9 m of Wittering Formation resting on Whitecliff Sand with an intervening pebble bed. The formation consisted of:

	Thickness m	Depth m
Clay, soft to firm, brown, silty	0.3	2.3
Clay, stiff, dark grey, silty and sandy	2.3	4.6
Clay, stiff, dark grey, thickly laminated and thickly layered with fine- and medium-grained sand and thin layers and fragments of lignite	7.4	12.0
Clay, stiff, dark grey, very sandy, with round black flint pebbles	0.9	12.9

Exposures [4282 1357] in a bank near Portswood Park show the following section at the base of the formation:

	Thickness m
Sand, orange and greyish brown, laminated; and sand, lignitic, clayey	0.40
Sand, yellowish brown, fine- to medium-grained, with interbeds of clay, brown, lignitic, extremely sandy	4.05
Sand, yellowish brown, very lignitic	0.50

Sand, greyish brown and olive, clayey, fine- to medium-grained, with a band of flint pebbles 0.6 m below the top	0.85

Site-investigation boreholes [4595 1514 to 4697 1502] near West End proved the top 16 m of the formation to be predominantly laminated clay, and the lower 7 m to be predominantly sand with some clay layers. The Earnley Sand rests almost directly on the Whitecliff Bay Bed, suggesting that the upper part of the Wittering Formation is missing in that area.

Excavations and site-investigation boreholes for the M27 motorway around Netley Hill [481 123] have demonstrated that the lower 25 m of the formation consists of two main lithologies, laminated clay; and sand with clay layers. The two lithologies commonly interfinger over horizontal distances of less than 20 m (Figure 21). Outcrop and augering data from the area immediately SW of the Netley Hill cutting indicate that the upper part of the formation consists mainly of laminated clay in that area.

Chilling

The full thickness of the Wittering Formation was cored in the Chilling Farm Borehole [5098 0443] between 85.59 and 41.50 m depth (Appendix 1). The lower 18.7 m of the sequence is predominantly olive-grey to greenish grey fine-grained sand, locally with clay laminae and beds, scattered lignitic material and a sparse to moderate glauconite content. The topmost 25.4 m of the formation is predominantly clay, locally with silt and very fine-grained sand laminae and beds. The Whitecliff Bay Bed (53.8 to 46.0 m) consists mainly of olive-grey silty to silt-free seatearth clays penetrated by subvertical rootlets.

EARNLEY SAND

The main outcrop of the Earnley Sand (Earnley Formation of King and King, 1977) extends from Nomansland in the north-west, south-eastwards through Southampton Docks to Hamble. Outliers between West Wellow and Chandler's Ford, and between West End and Botley, occupy synclinal structures north of the Portsdown Anticline (Figure 22). Over much of the district, the Earnley Sand gives rise to moderately pronounced hills and ridges that rise above the more subdued ground underlain by the dominantly clayey Wittering Formation. Exposures are few and the formation, being of low economic value, has been little dug, although there are pits for moulding sand near Hound (p.48). It was cored in the Bunker's Hill, Shamblehurst, and Chilling Farm boreholes (Appendix 1).

The formation is lithologically fairly uniform throughout the district and comprises mainly green, glauconitic, bioturbated, clayey, silty, fine-grained sand and sandy silt, locally with an abundant and diverse macrofauna of marine invertebrates. The glauconite, as mammilated and lobate grains, is commonly an abundant constituent, and locally patches and streaks consist almost entirely of glauconite. Few sedimentary structures are visible owing to the intense bioturbation, but cross-bedding is present near the base of the formation at some localities. Spheroidal calcareous nodules, commonly 0.9 to 1.2 m in diameter, occur in places.

The transgressive base of the Earnley Sand is marked by a sharp lithological contrast between relatively structureless glauconitic sands and the underlying laminated and thin-bedded clays and sands of the Wittering Formation. The junc-

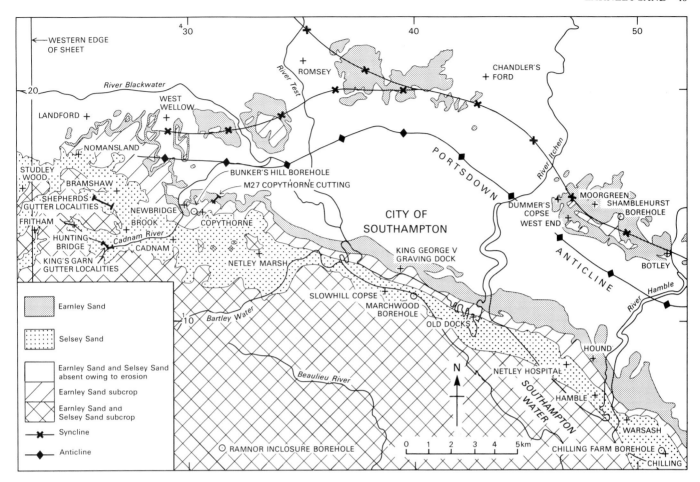

Figure 22   Distribution of Earnley Sand and Selsey Sand in the Southampton district, showing also the main localities and boreholes referred to in the text

tion is commonly burrowed, and scattered flint pebbles locally rest on the sedimentary surface that marks the base of the Earnley Sand.

The formation is mostly 4 to 8 m thick in the western part of the outcrop between Nomansland and Copythorne; it dies out just west of Nomansland. Elsewhere in the district the formation is mostly between 15 and 18 m thick at outcrop; a thicker sequence (24 m) was recorded in the subcrop in the Ramnor Inclosure Borehole.

East of the River Itchen, the formation contains an abundant marine macrofauna. At Bracklesham Bay, West Sussex, Curry and others (1977), following Dixon (1850) and Fisher (1862) recognised five faunal marker units in the Earnley Sand, and these have been recorded in the Shamblehurst Borehole. The units are, in ascending order, the Cardita (Venericardia) Bed, Turritella Bed, Palate Bed and Nummulites laevigatus Bed. The Callista Bed, lying beneath the Cardita and Turritella Bed, was first named by King and Kemp (1982) at Gosport. The bivalve *Callista proxima bruxellensis* is common in the Callista Bed together with *Cardita spp. Pitar sp.*, and *Turritella sp.*. Kemp (1984b) recorded common vertebrate remains from the Callista Bed near West End, mainly teeth of sharks and rays, and many fish teeth. The Cardita Bed contains very common *Venericor [Cardita] planicosta*; this bed has a patchy distribution in the

Hampshire Basin, being present at Shamblehurst and Bracklesham Bay, but absent at Gosport (King and Kemp, 1982) and West End (Kemp, 1984b). Abundant *Turritella conoidea* and common *Venericardia carinata* occur in the Turritella Bed at Shamblehurst and at Bracklesham Bay. Near West End, the Turritella Bed contains abundant crushed molluscs dominated by *Turritella sp.* and *Cardita sp.*, together with sharks' teeth (especially '*Lamna*' *lerichei*) and reptile bones (Kemp, 1984b). The Palate Bed—named from the occurrence in it at Bracklesham Bay of palates of rays (Dixon, 1850)—is lithologically distinctive, consisting of intensely bioturbated very glauconitic clayey sandy silt with patches and lenses of clay. Fossils from the bed near West End include decalcified moulds of *Venericardia sp.*, vertebrates (including sharks' teeth), and abundant *Nipa* fruit remains (Kemp, 1984b). At Shamblehurst the Palate Bed is unfossiliferous, but lithological correlation can be made with the Bracklesham Bay and Gosport sections. A lithologically similar bed was recognised in the Earnley Sand in the M27 motorway cutting at Copythorne by King and King (1977). The older faunal marker units cannot be recognised that far west in the district.

The Nummulites laevigatus Bed forms the most widespread and distinctive faunal marker unit in the Earnley Sand. It commonly occurs near the top of the formation and

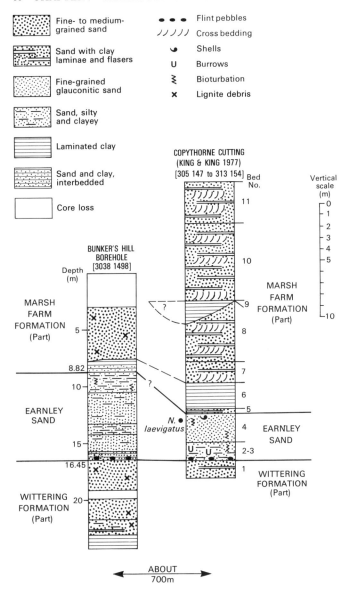

Figure 23 Correlation of the Marsh Farm Formation, Earnley Sand, and topmost Wittering Formation in the Bunker's Hill Borehole and M27 Motorway Copythorne cutting. See Figure 22 for location

is characterised by the presence of the large foraminifer *N. laevigatus*. The unit has been recorded as far west as Copythorne, where the name fossil is found only as moulds.

The Earnley Sand contains moderately diverse dinoflagellate assemblages. In the West End area the floras are indicative of the *comatum* and *arcuatum* zones; the *comatum* Zone is present in the Bunker's Hill Borehole and the *comatum* and *arcuatum* zones are present in the Earnley Sand at Whitecliff Bay in the Isle of Wight (Eaton, 1976; Bujak and others, 1980). However, in the Shamblehurst Borehole, the Earnley Sand has yielded *laticinctum* Zone floras, and in the Ramnor Inclosure Borehole *abbreviatum* Zone floras.

Kaolinite is plentiful (up to 30%) in the < 2 μm fraction of the Earnley Sand in the Ramnor Inclosure Borehole, where the clay-mineral assemblage illite > kaolinite > smectite occurs. In the Bunker's Hill Borehole, a sample from the lower part of the formation contains illite, kaolinite and smectite in subequal proportions. A single sample from the Earnley Sand of the Shamblehurst Borehole is dominated by illite, with about 25% smectite and 10% kaolinite.

The heavy-mineral assemblages in the Earnley Sand belong to Morton's Unit 5. The base of Unit 5 was considered by Morton (1982) to coincide with the base of the Earnley Sand. This is apparently the case in the north-east of the district, in the Shamblehurst Borehole (Figure 20) and on Baddesley Common, but in the Bunker's Hill Borehole (Figure 24) Unit 5 extends down into the Wittering Formation.

Most of the sands in the Earnley Sand (53 samples analysed) are clayey, silty, fine-grained to very fine-grained quartz sand. The mean grain size ranges from medium-grained sand to silt (1.71 to 4.53ϕ). The finest-grained samples were recorded in the Shamblehurst Borehole in the east of the district. There, 12 samples have a mean-grain-size range of 3.04ϕ to 4.53ϕ; coarser-grained sands (mean grain size >2ϕ) tend to be restricted to the north-west of the district. The sands are mostly moderately sorted to poorly sorted, but well sorted to very well sorted sands occur near the base of the formation in the north-west of the district. These last named combine good sorting with near symmetrical grain-size distributions and are clean sands from which the fines were probably removed by winnowing during the early stages of the transgression of the formation. In the eastern part of the district, a moderately well sorted sand was recorded from just above the base of the formation in the Shamblehurst Borehole; samples from higher in the sequence were poorly to very poorly sorted. The basal sample is also the cleanest, in contrast to the overlying samples which possess substantial amounts of silt and clay and are fine-skewed to strongly fine-skewed. Apart from the basal samples, most sands in the formation are fine-skewed to strongly fine-skewed.

The diverse marine fauna and abundant glauconite indicate that the formation was deposited in a shelf sea which Plint (1983) estimated was between 10 and 30 m deep. A coastline fringed by tidal flats, marshes, and lagoons lay just west of the district at the time of deposition of the Nummulites laevigatus Bed.

Details

Landford – Copythorne

Excavations [2645 1880] on Landford Common revealed 1.0 m of yellowish brown, clean, very well sorted, medium-grained sand with scattered glauconite. Small exposures [2827 1716, 2839 1709] NW of Moor Bridge Farm, Canada Common, show up to 0.6 m of greyish green, well sorted to moderately sorted, glauconitic, fine-grained sand, beneath up to 1.0 m of drift. A piston-sampler borehole [2956 1781] on Black Hill, West Wellow, proved the formation to consist of 5.4 m of greyish green, glauconitic, clayey, silty, fine-grained sand. A road cutting [2986 1502] just east of South Brook Farm, Newbridge, shows poor exposures of up to 2.0 m of greenish brown, glauconitic, clayey silty sand. The section is continued downwards west of the road where the following sequence was recorded in another cutting [2985 1498];

	Thickness m
TOPSOIL	
Soil, greyish brown, with flints	0.3
EARNLEY SAND	
Sand, orange and greyish green, glauconitic, clayey	1.5
Sand, greyish green, glauconitic, clayey, silty, with some thin clay bands; well rounded flint pebbles at the base	c.1.0
WITTERING FORMATION	
Sand, pale grey, fine-grained	0.3

In the Bunker's Hill Borehole [3038 1498], Copythorne, the Earnley Sand is 7.63 m thick, and consists of greenish grey, bioturbated, silty clayey fine-grained glauconitic sand, with some beds of greenish grey extremely sandy clay; details are given in Appendix 1. The basal 6 m contains a few moulds of *Caryocorbula*, *Macrosolen* and *Venericardia*. The microflora consists dominantly of pollen, and sparse but well preserved dinoflagellates indicative of the *comatum* Zone. The following thinner (4.04 m) sequence was recorded by King and King (1977) in the Copythorne Cutting [303146 to 309150] of the M27 motorway:

	Thickness m
EARNLEY SAND	
Nummulites laevigatus Bed: Sand, green, glauconitic, mottled and bioturbated, fine-grained. Shell moulds are abundant in the upper part, the better preserved forms being: the foraminifer *Nummulites laevigatus*, the gastropods *Calyptraea sp.*, *Scaphander edwardsii* and *Turritella sulcifera*, and the bivalves *Barbatia appendiculata*, 'Corbula' gr. *striata*, *Crassatella sp.*, *Macrosolen hollowaysii*, *Solen (Eosolen) sp.*, *Venericardia sp.*, *Venericor planicosta*, and a Venerid, probably *Pitar sp.*	2.46
Palate Bed: Sand, greyish green, glauconitic, bioturbated, clayey, silty, with numerous sandy silt and sandy clayey silt mottles; ramified throughout by a galleried, tubular, unwalled burrow system (average burrow diameter 30mm). Contains rare moulds of molluscs, including corbulids and *Venericor planicosta*	1.53
Sand, pebbly, consisting of white rounded flint pebbles scattered in a matrix of very glauconitic sand, mottled with clay streaks and patches	0.05
WITTERING FORMATION	
Sand, fine- to medium-grained, with a few thin clay beds	1.46

The fossils from the upper part of this section suggest a correlation with part of the Nummulites laevigatus Bed at Bracklesham Bay (bed E7 of Curry and others, 1977). A correlation of the Earnley Sand in the Bunker's Hill Borehole and in the M27 Copythorne Cutting is included in Figure 23.

Ramnor Inclosure Borehole [3114 0475]

Geophysical logs indicate that the formation, 22.84 m thick, was present between 254.45 and 231.61 m depth, but only the section between 254.45 and 247.00 m was successfully cored. The cores consist of olive-grey, glauconitic, bioturbated, silty to very silty clay with a little clayey silty sand. Calcareous concretions were cored at three levels. Dinoflagellates indicate that the formation lies entirely within the *abbreviatum* Zone.

Romsey – West End – Hedge End

Exposures [3678 2177 to 3678 2165] near Harefield, Romsey, show 2.4 m of glauconitic sand, cross-bedded in places, and with horizons of paler less clayey sand. A sample from the basal 0.4 m is greenish grey, glauconitic, moderately sorted, fine- to medium-grained sand. One cross-bedding measurement indicated transport from the NE.

Kemp (1984b) examined motorway cuttings [4611 1535 to 4716 1526] between Dummer's Copse and Quob Lane, north and NW of West End, and recorded the following composite section in the lower 12.9 m of the Earnley Sand:

	Thickness m
Nummulites laevigatus Bed: Sand, green-brown, dense, fine- and medium-grained, decalcified at outcrop but originally fossiliferous	3.30
Sand, dark grey, dense, fine-grained, glauconitic, with abundant *Nummulites laevigatus* and *Venericor planicosta*, with many other small molluscs	2.88
Sand, dark grey and green, clayey, fine-grained, glauconitic and decalcified except just below cemented sandy concretions which occur in the upper part; there, the abundant concentrated molluscs included *Venericor planicosta*, *Macrosolen sp.*, *Turritella sulcifera*, with common *N.laevigatus* and vertebrate remains	1.32
Palate Bed: Clay, dark green-grey, sandy, stiff, very glauconitic, with pockets of green fine-grained sand, intensely bioturbated throughout, originally fossiliferous with many decalcified moulds of *Venericardia sp.*, and abundant vertebrate remains including teeth of the sharks *Jaekelotodus trigonalis*, 'Lamna' *lerichei*, *Eugomphodus macrotus*, and abundant *Nipa* fruit remains	3.31
Turritella Bed: Sand, blue-green, clayey, glauconitic, with abundant crushed molluscs dominated by *Turritella spp.*, *Cardita sp.*, and vertebrate remains, particularly teeth of the shark 'Lamna' *lerichei* and reptile bones	0.55
Callista Bed: Sand, dark grey-green, clayey, very dense, slightly glauconitic, with abundant slightly crushed molluscs, principally *Callista proxima*, *Cardita spp.*, *Pitar sp.*, *Turritella spp.*, and vertebrate remains, mainly teeth of sharks and rays including *Eugomphodus spp.*, 'Lamna' *sp.*, *Scyliorhinus spp.*, *Galeorhinus sp.*, *Myliobatis striatus* and many fish teeth	1.25
Clay, dark grey-green, sandy, indurated with stiff grey clay, rare glauconite in shelly patches. Sharp base on Wittering Formation	0.30

Fine-grained gravel was recorded from near the base of the formation in boreholes [4626 1527, 4682 1531] west of Quob Farm, West End. A shell-bed (?Callista Bed) near the base, penetrated in a borehole [4627 1534] in Dummer's Copse, contained *Sigmesalia fasciata* and *Turritella* gr. *imbricataria*. Dinoflagellates from the same horizon are indicative of the *comatum* or a younger zone. A shaft [4683 1531] dug for a sewerage pipeline penetrated, just above the base of the formation, the Callista Bed with *Callista proxima bruxellensis*, *Sigmesalia sp.*, *Turritella sp. indet* and *Venericor* cf. *planicosta*.

At Moorgreen, a borehole [4770 1492] penetrated 12.5 m of Earnley Sand beneath 10.4 m of Marsh Farm Formation. The Earnley Sand was mainly greyish green, glauconitic, slightly clayey to very clayey, fine-grained sand and contained abundant *Nummulites laevigatus* 3.8 to 6.1 m below the top. The same interval yielded *Corbula spp.*, *Crassostrea sp.*, *Euspira sp.*, *Sigmesalia sp.*, *Crassostrea*

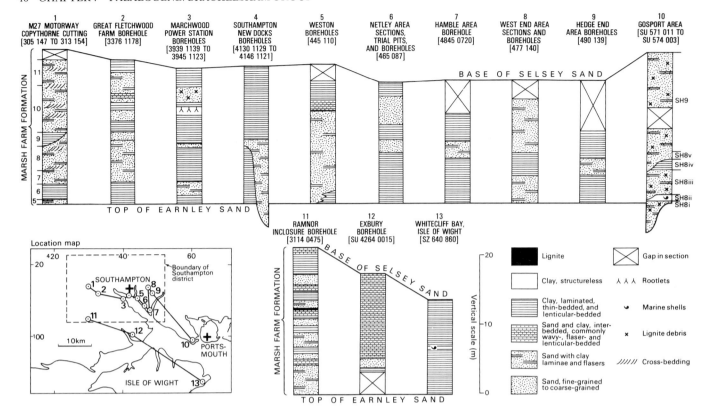

Figure 24   Lithological variation of selected sections in the Marsh Farm Formation of the Hampshire Basin. Bed numbers and section in column 1 are after King and King (1977), and bed numbers and section in column 10 are after King and Kemp (1982)

sp., *Turritella sp.*, and *Venericardia elegans*. Dinoflagellates include *Areoligera undulata*, *Homotryblium oceanicum* and *Turbiosphaera magnifica* which indicate an *arcuatum* or younger zone.

The Shamblehurst Borehole [4927 1456] penetrated 20.95 m of Earnley Sand, mainly greenish grey glauconitic, bioturbated, clayey silty very fine-grained sand, and clayey sandy silt. The lowermost 9.6 m is very fossiliferous, and the Callista Bed, Cardita Bed, Turritella Bed, Palate Bed, and Nummulites laevigatus Bed can be recognised. The sequence is summarised in Appendix 1.

Marchwood–Southampton Docks–Hound

The Marchwood Borehole [3991 1118] was uncored, but geophysical logs and cuttings indicate that the Earnley Sand was 32.3 m thick, penetrated between depths of 63.4 to 31.1 m. The formation was greyish green to bright emerald-green, fine- to medium-grained sand, very glauconitic in parts, especially between 51.5 and 44.5 m. Bivalves, gastropods, and scaphopods were reported but not identified; specimens of *Nummulites laevigatus* were recovered from 42.4 m.

Excavations [3930 1260 to 3940 1225] for the King George V graving dock exposed part of the Earnley Sand, estimated to be up to 18 m thick. The following section [c.393 124], adapted from that given in Wrigley (1933), rests on Wittering Formation:

	Thickness m
Sand, grey, clayey, with *Nummulites laevigatus* abundant throughout, and *Anomia, Calyptraea, Corbula, Natica* and *Venericardia elegans* abundant in the upper part	7.62
Sand, firm, green, clayey, containing similar molluscs to the overlying bed, with the addition of *Callista* aff.	

proxima; the lower part contains spherical concretions about 0.9 m across   6.10

Later excavations and boreholes [3950 1222 to 4151 1120] along the new dock wall (Anderson, 1933), extending from the King George V graving dock towards the older part of Southampton, showed the lower part of the Earnley Sand to be apparently unfossiliferous, bright green, clayey sand, averaging 9 m thick, that rested on laminated clays of the Wittering Formation. This sand is overlain by about 3 m of extremely fossiliferous, grey and green, sandy clays with abundant *Venericor planicosta* and *Nummulites laevigatus*, less common *Turritella imbricataria* in the upper part, and abundant *Macrosolen hollowaysii* in the lower part. *Macrosolen* is most abundant and best preserved in the spheroidal calcareous concretions, 0.9 to 1.2 m in diameter, which are common at this stratigraphical level. Similar concretions have been encountered during dredging in Southampton Water, and examples are displayed on the Royal Pier, Southampton.

Near Hound, a pit [4792 0865] worked for moulding sand exposes over 3 m of yellowish green and greyish yellow, highly glauconitic, bioturbated, slightly clayey fine-grained sand with some disrupted layers of laminated clay. Moulds of molluscs are common, including *Macrosolen hollowaysii* and *Venericor planicosta*.

Chilling

The full thickness of the Earnley Sand was cored in the Chilling Farm Borehole [5098 0443] between 41.5 and 25.9 m depth. The formation is predominantly greyish green glauconitic silty to very silty variably clayey fine-grained sand, locally with an abundant bivalve and gastropod fauna. *Nummulites laevigatus* is present near the top of the formation (27.5 to 26.4 m depth).

MARSH FARM FORMATION

The Marsh Farm Formation (King and King, 1977) crops out in an area stretching from Nomansland in the north-west through Totton and Southampton Docks to Warsash in the south-east (Figure 19). In the extreme north-west of the district the formation rests on the lithologically similar Wittering Formation; both formations pass westward into fluvial sands of the Bournemouth Group in the Fordingbridge district. A similar passage into Bournemouth Group sands occurs in the subcrop between the Ramnor Inclosure Borehole and Barton on Sea. It is probable that the Marsh Farm Formation does not extend farther west than the Brockenhurst area, although the Parkstone Clay of the Bournemouth–Poole area (Freshney and others, 1985) is probably equivalent to it. At Alum Bay in the Isle of Wight the formation is represented mainly by palaeosols, although some laminated clay is also present.

The Marsh Farm Formation contains two main lithologies in the present district; variably carbonaceous laminated clays with laminae and thin beds of fine-grained to very fine-grained sand and silt; and fine-grained to locally coarse-grained, sparsely glauconitic sand with a variable number of clay beds and laminae. Different sections show considerable variation in the proportions of the sand-dominant and clay-dominant facies (Figure 24). The base of the formation is usually well defined; laminated clay or fine-grained, sparsely glauconitic sand rests with marked lithological contrast on the highly glauconitic Earnley Sand.

Over most of the Southampton district the formation is 18 to 25 m thick. Elsewhere in the Hampshire Basin, it is 21.3 m thick at Gosport (King and Kemp, 1982), 13.5 m thick at Whitecliff Bay and 11.6 m thick at Selsey.

The formation shows rapid lateral and vertical variations in the proportions of sand and clay present. These variations are similar to those in the Wittering Formation, and can occur within lateral distances of a few tens of metres (Figure 25). At some localities the lithological changes are gradational, but elsewhere they are sharp, and sand is channelled into clay. Within the district there is a general facies change from sand-dominant west and north-west of the Calmore area to clay-dominant in the area of Southampton Docks and Fawley. Sand is again dominant in the Gosport area south-east of the district boundary (Figure 24). The sands are coarsest-grained in the north-west of the district and at Gosport, and finest-grained in the Ramnor Inclosure Borehole. The carbonaceous clays of the formation are almost silt- and sand-free, but most other clays are very silty or sandy.

Borehole data from the subcrop area at Marchwood, Fawley and Exbury and at Parkhurst and Whitecliff Bay in the Isle of Wight (Figure 24) suggest that laminated clays are the dominant lithology in the Marsh Farm Formation in the central part of the Hampshire Basin.

The laminations in the Marsh Farm Formation clays are usually 1 to 3 mm thick with the silt or sand partings commonly only one or two grains thick. The lamination is commonly lenticular; the lenticles vary from <1 cm to several centimetres in length and from <1 mm to 10 mm in thickness. Where a lenticle pinches out a silt or sand parting usually continues. Cross-lamination is commonly present within the thicker lenticles. Silt and sand lenticles have a distinct linearity that probably developed normal to the local current direction. Streaks of lignitic debris are common at the contact of the sand and clay.

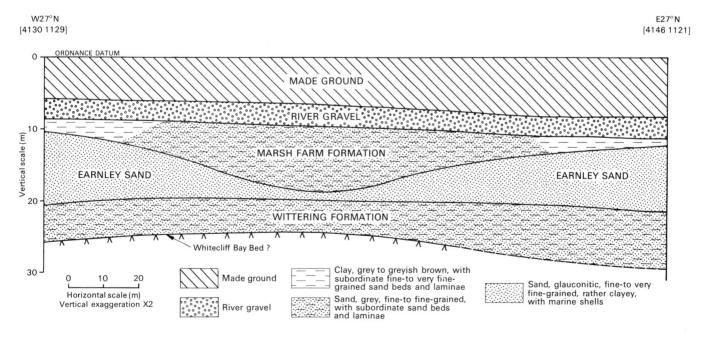

Figure 25   Cross-section through Marsh Farm Formation, Earnley Sand, and upper Wittering Formation at Southampton Docks

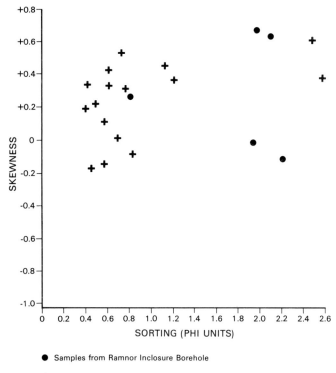

● Samples from Ramnor Inclosure Borehole

+ Other samples

Figure 26 Scatter-plot of skewness against sorting for Marsh Farm Formation sands of the Southampton district. See text, this page, for explanation

The coarser fractions of the clays consist mainly of very poorly sorted quartz ranging in size from 6.5ϕ to 1.0ϕ. The smaller grains are mainly angular to subangular and the larger are usually subrounded. Glauconite is commonly sparsely present, and fine-grained carbonaceous debris and marcasite are common.

Clay-mineral analyses of samples from the Ramnor Inclosure Borehole show the formation to consist of an illite > kaolinite > smectite assemblage in the lower part and an illite > smectite > kaolinite assemblage in the upper. Kaolinite contents of up to 35% occur in the lower part and smectite contents of up to 30% occur in the upper part.

The sands and silts of the formation at outcrop are dominantly quartz with sparse glauconite, and range in mean grain size from medium-grained sand (1.45ϕ) to fine- to very fine-grained sand (3.02ϕ). In the Ramnor Inclosure Borehole, however, the mean grain sizes are appreciably lower (mostly 4.5 to 6.4ϕ — coarse to medium-grained silt). The sand ranges from moderately sorted to well sorted in the Cadnam, Southampton city, and Gosport area, to poorly to very poorly sorted in the Ramnor Inclosure Borehole, with the skewness in both areas being mainly positive with a few negatively skewed samples (Figure 26). The sand grains range from angular to subrounded, the fine-grained sands being mainly angular to subangular. Some carbonaceous debris is commonly present, and occasionally some mica.

Most of the heavy minerals belong to Associations B and C of Morton (1982) and were derived from the south and the west respectively; the upper part of the formation contains an increasing proportion of Association A minerals derived from the north-east.

In the sand-dominant parts of the formation, such as in the Copythorne cutting of the M27 motorway and at Gosport, ripple, planar and trough cross-bedding are common, with the clay layers showing wavy and flaser bedding (King and King, 1977; King and Kemp, 1982). Megaripples and a conglomerate of clay clasts were recorded by King and Kemp (1982) at the base of a sand-filled channel at Gosport. Few exposures show sub-equal proportions of laminated clay and sand, but this combination is common in boreholes, including the Ramnor Inclosure Borehole. Thin sand units in that borehole show planar and cross-lamination. At Alum Bay, the Marsh Farm Formation contains lenticular-bedding, wavy-bedding, flaser-bedding and bipolar ripple lamination with crests oriented E–W (Plint, 1983).

Macrofossils are very rare in the Marsh Farm Formation. East of the district, at Gosport, King and Kemp (1982) noted turritellids low in the formation, and at Whitecliff Bay, Isle of Wight, a marine intercalation in the middle of the formation contains *Nummulites laevigatus* (Murray and Wright, 1974). The bivalves *Modiolus* and *Ostrea*, and the gastropod *Potamides cinctus*, all brackish-water tolerant, have been recorded near the southern edge of the district at Fawley (Curry and others, 1968). Elsewhere in the district the fauna is mainly confined to agglutinated foraminifera and sponge spicules (King and King, 1977). Trails 1 to 2 mm wide and subvertical burrows 3 to 10 mm in diameter are fairly common. The trails are in some examples connected to the burrows.

The pollens of the Marsh Farm Formation belong to form genera indicative of tropical rain forests; some appear to be related to modern mangrove swamp genera. One level, at about 212 m depth in the Ramnor Inclosure Borehole, contains a high proportion of *Tiliaepollenites* and is a useful floral marker level in the formation.

Conditions of deposition

The sedimentary and faunal characters of the Marsh Farm Formation suggest deposition in intertidal environments, possibly in lagoons or estuaries or in the interdistributary bays of a delta.

The lateral passage on a small scale from sand-dominant to clay-dominant lithologies probably indicates local variations in current strength. Sand-filled channels in the clays at Southampton Docks and Gosport are probably tidal channels. At Gosport, east of the Southampton district, the coarseness of the sand, and the presence of trough cross-bedding and mega-ripples led King and Kemp (1982) to suggest that the sands filled a distributary channel on a tide-dominated delta top.

In the western part of the district, King and King (1977) recorded channels plugged with clay at Copythorne. The occurrence there of agglutinating foraminifera indicates that the channels were still tidal. Farther west the Marsh Farm Formation passes into the fluviatile sands and subordinate clays of the Bournemouth Group. In the south-western part of the New Forest, the mixed sand and clay lithologies penetrated in the Ramnor Inclosure Borehole pass south-westwards into mainly fluviatile lithologies with palaeosols.

At Alum Bay, palaeosols are associated with intertidal clays. In the eastern part of the Hampshire Basin the presence of glauconitic shelly sands in the middle part of the formation indicates the presence of an open-marine environment in that area. Plint (1982) has suggested that a barrier separated this environment from the intertidal environments of the Southampton district, but the results of the present survey do not confirm this.

Figure 27 shows a suggested palaeogeography, in which much of the Hampshire Basin was the site of a large tidal basin that opened out to the sea in the south-east. Progradation in the Isle of Wight caused the development of palaeosols on pre-existing tidal flat sediments, while in the Bournemouth area it caused an influx of fluviatile sands which may have developed into deltas. The heavy minerals suggest derivation of most of the coarser sediments from the south and west, but with time an increasing amount of northerly-derived material appeared.

It is probable that the muddy tidal flats and scattered sand shoals of the central part of the basin were crossed by river-fed tidal channels that drained the area of fluviatile sedimentation that lay to the north-west and west. The sequence proved in the Ramnor Inclosure Borehole consists of a generally fining-upward succession upon which are superimposed 2 to 4 m thick coarsening-upward cycles. The overall fining-upward trend indicates a reduction of current velocity which may relate to progradation of a shoreline; the cycles may have been caused by short term, possibly seasonal, increases in the velocity of tidal currents (cf. Terwindt, 1971).

Details

Nomansland – Copythorne

The formation consists of 20 to 25 m of dominantly fine-, medium- and coarse-grained sands, commonly with dark grey clay and silt bands. Units of greyish brown laminated clay are present, but appear to be laterally impersistent. Exposures are extremely rare. The formation gives rise to pale grey sandy soils which underlie much of the open heathland of Plaitford Common, Canada Common, Furzley Common, and Cadnam Common.

An outlier of Marsh Farm Formation on Black Hill was proved in a piston-sampler borehole [2956 1781] to consist of 3.6 m of yellowish brown, medium-grained sand.

The following section was exposed in a small disused sandpit [2845 1529] on Cadnam Common:

	Thickness m
Soil, dark brown, sandy, with flints	0.3
Clay, very sandy, yellowish brown to grey	0.6
Interbedded sand and clay	0.3
Sand, white, clay-free, fine- to medium-grained	0.3

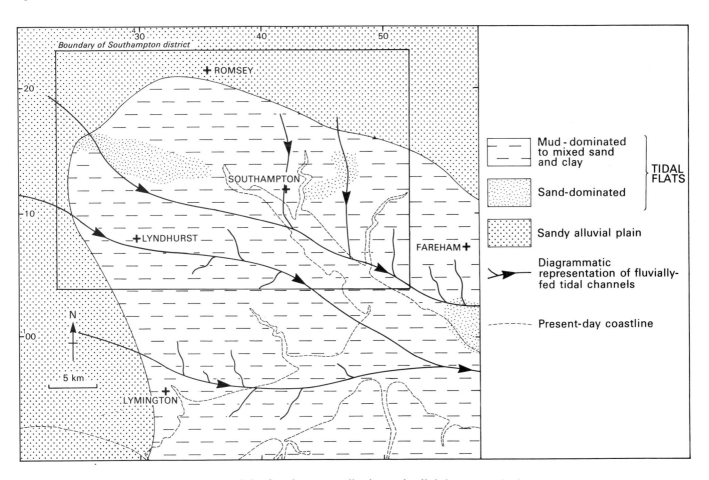

Figure 27 Possible palaeogeography of the Southampton district and adjoining areas during deposition of the Marsh Farm Formation

During the construction of the Copythorne cutting [c.305 147 to c.313 154] of the M27 Motorway, up to 21 m of Marsh Farm Formation was exposed. The section given below, and using their bed numbers, was recorded by King and King (1977). A generalised graphic section is given in Figure 23.

Bed No.		Thickness m
11	Sand, fine- to medium-grained, cross-bedded; with occasional dark organic laminae	3.68
10	Sand, interbedded, cross-bedded to laminated, fine- medium- and coarse-grained, with dark grey plant-rich silty and clayey laminae throughout. Ripple, planar and trough cross-bedding common, silt and clay laminae commonly wavy-, flaser- and convolute-bedded. Very rare tubular sand-filled burrows	6.90
9	Silt, clayey; and clay, silty, grey, thin-bedded and laminated. Only locally present, probably fills a channel	0 – 2.00
8	Sand, as Bed 10	5.42
7	Sand, grey, fine- and medium-grained, with occasional dark greyish brown silty organic-rich laminae, and some low-angle bedding	2.00
5	Sand, grey, medium-grained, with dark grey wavy- and flaser-bedded organic silty clays. Sharp base on Earnley Sand	0.46

All the beds are decalcified; plant debris is common in beds 5 to 10 and includes fruits and seeds; the seed *Scirpus lakensis* is common in Bed 6. One sample from Bed 6 yielded rare agglutinating foraminifera (*Ammodiscus sp.*, and *Trochammina sp.*), and rare pyritised centric diatoms (*Coscinodiscus sp.*). Pyritised and siliceous sponge spicules (*Geodia sp.*), and megasclere spicules are common in Bed 6.

Grain-size analyses of seven samples from beds 7 to 11 indicate a mean size range between 1.45 and 2.78ϕ (medium- to fine-grained sand). The fine-grained sands are moderately well sorted and the medium-grained sands well sorted. Skewness is variable but most samples are fine-skewed.

In the Bunker's Hill Borehole [3038 1498], Marsh Farm Formation was penetrated from ground level to 8.82 m depth. The lower beds (8.82 to 7.62 m depth) are dominantly brownish grey laminated clays, interbedded sands and clays, and greenish grey extremely sandy clays. These beds are tentatively correlated with beds 5 and 6 of the M27 Copythorne cutting section (Figure 23). The topmost 7.62 m were not cored, but consist of yellowish brown fine- to medium-grained sand with some scattered lignitic debris. The base of the sand is apparently channelled into the underlying clay.

Netley Marsh

A graphic log, compiled from cuttings and a gamma-ray log, of a borehole [3376 1178] at Great Fletchwood Farm is shown in Figure 24. The borehole contains proportionately more laminated clay than do the sections at and west of Copythorne.

Marchwood

Boreholes [3939 1139 to 3945 1123] on the site of Marchwood Power Station show complex lateral lithological changes within distances of tens of metres from predominantly laminated clay to predominantly sand with a few clay beds and laminae. A zone of high sand content with an alignment around WSW–ENE may represent a sand-filled channel cut through laminated-clay-rich beds. The Marchwood site shows a continuation of the trend towards a more clay-rich facies in an easterly direction.

Southampton Docks

Strata penetrated in boreholes [4130 1129 to 4146 1121] on the site of Southampton New Docks are shown in Figure 25. There is evidence of channelling; one sand-filled channel, probably with a near E–W trend, cuts down through the underlying Earnley Sand almost to the Wittering Formation. Away from this channel, boreholes show the succession to consist dominantly of laminated clays with thin beds and laminae of very fine-grained to fine-grained sand.

Netley area

A composite section compiled from a road cutting exposure [4652 0879], sequences proved in trial-pits [4682 0889 and 4695 0898] and wells [4634 0818 and 4651 0778] at Royal Victoria Hospital is shown in Figure 24. The lower part of the sequence consists mainly of laminated clays, and has been worked for brick making. This passes up into an upper sequence of fine-grained sand with clay laminae. A similar sequence is present in a borehole [4845 0720] beside the River Hamble.

West End – Hedge End

An outlier of Marsh Farm Formation at West End is associated with the north-facing steeper limb of the Portsdown Anticline, and an outlier at Hedge End is associated with its attendant syncline.

A pit [4718 1405] at West End exposes 2 to 3 m of buff fine-grained sand with scarce thin clay laminae. Sections [47675 1394 and 4775 1400] near Hickley Farm exposed fine-grained sand with many clay layers. At the first of these, some of the clay layers are disrupted to form a clay-clast conglomerate with flat pebbles. Similar lithologies were seen at the top of a shaft [4709 1494] north of West End where up to 3 m of sand with clay layers rested on glauconitic Earnley Sand.

Laminated clays are dominant in the outcrop that extends from Moorgreen Hospital towards Hedge End. Many of the site-investigation boreholes from the M27 Motorway in that area showed sequences of laminated clays with layers and partings of fine-grained sand. This lithology occurred overlying Earnley Sand in a shaft [4990 1326] and in nearby boreholes [490 139] (Figure 24).

Ramnor Inclosure Borehole

The Marsh Farm Formation sequence proved in the Ramnor Inclosure Borehole [3114 0475] is summarised in Figure 24. The lithologies of those parts of the sequence that were washed away during drilling have been deduced from the gamma-ray log. Sand with thin layers and laminae of clay dominates the sequence, although not to the same extent as at Copythorne. The borehole sequence is carbonaceous at some levels and contains one lignite band; traces of gas were encountered during drilling.

Fawley area

The sequences proved by extensive drilling and in a tunnel under Southampton Water from Fawley [SU 477 028] to Chilling [501 041] were described by Curry and others (1968). Only the upper 18 m of the Marsh Farm Formation was penetrated in the boreholes; it consists of very stiff, pale olive to pale olive-grey, sandy clay with thin beds and laminae of sand with some lignite and shell fragments (Bed A of Curry and others, 1968).

Chilling

The full thickness of the Marsh Farm Formation was cored in the Chilling Farm Borehole [5098 0443] between 25.9 and 8.5 m depth. (Appendix 1). The lower 9.2 m is predominantly brownish olive-grey to olive-grey clay with partings, impersistent laminae, and a few thicker beds of very fine-grained sand and silt. Near the base of the formation low gamma-ray counts indicate that a core loss between 25.56 and 22.07 m was probably sand. The upper 8.2 m of the formation was mostly uncored; the gamma-ray log and cores indicate that this interval is predominantly sand, possibly with a few clay beds or intervals of interbedded sand and clay.

SELSEY SAND

The Selsey Sand consists dominantly of glauconitic, bioturbated, commonly shelly, sandy silt to silty fine-grained sand with a variable clay content. Greenish grey and olive-grey clays with a high silt and sand content also occur. Carbonate concretions are common at certain levels.

Selected lithological sequences in the Selsey Sand of the district together with biostratigraphical correlations with selected sections elsewhere in the Hampshire Basin are given in Figure 29.

The base of the formation is taken at a transgression surface that marks an abrupt lithological change from Marsh Farm Formation laminated clays or sands with clay layers, to glauconitic Selsey Sand; the basal bed is locally pebbly. The upper boundary of the Selsey Sand is diachronous with respect to the recorded range of the foraminifer *Nummulites variolarius*.

The Selsey Sand shows vertical and lateral variations in the relative amounts of clay and sand, but no regional pattern of change has been detected. A lithologically distinctive very fine-grained sand with an abundant nummulitid microfauna occurs in the topmost part of the formation in an area stretching from Studley Wood, near Fritham in the north-west of the district, to Parkhurst in the Isle of Wight.

The Selsey Sand crops out in a belt that stretches from Nomansland in the west via Netley Marsh, Marchwood and along Southampton Water to Chilling in the south-east (Figure 22). The formation is 50 m thick in the Ramnor Inclosure Borehole; elsewhere in the district it is between 30 and 50 m thick. Tentative isopachytes for the Selsey Sand are shown in Figure 28. These indicate the presence of a NW–SE-trending depositional basin south-west of which the marine Selsey Sand apparently passes into the fluviatile and intertidal upper part of the Bournemouth Group.

The sands which form the bulk of the formation are composed mainly of subrounded to subangular quartz with variable amounts of glauconite, silt, and clay. The Selsey Sand is characterised in its lowest part by an influx of heavy minerals of northerly origin (Association A of Morton, 1982). This association is replaced first by Association B, of

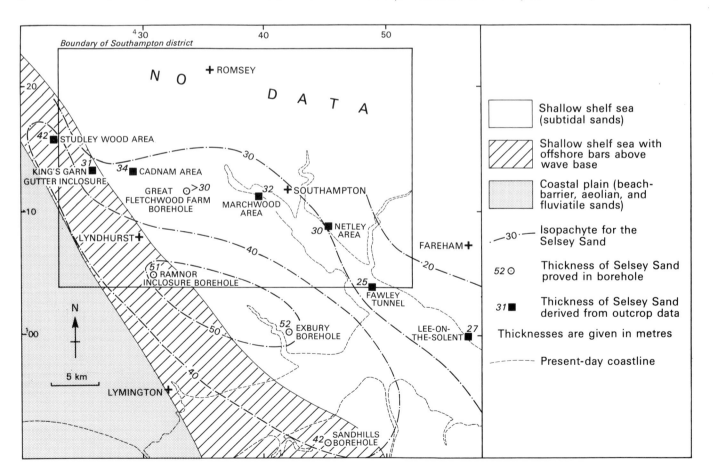

Figure 28 Isopachyte map and possible palaeogeography of the Southampton district and adjoining areas during deposition of the Selsey Sand

Armorican origin, and then, in the top part of the formation, by Association C of Cornubian origin.

The mean grain size of the sands and silts varies between 3ϕ and 5ϕ (fine-grained sand to medium-grained silt). The coarsest sands occur in the western part of the district at the top of the formation; they show the best sorting (0.6ϕ to 0.75ϕ) and the lowest skewness values ($+0.15$ to $+0.36$). The silts and silty sands that make up most of the formation are poorly sorted ($>1.0\phi$) and strongly positively skewed ($> +0.5$).

Bedding structures are rarely visible owing to intense bioturbation, but Plint (1983) recorded cross-bedding from near the base of the formation at Whitecliff Bay, Isle of Wight.

The $2\mu m$ clay fractions of samples from the Ramnor Inclosure Borehole consist mainly of illite > smectite > kaolinite assemblages. Kaolinite contents are low (10%) at the base of

the formation, rise to around 20% in the middle and fall to around 15% towards the top. The coarser clastic content of the clays consists mainly of poorly sorted angular to subrounded quartz grains ranging in size from 3.8ϕ to 1.2ϕ. Glauconite is very common, both as well rounded grains and as globular aggregates. Marcasite is fairly common, and mica occurs sparingly. Shell debris is common and lignite debris is rare. The clays are strongly bioturbated and seldom show lamination.

The formation contains an abundant and diverse marine macrofauna in which bivalves and gastropods are especially common and bryozoans, solitary corals, cephalopods, scaphopods, serpulids and fish are also present.

Fisher (1862) described several units with characteristic fossil assemblages, which he named in ascending order the 'Brook Bed', 'Shepherds Gutter Bed' and 'Hunting Bridge Bed', in the upper part of the Selsey Sand within the New

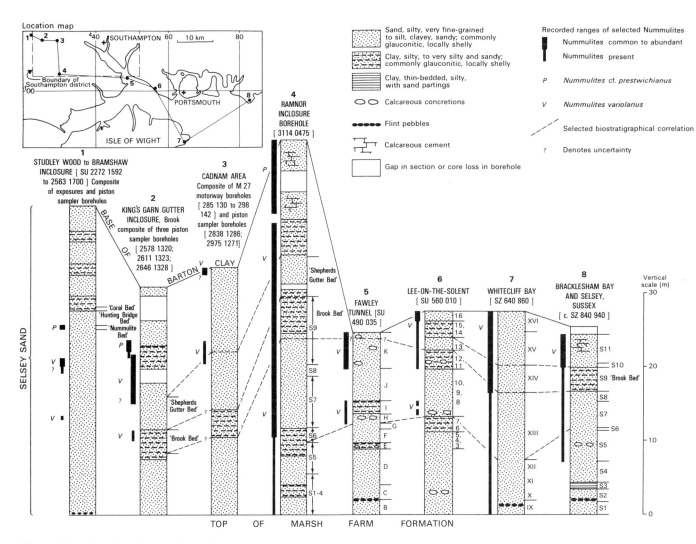

Figure 29 Stratigraphy and correlation of selected sections in the Selsey Sand of the Hampshire Basin.

In column 4, faunal units S1 to S9 indicate correlation with similarly numbered units at Bracklesham Bay; in column 5, section and bed letters are after Curry and others (1968); in column 6, section and bed numbers are after Fisher (1862); in column 7, section is after Fisher (1862) and Plint (1983) and bed numbers after Fisher (1862); and in column 8, section and bed number are after Curry and others (1977)

Forest of the present district. The faunal characters of these 'beds' have been shown to be laterally persistent over large areas in the Hampshire Basin, making them useful for correlation (Figure 29).

The Brook Bed was named by Fisher (1862, p.83) from the village of Brook, south-west of which were small exposures [2631 1352] (now mainly concealed) in the banks of King's Garn Gutter. Most of the earlier rich fossil collections were obtained by digging special pits adjacent to the stream (e.g. Elwes, 1887). The best exposures at present are in the banks [2662 1326] of Coalmeer Gutter, just above its junction with King's Garn Gutter (Stinton, 1970). The Brook Bed is 3 to 5 m thick in the type area and consists of very sandy clay and clayey sand. It contains an abundant fauna, and Elwes (1887) noted that 135 species had been recorded. It is distinguished by the great abundance of the bivalve *Corbula* (*Varicorbula*) *wemmelensis* in its upper part, the abundance of the gastropod *Turricula attenuata* (elsewhere rare), and the presence of the gastropod *Athleta* (*Volutospina*) *horridus* and *A.*(*V.*) *nodosus*. Other characteristic species include the gastropods *Sassia expansa*, *Tibia* (*Eotibia*) *sublucida*, and *Turricula inarata*.

Faunas characteristic of the Brook Bed have been recognised elsewhere in the district in boreholes in King's Garn Gutter Inclosure (p.57) and in the Ramnor Inclosure Borehole (p.58). Outside the district the Brook Bed fauna is represented in beds L and (in part) K in the Fawley Transmission Tunnel (Curry and others, 1968); in Bed 13 of Fisher (1862) at Lee-on-the-Solent; in Bed 19 of Fisher (1862) at Bracklesham Bay (= Unit S9 of Curry and others, 1977) and in Bed XIV of Fisher (1862) at Whitecliff Bay (Figure 29).

In the New Forest, the Brook Bed is succeeded upward, either directly or after an interval of about 8 m of relatively unfossiliferous strata, by the Shepherds Gutter Bed, named by Fisher (1862) from small exposures [262 153] in the banks of Shepherds Gutter west of Bramshaw. The bed, 6 to 8 m thick, consists in the type area of sandy clay and dark grey clayey sand. The most characteristic species are the coral *Paracyathus*, the gastropods *Clavilithes contabulatus*, *Crassispira* [*Drillia*] *fisheri*, *Eopleurotoma scalarata*, and *Leptoconus* [*Conus*] *diversiformis*, and the bivalve *Crassatella lineatissima*. Small exposures [2604 1537 to c.2630 1500] are visible in the banks of Shepherds Gutter. The Shepherds Gutter Bed was penetrated in boreholes in King's Garn Gutter Inclosure and in the Ramnor Inclosure Borehole. Its representatives elsewhere in the Hampshire Basin include Bed M of the Fawley Tunnel section (Curry and others, 1968), Bed 16 of Fisher (1862) at Lee-on-the-Solent, and Bed 22 of Fisher (1862) at Bracklesham Bay (= Unit S11 of Curry and others, 1977). About 4 to 10 m above the Shepherds Gutter Bed in the New Forest is the Hunting Bridge Bed of Fisher (1862) (Huntingbridge Bed of Curry, 1958). The 'bed' was named from small stream bank exposures [c.251 143] in King's Garn Gutter near a locality (not named on the map) called Hunting Bridge. This 'bed' could not be found at this locality during the recent survey. Better exposures, described by Stinton (1970), are visible just west of the district boundary in the banks [2272 1592] of the Latchmore Brook

at the north end of Studley Wood. Characteristic fossils, listed by Curry (in Whittard and Simpson, 1958), are the gastropods *Ectinochilus planum*, *Galeodea calantica* and *Vermetus* cf. *cancellatus*, the scaphopods *Antalis grandis* and *Dentalium sp.*, and the bivalves *Bicorbula gallica*, *Costacallista laevigata* and *Miocardia isocardioides*. Elwes (1887) found 60 species at Hunting Bridge, of which 25 were different from species found in the Brook Bed.

Just below the Hunting Bridge Bed at the type locality and at Studley Wood is a thin (c.0.5 m) bed (the 'Nummulite Bed' of Stinton, 1970) containing abundant nummulitids referred by Stinton to *N.* cf. *prestwichianus*. Just above the Hunting Bridge Bed at Studley Wood a bed with the coral *Paracyathus* was called the 'Coral Bed' by Stinton (1970). Fisher (1862) described a similar bed with corals and '*Dentalia*' at the type locality.

The microfauna and microflora of the Selsey Sand include common foraminifera, ostracods, and dinoflagellates. Species of *Nummulites* common at certain levels can be useful indicators of stratigraphical level. *Nummulites variolarius* is common in the middle and upper part of the Selsey Sand. Two varieties of *N. variolarius* were recognised by Norvik (1969), and in the present survey; both are referred to here as *N. variolarius*. The name 'Nummulites variolarius Bed' has been widely used since its introduction by Fisher (1862), but it has never been precisely defined and is of limited stratigraphical value. The nummulite has been recorded sporadically throughout the lower part of the Selsey Sand in the Ramnor Inclosure Borehole, at Whitecliff Bay and at some other localities in the Hampshire Basin, but does not become abundant until the middle or upper part of the formation (Figure 29). The upper limit of its recorded range lies in the lower part of the Barton Clay at some localities. Nummulitids which are flatter than *N. variolarius* occur just below the Hunting Bridge Bed at the type locality, in the Studley Wood Nummulite Bed, and in an 11 m thick bed of calcareously-cemented sand at the top of the Selsey Sand in the Ramnor Inclosure Borehole. The Hunting Bridge Bed nummulites were referred to as a variety of *N. prestwichianus* by Curry (1937), and the Studley Wood nummulites to *N.* cf. *prestwichianus* by Stinton (1970). The Ramnor Inclosure specimens are similar but not conspecific with those from Hunting Bridge and Studley Wood. All these forms are referred here to *N.* cf. *prestwichianus*.

The Selsey Sand in the Ramnor Inclosure Borehole yielded dinoflagellates indicative of the *laticinctum*, *intricatum* and *arcuatum* Zones (Figure 6). At Slowhill Copse [3872 1148] near Marchwood, specimens from beds high in the Selsey Sand are indicative of the *intricatum* Zone.

In the Studley Wood area, Selsey Sand lithologies are present up to 21 m above the highest recorded *Nummulites variolarius*, at King's Garn Gutter similar lithologies occur up to 9 m above the highest recorded *N. variolarius*, and at Cadnam, *N. variolarius* occurs in typical Barton Clay. In the Ramnor Inclosure Borehole, the beds between the highest *N. variolarius* and the base of the Barton Clay consist of fine-grained sand. At Fawley, Lee-on-the-Solent, Whitecliff Bay and Selsey, the upper limit of *N. variolarius* is close to or spans the Selsey Sand – Barton Clay junction.

Conditions of deposition

The Selsey Sand is lithogically and sedimentologically similar to the Earnley Sand and is thought to have been deposited in similar environments in a shallow shelf sea with summer surface temperatures between 15° and 20°C. As in the Earnley Sand, shell concentrations in the Selsey Sand were possibly formed by storms. Lamination and herring-bone cross-lamination, recorded at Whitecliff Bay, may indicate intertidal conditions and tidal currents respectively. Figure 28 shows a suggested palaeogeography in which a NW–SE elongated arm of the sea had unrestricted access to open sea to the south-east. To the west and south-west lay an area of coastal beach-barrier, aeolian and fluviatile sands as suggested by Plint (1983). These sands were separated from the main body of the marine Selsey Sand by a belt of *Nummulites*-rich sand that is coarser grained, better sorted and more symmetrical in its grain-size distribution than the bulk of the Selsey Sand. These coarser grained sands are interpreted as having been deposited in an elongate mobile sand bar whose top was affected by the winnowing action of waves. No sediment has survived on the north-eastern side of the Selsey Sand depositional basin and the position of the shoreline in that direction is unknown. The lower part of the formation contains northerly-derived heavy-mineral assemblages that might indicate the presence of a NW-trending shoreline; higher parts of the formation contain southerly and westerly derived heavy-mineral assemblages that suggest the presence of a barrier to the north-east, perhaps caused by a rise of the Wealden and/or the Portsdown anticlines, that interrupted the heavy-mineral supply. This barrier was broken down during the deposition of the Barton Group.

Details

Studley Wood – Bramshaw Inclosure (Nomansland)

About 40 m of Selsey Sand, consisting of yellowish brown-weathering, greenish grey and green, bioturbated, glauconitic, extremely clayey silty sand, and sandy silt that grades into extremely silty sandy clay in many places, crops out in the Studley Wood area. About 450 m west of the district boundary, exposures [SU 2272 1592] near the headwaters of the Latchmore Brook, Studley Wood, have been described by Stinton (1970, pp.272–273), and Kemp and others (1979, fig. 5); the following section is a composite based on data from both publications.

	Thickness m
Coral Bed	
Clay, silty, sandy, with the coral *Paracyathus* and large calcareous annelid tubes	0.45
Clay, silty, sandy	1.60
Hunting Bridge Bed	
Silt, sandy; and silty sand, with abundant large specimens of *Antalis grandis*, *Turritella sulcifera*, *Thylacodes ornatus*, and numerous other molluscan species including *Bicorbula gallica* and *Spondylus rarispina*. Base glauconitic and locally pebbly	2.40
Nummulite Bed	
Silt, sandy, with common well preserved small molluscs, fish remains and other fossils; numerous examples of *Nummulites* cf.*prestwichianus*	seen 0.45

A cross section constructed between Bur Bushes [SU 2184 1618] in the Ringwood district and Bramshaw Inclosure [2563 1700] indicates that the Studley Wood Nummulite Bed lies 4 to 5 m above the upper limit of *N. variolarius* in that area. This upper limit was recorded in a seismic shothole [SU 2184 1618] at Bur Bushes. Just south of Appsey Copse, a piston-sampler borehole [2380 1627] penetrated the following strata:

	Thickness m	Depth m
BARTON CLAY		
Clay, very sandy	5.5	5.5
SELSEY SAND		
Sand, pale olive-grey and pale olive-brown, extremely clayey, silty	1.5	7.0
Clay, dark greenish grey, bioturbated, extremely silty, sandy, with patches of dark grey sand	1.0	8.0

The dinoflagellates from 8.0 to 7.7 m depth, *Areoligera undulata* and *Areosphaeridium multicornutum*, are indicative of the *intricatum* Zone. The Barton Clay yielded dinoflagellates indicative of the *porosa* Zone.

Shelly, greyish green, extremely clayey sand transitional to extremely sandy clay, in a stream exposure [2422 1643] in Ashens Hat, about 28 m below the top of the Selsey Sand, yielded *Nummulites* cf. *variolarius*. The dinoflagellates indicate the presence of the *coleothrypta* and *intricatum* zones on the presence of *Areoligera undulata*, *Areosphaeridium multicornutum*, and *Kisselovia coleothrypta*.

A piston-sampler borehole [2507 1686] near Nomansland proved, beneath 1.2 m of drift, shelly extremely sandy clay with patches of green clayey sand to 7.7 m depth. A sample from 7.7 to 7.3 m depth contained a few *N. variolarius*, and dinoflagellates that indicate the *intricatum* Zone. The same sample contained the serpulid *Ditrupa sp.*, the bryozoan *Orbitulopora petiolus*, the gastropods *Athleta (Volutospina) nodosus*, *Euspira sp.*, *Gemmula plebeia*, *Rissoina puncticulata* and *Sveltella microstoma*, and the bivalves *Barbatia appendiculata* and *Corbula wemmelensis* (abundant). A sample from 3.9 to 3.5 m depth contained abundant ostracods (not identified), and a very small number of nummulites, referred to *N.* cf. *prestwichianus*. A sample from 2.85 to 2.40 m depth contained the same macrofossils as the sample from 7.7 to 7.3 m, with the addition of the coral *Paracyathus sp.* and the bivalve *Lentipecten corneus*. The presence of the latter two species indicates a correlation with the Shepherds Gutter Bed.

Bramshaw – Brook

In Shepherds Gutter, Bramshaw, the Nummulite Bed (containing *N.* cf.*prestwichianus* as at Studley Wood) was recorded by Stinton (1970) in a trial boring [2604 1537], about 30 m upstream of the road bridge. Much of the section shown in Figure 30 (modified from Stinton, 1970, with additional observations) is visible in small exposures [2609 1535 to c.2680 1507] in the stream banks downstream from the road bridge; the remainder has been proved in auger holes. The section includes the type area of the Shepherds Gutter Bed (Fisher, 1862).

A temporary excavation [2695 1544] near Bramshaw Forge showed up to 2.0 m of very fossiliferous, greenish grey, extremely sandy clay with bands of dusky yellowish green, extremely clayey glauconitic sand. Fossils recorded included the corals *Paracyathus sp.*, adhering to *Clavilithes* and *Lentipecten* fragments, and *Turbinolia sp.*, the annelid *Protula extensa*, the bryozoan *Orbitulopora petiolus*, the gastropods *Clavilithes longaevus*, *Conomitra sp.*, *Gibberula [Marginella] bifidoplicata*, '*Pleurotoma*' *sp.*, *Turritella* aff. *conoidea*, *T. contracta*, and *T. sulcifera*, and the bivalves *Cardita sp.*, *Corbula wemmelensis* (common), *Crassatella sp.*, *Lentipecten corneus* (abundant), *Nemocardium* cf.

parile, and *Ostrea sp*. The abundance of *Lentipecten corneus* combined with the occurrence of *Turritella contracta* indicate that this exposure correlates with the basal *Lentipecten*-rich part of the Shepherds Gutter Bed. The dinoflagellates *Areoligera undulata* and *Areosphaeridium multicornutum* indicate the presence of the *intricatum* Zone.

Three piston-sampler boreholes were drilled in King's Garn Gutter Inclosure, near Brook; the composite sequence proved is given in Figure 29, together with the distribution of nummulitids. Thicknesses are uncertain owing to difficulties in correlating the three boreholes. In the stratigraphically lowest [2646 1328] of the three boreholes, the presence of *Eotibia sublucida* and *Athleta* (*Volutospina*) *nodosa* in the basal samples at 9.75 to 9.15 m depth indicates correlation with the interval 192 to 186 m (just below the Brook Bed) in the Ramnor Inclosure Borehole. Samples from between 7.35 and 5.75 m depth yielded a few *N. variolarius*. Samples from 6.95 to 6.15 m contain *Ditrupa sp.*, and compare with the interval 183 to 181 m (upper part of the Brook Bed) in the Ramnor Inclosure Borehole.

In the second borehole [2611 1323], samples from 7.35 to 5.55 m contain frequent to abundant *Lentipecten corneus* which, together with the associated fauna, including attached *Paracyathus sp.*, indicates correlation with the Shepherds Gutter Bed. *N. variolarius* is present in samples from 7.35 to 3.75 m depth.

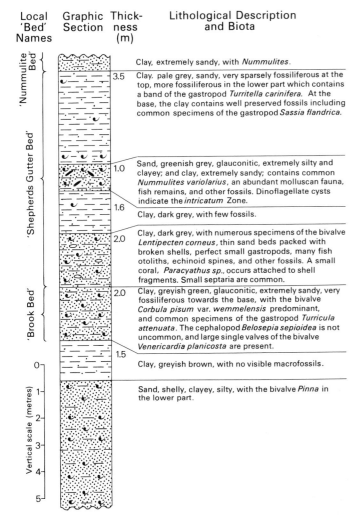

Local 'Bed' Names	Graphic Section	Thickness (m)	Lithological Description and Biota
'Nummulite Bed'			Clay, extremely sandy, with *Nummulites*.
		3.5	Clay, pale grey, sandy, very sparsely fossiliferous at the top, more fossiliferous in the lower part which contains a band of the gastropod *Turritella carinifera*. At the base, the clay contains well preserved fossils including common specimens of the gastropod *Sassia flandrica*.
'Shepherds Gutter Bed'		1.0	Sand, greenish grey, glauconitic, extremely silty and clayey; and clay, extremely sandy; contains common *Nummulites variolarius*, an abundant molluscan fauna, fish remains, and other fossils. Dinoflagellate cysts indicate the *intricatum* Zone.
		1.6	Clay, dark grey, with few fossils.
		2.0	Clay, dark grey, with numerous specimens of the bivalve *Lentipecten corneus*, thin sand beds packed with broken shells, perfect small gastropods, many fish otoliths, echinoid spines, and other fossils. A small coral, *Paracyathus sp.*, occurs attached to shell fragments. Small septaria are common.
'Brook Bed'		2.0	Clay, greyish green, glauconitic, extremely sandy, very fossiliferous towards the base, with the bivalve *Corbula pisum* cf. *wemmelensis* predominant, and common specimens of the gastropod *Turricula attenuata*. The cephalopod *Belosepia sepioidea* is not uncommon, and large single valves of the bivalve *Venericardia planicosta* are present.
		1.5	Clay, greyish brown, with no visible macrofossils.
			Sand, shelly, clayey, silty, with the bivalve *Pinna* in the lower part.

Vertical scale (metres): 0, 1, 2, 3, 4, 5

Figure 30 Section in the Selsey Sand, poorly exposed in the banks of Shepherds Gutter, Bramshaw [2604 1537 to c.2680 1507], modified after Stinton (1970)

In the stratigraphically highest borehole [2578 1320] two distinct nummulitid assemblages are present: samples from the bottom of the borehole at 9.65 m to 8.50 m yielded almost exclusively *N. variolarius*, but samples from the overlying strata (8.50 to 6.15 m depth) contain dominantly *N.* cf. *prestwichianus* with a gradual downward increase in the proportion of *N. variolarius* between 8.50 and 7.40 m. A similar distribution of nummulitid species was recorded in the uppermost Selsey Sand (171 to 160 m depth) of the Ramnor Inclosure Borehole. The presence of *N.* cf. *preswichianus* indicates correlation with the Studley Wood Nummulite Bed and the Hunting Bridge Bed. A diverse macrofauna, including *Lentidium sp.*, and '*Bittium*' *sp.*, in samples from 9.65 to 6.15 m, indicates the same correlation.

As reported by Stinton (1970, p.273), the Brook Bed is visible in the banks [2662 1326] of Coalmeer Gutter near its junction with King's Garn Gutter. It consists of about 0.6 m of very fossiliferous, greyish green, glauconitic clayey silty sand which has yielded dinoflagellates of the *intricatum* Zone, the bryozoan *Orbitulopora petiolus*, the gastropods *Athleta* (*Volutospina*) *nodosus*, *Conomitra sp. nov.*, *Eotibia sublucida*, *Gemmula plebeia*, *Pseudoneptunea sp.*, and *Ptychatractus interruptus*, and the bivalves *Corbula wemmelensis* (abundant), *Crassatella lineatissima*, and *Crassostrea plicata*. The presence of common *Athleta* cf. *nodosus* and *Eotibia sublucida* confirm Stinton's identification of the Brook Bed.

Brook brick-pit [276 140], now disused, shows poor sections in 1.5 to 2.0 m of brown and grey very sandy clay, overlying green very clayey glauconitic sand with the bivalves *Chlamys trigintaradiata*, *Crassostrea* cf. *plicata*, and common *Pinna sp*. Fish remains have also been recorded (Stinton, 1970, p.274). This bed was correlated by Stinton with a bed containing *Pinna* that underlies the Brook Bed in the Shepherds Gutter section (Figure 30); it is probably also equivalent to a bed with abundant *Pinna* in the Fawley Tunnel section (Bed K of Curry and others, 1968).

Cadnam – Copythorne

The Selsey Sand sequence established from site-investigation boreholes [285 130 to 298 142] for the M27 motorway in the Cadnam area consists mainly of glauconitic silty sand and sandy clayey silt, totalling 33.7 m (Figure 29). A 7.95 m-deep piston-sampler borehole [2838 1286] in Shave Green Inclosure proved 6.8 m of Barton Clay resting on 1.15 m of Selsey Sand. The latter consisted of greenish grey, fossiliferous, very clayey silty sand with *Nummulites variolarius*; the same nummulitid occurs in the overlying Barton Clay. A sample (7.95 to 7.20 m depth) from the Selsey Sand contained the bryozoan *Orbitulopora petiolus*, the gastropods *Conomitra sp. nov. subsp.A*, *Crassispira fisheri*, *Euspira sp.*, *Gemmula plebeia*, *Genota pyrgota* and *Turritella imbricataria*, and the bivalves *Corbula wemmelensis* (very common), *Crassatella lineatissima*, *Lentipecten corneus* (very common), and *Venericardia crebrisulcata*. The presence of *Conomitra sp. nov. subsp.A* and abundant *L.corneus* indicates correlation with the Shepherds Gutter Bed.

A piston-sampler borehole [2975 1271], 400 m south of Bartley Lodge, proved greenish grey, shelly, glauconitic extremely clayey silty sand and bioturbated extremely sandy clay with *Nummulites variolarius* present between 6.9 and 4.1 m depth. A rich dinoflagellate flora, including *Areoligera undulata* and *Melitasphaeridium asterium*, indicates the presence of the *intricatum* Zone. A sample from 5.6 to 5.4 m depth yielded the gastropods *Conomitra sp. nov. subsp.A*, *Eopleurotoma gentilis*, *Gemmula plebeia*, *Raphitoma plicata* and *Rissoina puncticulata*, and the bivalves *Corbula wemmelensis*, *Lentipecten corneus*, and *Venericardia crebrisulcata*. A sample from 6.9 to 6.5 m depth contained the bryozoan *Orbitulopora petiolus*, the gastropods *Conomitra sp. nov. subsp.A*, *Crassispira fisheri*, *Gemmula plebeia*, and *Turritella imbricataria*, and the bivalves *Corbula wemmelensis* and *Lentipecten corneus*. The presence of *Conomitra sp. nov. subsp.A* and *L. corneus* in both samples indicates correlation with the Shepherds Gutter Bed.

Marchwood

An excavation [3872 1148] for a boat dock at Slow Hill Copse showed the following section in the Selsey Sand, recorded by Kemp (1984a); bed numbers are those of Kemp:

		Thickness m
SC10	Clay, green, sandy, with some glauconite; contains *Nummulites* and a well preserved mollusc fauna dominated by the bivalve *Lentipecten corneus*	0.70
SC9	Clay, grey-green, sandy, with *Lentipecten* near base	1.02
SC8	Clay, stiff, grey-green, sandy; slightly slickensided contact with SC7; Corbulids common throughout	1.12
SC7	Clay, green, glauconitic, sandy, burrowed at base with abundant well preserved molluscs, some crushed, including *Venericor planicosta*, *Corbula* spp., *Turritella* spp., *Athleta* spp., *Sycostoma* and *Nummulites*. The vertebrates included *Eugomphodus* spp., and *Myliobatis*	0.94
SC6	Clay, stiff, grey, slickensided throughout, burrowed at the base; common small bivalves including *Corbula pisum*; *Nummulites variolarius* present	0.92
SC5	Silt, grey, glauconitic, sandy, clayey;burrowed throughout. Contains bored logs and abundant small Turrids, Corbulids and *Nummulites variolarius*; vertebrates (especially fish otoliths) common	1.26
SC4	Clay, stiff, grey, sandy, with abundant small molluscs including *Corbula*	0.47
SC3	Silt, grey-green, sandy, clayey, with glauconite present throughout; burrowed at base with less abundant molluscs and nummulites	0.60
SC2	Silt, grey, clayey, with *N. variolarius* and abundant molluscs, predominantly *Pinna*, *Corbula*, and *Turritella*	1.20
SC1	Silt, stiff, grey-green, clayey and sandy, glauconite content increasing towards the base; contains abundant well preserved molluscs; some *Nummulites* throughout; a few logs bored by *Teredo* preserved in large spherical concretions well developed in the uppermost 0.4 m	seen 3.25

Beds SC9 to SC10 were correlated by Kemp with Bed M, Bed SC6 with Bed L, and beds SC1 to SC5 with Bed K of the Fawley Tunnel section of Curry and others (1968).

Warsash area

A low cliff [5049 0389] exposes over 2 m of yellow, slightly glauconitic, clayey fine-grained sand. Sand in the upper part of the section contains decalcified concretions with casts of small bivalves and gastropods. Curry and others (1968) correlated this bed (assigned to Bed K of the Fawley Tunnel) with a clay with concretions (Bed 11 of Fisher, 1862) at Lee-on-the-Solent [SU 560 010] in the Portsmouth district.

Fawley Tunnel

The Fawley transmission tunnel under Southampton Water and its associated site-investigation boreholes revealed a complete section through the Selsey Sand (Curry and others, 1968). The top of the Selsey Sand is taken at the top of their Bed K (Figure 29). The formation there is 24.6 m thick, and consists mainly of glauconitic clayey silty fine-grained sand, with calcareous concretions in beds E, H, and K, and common shells, and two beds (E and I) predominantly of silty to very silty and sandy clay.

Ramnor Inclosure Borehole

The full thickness of the Selsey Sand was penetrated between 209.85 and 160.0 m in the Ramnor Inclosure Borehole [3114 0475]; the summary log is given in Appendix 1 and a graphic log in Figure 29. The base of the formation rests with sharp lithological break on clays of the Marsh Farm Formation. The lower 39 m of the sequence consists predominantly of glauconitic silty fine-grained sand, and silt, with sandy silty clay in the upper part. *Nummulites variolarius* is common to abundant between 200 and 172 m depth and then occurs sporadically to the base of the formation. The upper 10 m of the formation consists of almost clay-free, glauconitic, fine-grained sand which is calcareous-cemented between 164.04 and 162.8 m, and contains abundant *Nummulites* cf. *prestwichianus*. The following lithological and faunal units can be correlated with those in the Selsey Sand sequence at Bracklesham Bay described by Curry and others (1977). The numbering follows that of Curry and others.

Units S1 to S4 (209.7 to 205.1 m) contain a poorly preserved fauna including the gastropods *?Calyptraea*, a *?*strombid and *Turritella*, scaphopods, and the bivalves *?Cultellus*, *?*venerids, *Macrosolen hollowaysii* and *Nemocardium*.

Unit S5 (205.1 to 200.8 m) contains protulid worm tubes, the gastropods *Euthriofusus*, *Ficus* cf. *nexilis* and a nacreous archaeogastropod, and the bivalves *Corbula*, *Crassatella*, *Lentipecten corneus* and a venerid.

Units S6 and S7 (S6, 200.8 to 198.8 m; S7, 198.8 to 191.79 m) yielded protulid worm tubes, a bryozoan, the gastropods *Ancilla*, *Calyptraea*, *?Cryptochorda stromboides*, *Eotibia sublucida*, *Euthriofusus* sp., *Galeodea*, *Gemmula* sp., *Globularia* or *Crommium*, *Leptoconus selseiensis*, *Pterynotus* sp., *Turricula attenuata*, *Turritella* cf. *imbricataria*, *Turritella* cf. *sulcifera*, *Volutospina*, and *Xenophora* cf. *agglutinans*, and the bivalves *?Barbatia*, *Calpitaria*, cardiid, *Corbula*, *Crassatella*, *Cultellus* cf. *affinis*, *Lentipecten corneus*, *Nemocardium*, *Nucula*, *Panopea intermedia*, *?*tellinid, and a *?*venerid.

Unit S8 (191.79 to 190.25 m) contains a bryozoan, the gastropods *Eotibia sublucida*, *Leptoconus selseiensis*, *Sassia* sp., *Turritella sulcifera*, and *Volutospina* sp., and the bivalves 'Corbula', an oyster and a venerid.

Unit S9 (190.25 to 181.38 m) includes the Brook Bed; it contained the gastropods *Ancilla*, *Eotibia sublucida*, *Euspira*, *Galeodea* sp., *Gemmula* sp., *Globularia*, *Hemiconus*, *Oxyacrum inflexa*, pyramidellid, *Rimella* cf. *fissurella*, *Stellaxis* cf. *pulcher*, *Sycostoma*, *Turricula* sp., *Turritella sulcifera*, *Volutospina*, and *Xenophora agglutinans* with encrusting foraminifera, and the bivalves *Barbatia*, *Calpitaria*, *Corbula wemmelensis*, *Crassatella* cf. *sowerbyi*, *Cultellus* 'affinis', mytilid, *Nemocardium*, *Nucula*, oyster, and *Pinna*.

The Shepherds Gutter Bed (181.38 to 175.53 m) yielded common *Nummulites variolarius*, a paracyathid coral, bryozoans, the gastropods *Calyptraea*, *?Clavilithes*, *Eopleurotoma obscurata*, *Euspira*, *Fusinus*, *Globularia* cf. *grossa*, *?Leptoconus*, *Mitreola* cf. *labratula*, *Oxyacrum inflexa*, *Pterynotus tricarinatus*, *Sinum clathratum*, *Turritella* cf. *imbricataria*, *Turritella sulcifera*, and *Volutospina athleta*, a scaphopod, and the bivalves *Anomia*, *Bucardiomya*, *Calpitaria*, carditid, *Corbula*,

Crassatella, *Cultellus* cf. *affinis*, *Lentipecten corneus*, *Nemocardium*, *Nuculana*, oyster, pholads in wood, solenid, teredinid pallets, and ?*Thracia*.

The Nummulite Bed (170.98 to 160.0 m) yielded *Nummulites* cf. *prestwichianus*, the gastropods *Ancilla* cf. *canalifera*, *Calyptraea*, ?*Galeodea*, *Hipponyx dilatatus*, an opisthobranch, a scaphopod, and the bivalves *Calpitaria* cf. *sulcataria*, 'Corbula', *Crassatella*, *Tellina*, and a tellinid.

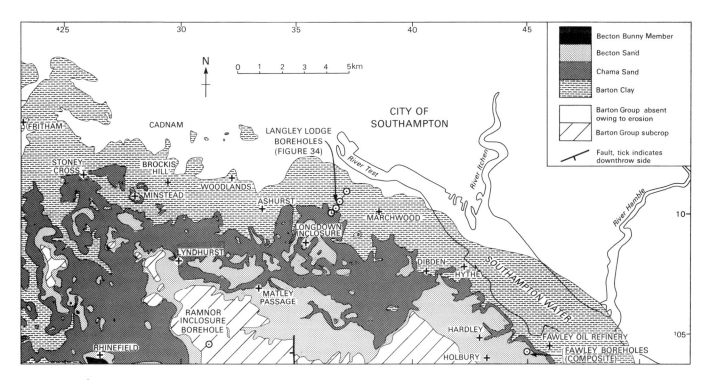

Figure 31 Distribution of the Barton Clay, Chama Sand, Becton Sand, and Becton Bunny Member in the Southampton district, showing also the main localities and boreholes referred to in the text

CHAPTER 8

Palaeogene: Barton Group

The Barton Group can be divided into a lower predominantly argillaceous part referred to as the Barton Clay on the 1899 geological map and the present map, and an upper predominantly arenaceous part referred to as the Barton Sand on the 1899 map and divided into a lower Chama Sand Formation and an upper Becton Sand Formation on the present map. The lower part of the Barton Clay as defined in this memoir includes strata formerly included in the Bracklesham Beds (see p.11). The Becton Sand locally contains a lenticular bed of clay and clayey sand named the Becton Bunny Member. The Barton Group coarsens upward from the Barton Clay via the clayey fine-grained sands of the Chama Sand to the relatively clay-free sands of the Becton Sand. Small coarsening-upward cycles occur within the group and probably result from a number of rapid marine transgressions and slower regressions similar to those that occurred during the deposition of the London Clay. The 3-dimensional relationships of the clays and sands in the Barton Group suggest that a shoreline prograded southeastwards during regressive phases. During the deposition of the Barton Clay this shoreline reached as far east as Fordingbridge and Barton on Sea, but it remained to the west of the Southampton district. It reached the district during deposition of the Chama Sand.

BARTON CLAY

The Barton Clay consists mainly of yellow-weathering, greenish grey to olive-grey, usually bioturbated clay with a variable content of glauconite and very fine-grained sand that occurs scattered throughout the clay and in discrete bands. Where unweathered, the clays are commonly shelly, the upper part of the formation being particularly rich in bivalves and gastropods. The formation crops out in a continuous belt that crosses the district from Fritham to Fawley via Minstead, Ashurst and Hythe (Figure 31).

The base of the formation is taken at an upward increase in clay content in comparison with the underlying Selsey Sand This lithological change is diachronous with respect to the nummulitid and molluscan faunas. In the south-eastern part of the district, in the Cadnam, Ashurst, and Fawley areas, the base of the Barton Clay is difficult to recognise because of the presence of silty glauconitic very fine-grained sand in the lower part of the formation.

The Barton Clay varies in thickness from about 55 to 80 m in the Southampton district, and from about 50 to 90 m in the Hampshire Basin as a whole (Figure 32). The thicker deposits lie beneath the Solent and the Isle of Wight.

There is little lithological variation in the Barton Clay, other than local variations in sand content. When traced south-westwards, the lower part of the Barton Clay is replaced by coastal and estuarine sands (the Boscombe Sand) at Hengistbury Head [SZ 178 904], Dorset (Figure 33). A similar transition occurs between the Southampton district and Alum Bay [SZ 305 855], Isle of Wight.

The clay fractions of Barton Clay samples from the Ramnor Inclosure Borehole show illite and smectite to be dominant over kaolinite at most levels. Very high smectite contents occur at some levels (for example, 60% in the middle part of the formation at 137.1 m depth); contents of up to 45% occur in the middle and upper parts of the formation. Kaolinite contents of the $<2\mu m$ fractions, around 10% at the base, fall to 3% at 137.1 m, but rise fairly steadily to around 20% at the top of the formation. Other analyses from the district confirm Gilke's (1978) conclusion that kaolinite contents decrease eastwards and northwards in the Hampshire Basin and that smectite contents rise in the same directions.

The sand fraction of the Barton Clay consists mainly of quartz which ranges in size from 3.2ϕ to 0.5ϕ m, although the larger grains are rare. The grains are angular to subangular in the smaller grain sizes, and well rounded in the larger. Glauconite is common, usually in the same size-range as the quartz grains, and is mainly rounded to subrounded. At many levels comminuted shell debris and foraminifera are very common.

The lower part of the Barton Clay contains both a zircon-garnet-tourmaline heavy-mineral assemblage of southern origin and a tourmaline-zircon-garnet assemblage of Cornubian origin: interplay between these two sources is highly variable (Morton, 1982). At higher stratigraphical levels in the Barton Clay in the Ramnor Inclosure Borehole, the heavy minerals include garnets and epidotes of northern origin.

The Barton Clay at outcrop in the Southampton district is commonly decalcified and shelly fossils are rarely seen, but unweathered samples from boreholes contain an abundant fauna dominated by bivalves and gastropods. The bivalves include carditids, *Corbulids* and *Crassatella*, and the gastropods include turritellids. Corals, echinoids, serpulids, scaphopods and fish vertebrae and teeth are also present. At Barton on Sea, Burton (1933) divided the bulk of the Barton Clay into 9 'Horizons' lettered A1 to G in ascending order, distinguished on lithological and faunal characters. Most of these 'Horizons' can be recognised in the Ramnor Inclosure Borehole (Figure 33) where the sequence is 50% thicker than at Barton on Sea.

Because of the diachronous nature of the base of the Barton Clay, faunal marker units such as the Hunting Bridge Bed and Coral Bed (p.55) occur in the Barton Clay in the Ramnor Inclosure Borehole and in the Selsey Sand in the north-west of the district (Figure 33). The 'Rimella canalis Bed' of Curry (1942), characterised by the presence of the gastropod *Ectinochilus planum* (formerly *Rimella canalis*), overlies the Coral Bed in the Ramnor Inclosure Borehole. It has not been recognised elsewhere in the district.

Nummulitids occur at several levels in the Barton Clay. *Nummulites variolarius* is mostly confined to the Selsey Sand, but at Cadnam, Fawley and in the Isle of Wight it ranges up into the Barton Clay. The Rimella canalis Bed in the Ramnor Inclosure Borehole yielded very poorly preserved nummulitids referred to by Mr C. King as *Nummulites* cf. *variolarius*. Elsewhere in the Hampshire basin, the Rimella canalis Bed of the Isle of Wight has yielded forms which Curry (1942) termed '*N. variolarius* (Lamarck) *var.*'. *Nummulites prestwichianus* is restricted to a thin (<2m), well defined interval within the Barton Clay that has been recognised at many localities throughout the Hampshire Basin. This level was used by Keeping (1887) to define the base of the Barton Group; it has generally been called the '*Nummulites prestwichianus* Bed', (e.g. Curry, in Whittard and Simpson, 1958). Its distribution in selected sections in the Hampshire Basin is shown in Figure 33; within the Southampton district it has been recorded only in the Ramnor Inclosure Borehole.

Between 2 and 12 m above the recorded highest level of occurrence of *N. prestwichianus* lies a 2 to 9 m-thick interval rich in *Nummulites rectus* (Curry, 1937). The distribution of strata containing *N. rectus* at selected sections in the Hampshire Basin is shown in Figure 33. It was recorded from the Ramnor Inclosure Borehole from a level about 2 m above the highest occurrence of *N. prestwichianus* and was seen in samples from boreholes at Brockis Hill, Cadnam (p.63) and at Woodlands (p.63). This is the highest stratigraphical level

at which nummulitids have been recorded in the Hampshire basin.

Bujak and others (1980) divided the Barton Clay into three dinoflagellate assemblage zones, from top to bottom, the *Rhombodinium porosum* Assemblage Zone, the *Areosphaeidium fenestratum* Assemblage Zone, and the *Heteraulacarcysta porosa* Assemblage Zone. In some Hampshire Basin sections, such as that at Whitecliff Bay, higher zones extend down into the Barton Clay. The *Cyclonephelium intricatum* Assemblage Zone of Bujak and others (1980), which formed their top zone of the Bracklesham Group, lies within the Barton Clay of this account.

The lithological and faunal characters of the Barton Clay and Becton Bunny Member are indicative of deposition below wave base on a marine shelf. The low diversity shelly fauna and the presence of diatoms (Curry and others, 1968) suggest a salinity less than normal for the Barton Clay below the lowest occurrence of *N. prestwichianus*. The presence of silty sand in this part of the formation may indicate an influx of fresh water from the surrounding land areas. In the Ramnor Inclosure Borehole a change in probable salinity occurs just above the upper limit of *N. rectus*, about 35 m above the base of the Barton Clay. This is accompanied by a change in the heavy-mineral assemblages. Mixed Cornubian/Armorican assemblages in the lower part of the formation are replaced at this level by Scottish assemblages. This change probably

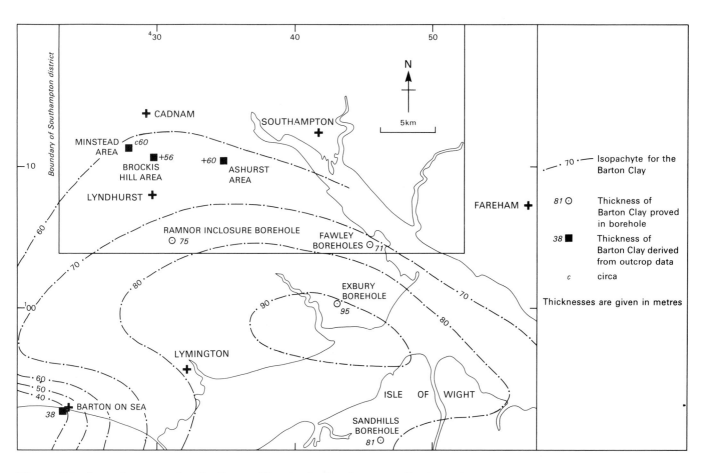

Figure 32 Isopachyte map for the Barton Clay in the Southampton district and adjoining areas

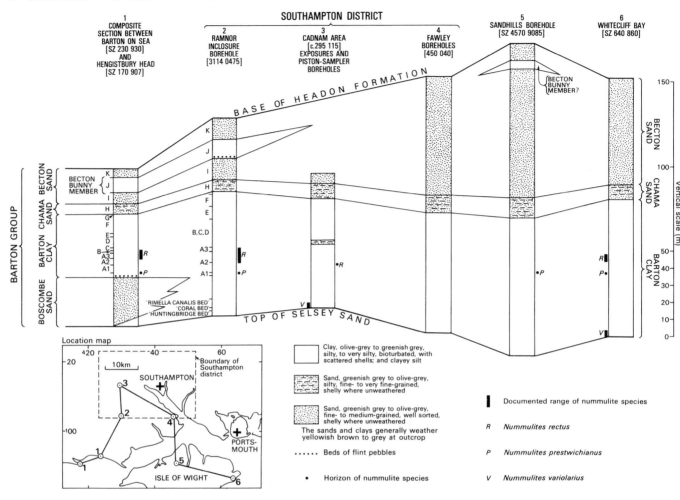

Figure 33 Stratigraphy and correlation of selected sections in the Barton Group of the Hampshire Basin

In column 1, the section above the Boscombe Sand is based on the Barton on Sea section of Burton (1933). Units lettered A to K in the Barton on Sea (column 1) and Ramnor Inclosure (column 2) sections are the faunal 'Horizons' of Burton (1933)

reflects the cessation of sediment supply from the south and west because of the establishment of a stable, linear shoreline which enabled longshore drift to supply northerly-derived heavy minerals. In the early part of the Barton Clay the shape of the shoreline was probably complex, with small rivers emptying into shallow hyposaline embayments that had restricted access to the sea.

Details

Brockis Hill area

A piston-sampler borehole [2955 1148] on Brockis Hill proved the following sequence:

	Thickness m	Depth m
Drift deposits	1.5	1.5
BARTON CLAY		
Sand, pale yellowish brown, pale orange-brown and greenish grey, somewhat clayey, fine-grained	0.2	1.7

Clay, stiff, pale orange-brown and pale olive-grey, very silty and finely sandy	c.2.3	c.4.0
Clay, stiff, olive-grey to dark greenish grey, slightly sandy, with scattered shelly material (very sandy clay from 7.4 to 7.8 m depth)	6.75	10.75

A sample from 10.75 m yielded a dinoflagellate assemblage indicative of the *coleothrypta* and *intricatum* zones. Samples from between 9.60 and 4.85 m yielded *Cordosphaeridium funiculutum*, *Cyclonephelium semitectum*, *Distatodinium paradoxum*, *Hystrichosphaeropsis rectangularis*, *Lentinia serrata*, *Phthanoperidinium levimurum*, *Rhombodinium draco* and *Selenopemphix armata*, indicative of the *draco* Zone. A sample from 6.65 m contained poorly preserved molluscs, partly preserved as pyrite moulds, including the gastropod *Turritella sp.*, and the pteropod *Skaptotion bartonense*. Samples from 10.75 to 7.80 m depth contained agglutinated foraminifera including *Glomospira irregularis*, *Trochammina sp. nov.*, and *Verneuilina sp.*; the last named is present in the Ramnor Inclosure Borehole only in the Barton Clay above the level of occurrence of *N. prestwichianus*. Rare pyritised *Coscinodiscus* were also present. Molluscs from the same interval (10.75 to 7.80 m) were mostly corroded and poorly preserved; they included the gastropod *Conomitra sp.*, the pteropod

Skaptotion bartonense, and the bivalves *Corbula*, *Crassostrea* cf. *plicata* and *Nemocardium sp.*.

A piston-sampler borehole [2960 1163], on the Barton Clay outcrop north of Brockis Hill showed the following strata:

	Thickness m	Depth m
BARTON CLAY		
Clay, weathered, yellowish brown to greyish green, slightly silty	3.70	3.70
Clay, dark greenish grey, sandy to very sandy, with thin bands and patches of very clayey sand	2.75	6.45
Clay, stiff, greenish grey to olive-grey, slightly sandy to sandy, with some rare scattered small shell fragments	3.80	10.25

The nummulite *N.* cf. *rectus* is present in a sample from 4.85 m. Samples from between 6.45 and 4.85 m contained a sparse but well preserved assemblage of calcareous foraminifera including *Brizalina* cf. *cookei*, *Buccella propingua*, *Cibicides fortunatus*, *C. pygmeus*, *C. tenellus*, *Elphidium minutum*, *Fursenkoina schreibersiana*, *Globorotalia danvillensis*, *Globulina gibba*, and *G. gravida*. Between 8.40 to 7.85 m the foraminifera were mainly agglutinated forms: *Trochammina sp. nov.* and large calcareous foraminifera including *Globulina gibba and G. gravida*. The sample at 7.85 m contained the ostracods *Cytherella compressa* and *Cytheretta laticosta*. At 9.4 m a sample contained the foraminifera *Bolivina*, *Cibicidoides*, *Elphidium*, *Fursenkoina*, and *?Globorotalia danvillensis*, the pteropods *Skaptotion bartonense* and *?Spiratella nemoris* and the bivalve *Corbula* (*Varicorbula*) cf. *pisum*.

A piston-sampler borehole [2984 1184] 400 m NE of Brockis Hill penetrated the junction of the Barton Clay and Selsey Sand. The Barton Clay consisted of 3.65 m of yellowish brown to pale grey-weathered slightly sandy to sandy clay with patches of clayey fine-grained sand, overlying 4.75 m of Selsey Sand (greenish grey glauconitic clayey to very clayey sand).

Woodlands area

A piston-sampler borehole [3364 1079] penetrated the following strata:

	Thickness m	Depth m
Sand, buff, very clayey, with some patches of yellow-orange staining and rough banding	2.05	2.05
Sand, olive-grey, very clayey, with some clayey sand bands at the top	0.80	2.95
Sand, greenish buff, clayey, some yellow stain at the top; olive-grey clay bands at the base	0.50	3.45
Clay, extremely sandy, greenish grey, bioturbated, with dark marcasitic stains	1.40	4.95
Clay, greenish grey, marcasite-stained, sandy, plastic, bioturbated, with small sand bodies	1.00	5.95
Clay, greenish grey, sandy, plastic, bioturbated with small sand bodies stained with marcasite	3.10	9.05
Clay, greenish grey, sandy, plastic, bioturbated with sand laminae, stained with marcasite	0.70	9.75

Nummulites rectus was present between 9.05 and 9.75 m. The dinoflagellate flora indicates the *porosum* Zone.

Langley Lodge, Marchwood area

Four piston-sampler boreholes [3650 1021; 3670 1041; 3686 1071; 3714 1112] drilled across the Barton Clay outcrop near Langley Lodge west of Marchwood penetrated the formation from a level approximately 8 m below the lowest occurrence of *Nummulites prestwichianus* to the base of the Chama Sand. The lithostratigraphy and dinoflagellate biostratigraphy of the composite section are shown on Figure 34.

Ramnor Inclosure Borehole

Barton Clay was penetrated between 160.0 and 85.0 m in the Ramnor Inclosure Borehole; a lithological log is given in Appendix 1 and a condensed graphic log is shown in Figure 33, with a suggested correlation with the Barton on Sea section.

The formation consists of dark greenish grey to olive-grey silty to very silty clay, clayey silt, and sandy clayey silt, glauconitic, commonly bioturbated, and with shelly fossils common at many levels. The base is sharply defined by a marked decrease in grain size from

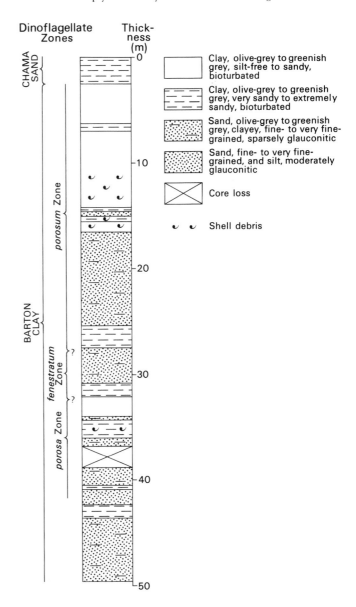

Figure 34 Lithostratigraphy and dinoflagellate biostratigraphy of part of the Barton Group penetrated in boreholes [3650 1021; 3670 1041; 3686 1071; 3714 1112] near Langley Lodge, about 2 km west of Marchwood. See Figure 31 for location of the boreholes

the very fine-grained calcareous sand of the Selsey Sand to sandy clayey silt of the Barton Clay. The beds between this junction and the lowest occurrence of *N. prestwichianus* at 134.8 m represent the 'Huntingbridge Division' of Curry and others (1977). Within this interval the Hunting Bridge Bed (160.0 to 156.4 m) Coral Bed (156.4 to 155.2 m) and *Rimella canalis* Bed (155.2 to 150 m) are present.

The Hunting Bridge Bed yielded the gastropods *Bathytoma*, buccinid (small), *Calyptraea*, cerithiid, *Ectinochilus planum*, *Eopleurotoma* cf. *scalarata*, *Fusinus sp.*, naticid, ?rimellids, *Strepsidura turgida*, ?*Sycostoma* or *Athleta selsiensis*, *Turritella sulcifera*, and *Volutospina* cf. *scalaris*, and the bivalves *Amusium corneum*, ?*Anomia* or *Amusium*, ?*Barbatia*, *Bicorbula gallica*, ?*Calpitaria*, ?cardiid, *Corbula*, *Eosolen plagiaulax*, ?*Limopsis*, *Nemocardium*, oyster, ?*Pinna*, and a large venerid. The Coral Bed contained paracyathid corals, ?opisthobranch and turrid gastropods, a scaphopod, the bivalves *Barbatia*, *Calpitaria*, a carditid, *Chlamys*, ?*Nemocardium*, and *Nuculana*, and fish scales. The Rimella canalis Bed yielded the gastropods ?*Capulus* or *Calyptraea*, *Ectinochilus planum* (formerly *Rimella canalis*), a naticid, a scaphopod, the bivalves *Crassatella*, *Nemocardium* and *Nuculana*, and fish debris. *Nummulites* cf. *variolarius* occurs between 153.80 and 152.45 m.

Nummulites prestwichianus was recorded between 134.8 and 132.9 m, and *Nummulites rectus* between 127.15 and 118.0 m.

Several of Burton's (1933) 'Horizons' were recognised in the borehole in the beds above the level of *N. prestwichianus*. These include Horizon A1 at 134.8 to 132.7 m which yielded a sparse bivalve fauna including *Corbula*, ?*Cubitostrea plicata*, ?*Lentipecten corneus*, *Nuculana*, and oysters. Horizon A2 at 132.7 to c.121 m contained the gastropods *Calyptraea*, ?fusinid, Naticid, *Volutospina sp.*, and ?*Xenophora*, a scaphopod, the bivalves *Calpitaria*, carditid, *Corbula*, *Crassatella*, *Musculus/Crenella*, mytilaceans, *Nemocardium*, *Nucula*, *Nuculana*, oysters, *Venericardia simplex*, and fish otoliths, scales, and bones. Horizon A3 may be represented in the uncored interval 120.2 to 118.4 m.

Horizons B,C, and D are probably represented between c.118 and 101.4 m, but few fossiliferous samples were present. The fauna included the gastropods *Bathytoma*, and *Sycostoma*, and the bivalves ?*Calpitaria*, carditid, *Corbula*, *Crassatella* cf. *sulcata*, *Cubitostrea plicata*, ?*Garum*, *Glycymerita*, *Nuculana*, oyster, and *Pectunculina scalaris*.

Horizon E at 101.4 to 93.8 m contained the serpulid *Ditrupa plana*, the gastropods *Bathytoma turbida*, *Calyptraea*, *Conomitra parva*, naticid, *Sycostoma pyrus*, *Turritella*, *Volutospina* cf. *athleta* and *Xenophora agglutinans* (very common), the scaphopod *Dentalium bartonense*, the bivalves *Calpitaria transversa*, *Cardiocardita sulcata*, carditid, *Corbula*, *Crassatella* cf. *sulcata*, *Cubitostrea plicata*, *Glycymerita deleta*, ?*mytilid*, *Nemocardium*, ?*Orthocardium porulosum*, oyster, and ?tellinid, and a fish vertebra.

Horizon F at 93.8 to 86.4 m contained corals, *Graphularia*, the gastropods *Adeorbis sp.*, *Ancilla canalifera*, architectonicid, *Bathytoma turbida*, ?*Conomitra parva*, *Euspira*, ?*Euthriofusus*, *Hippochrenes* (very juvenile), opisthobranch, *Rimella*, *Sycostoma* cf. *pyrus*, turrids, *Turritella sp.*, *Turritella* intermediate between *edita* and *imbricataria*, *Volutospina* cf. *luctator*, and *Xenophora* cf. *agglutinans*, the scaphopod *Dentalium bartonense*, the bivalves *Anomia sp.*, *Calpitaria*, carditids, *Corbula*, *Crassatella*, *Cubitostrea plicata*, *Nucula*, *Nuculana*, tellinid, and echinoid fragments.

Horizon G, a thin shell bed in the coastal exposures, is not represented in the borehole. The base of Horizon H at 85 m is the base of the Chama Sand.

CHAMA SAND

The Chama Sand consists of greenish grey to grey, slightly glauconitic, clayey silty very fine-grained sand and extremely sandy clay. At Barton on Sea, it is equivalent to Horizon H of Burton (1933). Where unweathered, it is commonly shelly; *Chama squamosa* and turritellid gastropods are the commonest fossils. The formation is highly bioturbated. It remains lithologically uniform throughout the Hampshire Basin. The base of the Chama Sand is taken at a change from relatively sand-free clay (Barton Clay) to glauconitic clayey sand (Chama Sand). This junction commonly gives rise to a topographical feature and a spring line. The formation coarsens upward into the Becton Sand.

The Chama Sand shows little variation in thickness in the Hampshire Basin. In the Southampton district it is 8 to 12 m thick in the Lyndhurst area, 7 m thick in the Ramnor Inclosure Borehole, 9 m thick at Fawley, 11 to 12 m thick in the Dibden to Longdown Inclosure area and may locally be 15 m thick west of Lyndhurst. On the Isle of Wight the thickness varies between 4.5 m at Whitecliff Bay and 7 m at Alum Bay.

The clay-mineral assemblages of the Chama Sand are a continuation of the illite-smectite-kaolinite assemblages of the Barton Clay, and maintain the upward increase in kaolinite content. Smectite replaces illite as the dominant mineral at the top of the Chama Sand. A small amount of vermiculite is also present.

The coarser-grained clastic material of the Chama Sand is dominantly quartz with some glauconite. The quartz grains are angular to subrounded and the glauconite is subrounded. Mica is also fairly common, with flakes up to 200 μm occurring at some levels in the Ramnor Inclosure Borehole. Mean grain sizes range between 3.3ϕ and 5ϕ. Sorting is moderately good to very poor (0.5 to 2.3ϕ). Grain-size distributions are strongly positively skewed ($+0.5$ to $+0.8$).

The heavy minerals of the Chama Sand fall within Association A of Morton (1982), a garnet-epidote assemblage derived from a northern metamorphic basement.

The Chama Sand is mostly decalcified at outcrop, but yielded many bivalves including *Chama squamosa*, species of *Cardita* and *Crassatella* and gastropods such as *Turritella* cf. *edita*, in the Ramnor Inclosure Borehole. Surface exposures such as the road cutting [2514 1135] near Stoney Cross yielded *Chama squamosa* and *Athleta solandri* and seismic shot holes [247 072] in the Knightswood area also yielded *Chama squamosa*.

The relatively high permeability of the Chama Sand and the consequent more intense weathering of the formation causes the yield of dinoflagellates to be poor except in boreholes. The Chama Sand usually lies within the *Homotryblium variabile* Assemblage Zone of Bujak and others (1980), although at Whitecliff Bay, Isle of Wight, the Chama Sand lies in the zone above, that of *Polysphaeridium congregatum*.

The Chama Sand was probably deposited below fair-weather wave base on a lower shoreface. This is indicated by the poor sorting of the sands, the strong positive skewness of their grain-size distributions, and their shelly fauna.

Details

Stoney Cross Plain

Road cuttings [2488 1121 to 2523 1140] on the west side of Stoney Cross Plain showed exposures of Chama Sand, partly beneath Older River Gravels and Made Ground. A section [2514 1134] in one cutting showed the following strata:

	Thickness m
Sand, orange- and buff-weathered, very clayey, silty very fine-grained	2.0
Sand, greyish green, clayey, silty, very fine-grained, with somewhat calcareous concretions of pale greenish grey very fine-grained sand, containing oyster shells and moulds of other fossils	1.0 seen

Casts made from the fossil moulds using latex rubber show finely detailed ornaments. The following fauna was identified: the poorly preserved foraminifera *Cibicides ungerianus*, *Globulina gibba* and *Pararotalia? inermis*, the gastropods *Athleta* cf. *solandri*, *Bathytoma sp.*, *Eopleurotoma sp.*, *Globularia patula*, naticid indet., *Pollia lavata*, *Rimella rimosa* (common), *Surculites sp.*, and *Volutocorbis scabricula*, scaphopod fragments (common), and the bivalves *Cardiocardita* cf. *sulcata*, *Chama squamosa*, *Chlamys sp.*, *Corbula sp.*, *Cubitostrea plicata* (abundant), and *Panopea sp.*

Ramnor Inclosure Borehole

Chama Sand was penetrated between 85 and 78 m depth in the Ramnor Inclosure Borehole and is correlated with Horizon H of the Barton on Sea section (Burton, 1933). A generalised graphic log and correlation with other sections is shown in Figure 33; a detailed log is given in Appendix 1. The formation consists of highly bioturbated greenish grey clayey very fine-grained sand to coarse-grained silt. Shelly debris is common and the following fossils were identified: foraminifera, corals, the serpulid *Ditrupa*, bryozoa, the gastropods *?Alvania/Turboella*, *Ampullonatica ambulacrum*, ancillid, *Bathytoma*, *Bittium*, *Bonellitia*, *Calyptraea*, *Euspira*, *?Euthriofusus*, *Hemiconus scabriculus*, *Hemipleurotoma sp.*, *Marginella*, naticid, *Pollia*, *Rimella rimosa*, *Rimella sp.*, *Ringicula*, rissoid?, *Roxania*, *Sycostoma pyrus*, *Tornatellaea simulata*, *Turritella* cf. *edita*, *?Unitas*, *Volutocorbis scabricula*, and *Volutospina* cf. *luctator*, the scaphopod *Dentalium*, the bivalves *?Anomia*, *Barbatia*, *Cardita*, *Chama squamosa*, *Chlamys*, *Corbula*, *Crassatella* cf. *sulcata*, *Cubitostrea plicata*, *Glans oblonga*, *Nuculana*, *Ostrea*, *Pectunculina scalaris*, and a solenid, and fish spines.

BECTON SAND

At outcrop, the Becton Sand consists of yellow- to pale grey-weathering, well sorted, fine-grained to very fine-grained sand. At Barton on Sea it was divided by Burton (1933) into three Horizons—I, J, and K in ascending order. Well developed cross-bedding is present at a few localities. Where unweathered in boreholes, the sand is greenish grey, and the lower part is bioturbated and shelly. Burrowed horizons have been recorded in the Becton Sand in coastal sections elsewhere in the Hampshire Basin (for example, Burton's (1933) Horizon I at Barton on Sea) but the sections within the Southampton district are too deeply weathered for these to have been recognised. In that part of the district west and south-west of Lyndhurst a laterally impersistent clay and clayey sand (the Becton Bunny Member) can be mapped in the middle part of the formation (Figure 31).

The sand below the Becton Bunny Member contains slightly more clay than that above it. Flint pebbles, usually well rotted and well rounded, occur near Holbury and have been reported from near Lyndhurst and at Matley Passage [335 070] (Reid, 1902). Fossil rootlets occur in the upper part of the sand in the Ramnor Inclosure Borehole.

The junction of the Chama and Becton sands cannot be precisely defined because in unweathered sections there is a gradational upward decrease in clay content from the Chama Sand into the Becton Sand over a vertical distance of several metres. For practical purposes when mapping the boundary between the two formations it was found that the plasticity of the sand was a good guide to its clay content. Sand that could not be moulded by hand was classified as Becton Sand. The junction is easier to place in geophysical logs that are sensitive to variations in clay content.

The Becton Sand varies in thickness in the Hampshire Basin, being 93 m thick in the Sandhills Borehole [SZ 4570 9085] in the Isle of Wight and less than 20 m thick in parts of the present district (Figure 35). The greatest thickness variations occur in the sand below the Becton Bunny Member; the upper sand shows little variation. The thickest sequence proved in the present district, 71 m at Fawley Oil Refinery, contains several beds of clayey fine-grained sand and extremely sandy clay. Similar clay bands are present in the thick Sandhills Borehole sequence.

Clay-mineral assemblages from the Becton Sand penetrated in the Ramnor Inclosure Borehole show a gradual upward reduction in smectite and a corresponding upward rise in illite contents. An abnormally high smectite content of 44% occurs in the middle part of the formation. Kaolinite levels are relatively constant at around 15%.

The sand fractions of the Becton Sand are composed dominantly of angular to subrounded quartz. Mean grain sizes vary between 2.4ϕ and 3.7ϕ and sorting from very well to moderately sorted (0.18ϕ to 0.90ϕ) (Figure 36).

Where unweathered, the formation contains grains of well rounded glauconite. Mica flakes are common, particularly in the upper sand where they are up to 500 μm across, together with fine-grained lignitic debris. The heavy-mineral assemblages are characterised by garnet and epidote derived from a northern source.

The Becton Bunny Member is confined within the present district to a small area of outcrop around Rhinefield, south-west of Lyndhurst. It was also proved in the Ramnor Inclosure Borehole and appears to be present in a well [SU 4264 0015] at Exbury in the adjacent Lymington district. At outcrop, it consists of highly bioturbated, carbonaceous, clayey, very fine-grained sand and silt that passes eastward into clay-free sand. In the Ramnor Inclosure Borehole it consists of shelly sandy clay and clayey very fine-grained sand and silt that is lithologically similar to the Barton Clay.

The Becton Bunny Member is thickest between Exbury and the Ramnor Inclosure Borehole (Figure 35). The sand in the Becton Bunny Member is similar in composition to the rest of the formation but is finer grained and less well sorted. Mean grain size averages 4.3ϕ and the sorting is poor (average 1.6ϕ).

At outcrop the Becton Sand is unfossiliferous, probably due to decalcification, but in the Ramnor Inclosure Borehole the lower sand and the Becton Bunny Member yielded a moderately diverse fauna (listed in the details of the Ramnor Inclosure Borehole), mainly of bivalves and gastropods, indicative of shallow marine conditions. Although bioturbated, the upper sand contains no shelly fauna and the only organic remains are rootlets.

The Becton Sand yields few dinoflagellates because the sands at outcrop are usually intensely weathered, and only in the Ramnor Inclosure Borehole were good floras recovered. In this borehole all the floras belonged to the *Wetzeliella* (*R.*) *perforata* Zone of Costa and Downie (1976).

The Becton Sand is fine grained to very fine grained, well sorted and exhibits low positive to negative skewness. Comparison of the sorting/skewness scatter-plots (Figure 36) for samples of Chama Sand and Becton Sand shows a transition from one sand to the other. The lower part of the Becton Sand (equivalent to Burton's (1933) Horizon I) was probably deposited on the middle to upper shoreface. The Becton Sand sorting/skewness field probably reflects a gradual reduction in current winnowing with the increasing water depth, to a limit at around +0.80 skewness. Further increases in depth bring about a rapid decrease in sorting and a passage into the Chama Sand sorting/skewness field. In the central part of the Hampshire Basin, for example in the Ramnor Inclosure and Sandhills boreholes, clay-rich beds within the Becton Sand, including the Becton Bunny Member, resulted from minor transgressions. The grain-size characteristics, lack of shelly material, presence of bioturbation, and the occurrence of rootlet beds and fine-grained lignite debris indicate that the Becton Sand above the Becton Bunny Member was deposited on the upper shoreface and beach. It is possible that some aeolian sand is also present.

Details

Lyndhurst area

East of Lyndhurst an old, largely degraded sand-pit [3084 0800] shows several exposures of yellow and orange, fine-grained sand with some lamination, planar cross-bedding, and possible trough cross-lamination. Yellow fine-grained sand was augered in the floor of a nearby disused sand-pit [3346 0692].

Fawley area

Near Hardley a sand-pit [4258 0402] showed the following section:

	Thickness m
?SLIPPED HEADON FORMATION	
Clay, greenish grey, very sandy	0.3
BECTON SAND	
Sand, yellowish green, fairly clayey, with a little mica and some carbonaceous reddish brown seams at the base	1.4
Sand, yellow, orange and buff, fine-grained, with bands of hard ferruginous sand and very micaceous	

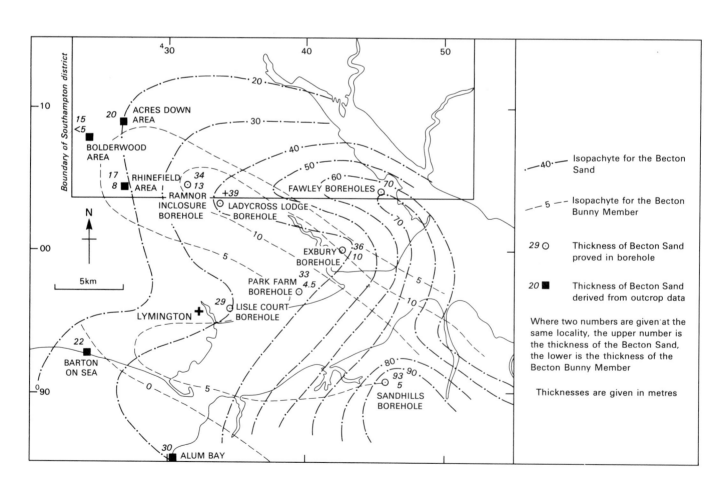

Figure 35 Isopachyte map for the Becton Sand and Becton Bunny Member of the Southampton district and adjoining areas

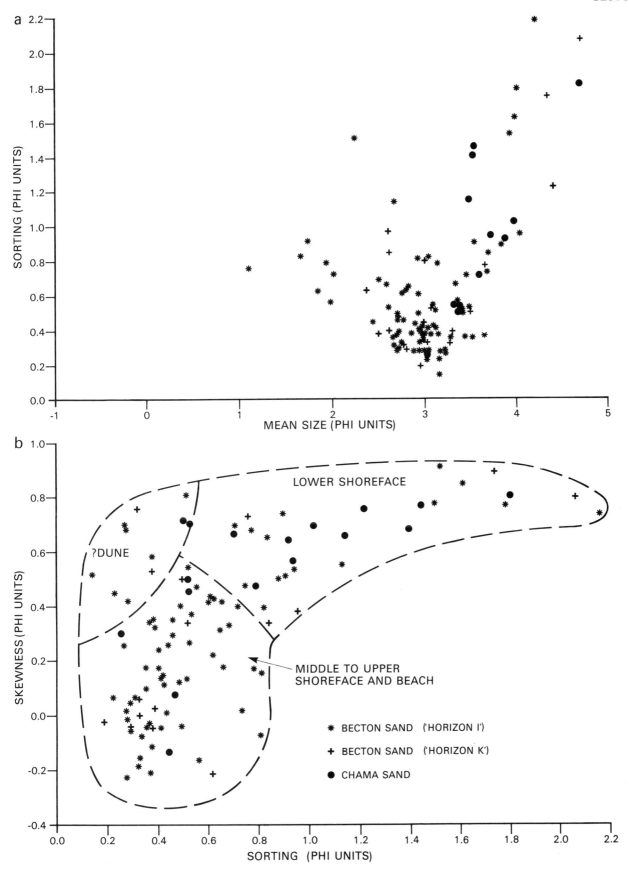

Figure 36 Scatter plot of (a) sorting against mean size and (b) skewness against sorting for the Becton Sand. See text, p.66, for explanation

	Thickness m
band. A few rotten flint pebbles. Planar cross-bedding indicates sand transport from 220°, 240° and 030°	6.4

A cutting [4549 0419] for an oil installation at Fawley Station showed the following Becton Sand sequence beneath c.2.0 m of very sandy gravel:

	Thickness m
Sand, greenish yellow, poorly laminated, clayey, with clay layers and layers containing clay clasts	0.8
Sand, yellow, fine-grained, with ferruginous layers and many joints and fractures containing ferruginous material	6.0

Ramnor Inclosure Borehole

A condensed log of the Becton Sand is given in Appendix 1. A number of gaps due to core loss occur in the section but the gamma-ray log suggests that these are occupied by sand. Suggested correlation with the Barton on Sea section is indicated in Figure 33.

Becton Sand was penetrated in the Ramnor Inclosure Borehole between 78.0 and 40.4 m depth. Three members are present; a lower sand member (78.08 to 65.68 m), correlated with Horizon I of the Barton on Sea section (Burton, 1933); a middle member (65.68 to 53.85 m), the Becton Bunny Member, correlated with Horizon J of the Barton on Sea section, and consisting of shelly clay and sand; and an upper sand member (53.85 to 40.40 m), correlated with Horizon K of the Barton on Sea section.

The topmost part of Horizon I (72.4 to 66.7 m) was mostly uncored, but geophysical logs indicate that sand was present. The cored lower part (78.0 to 72.4 m) consists of shelly silty very fine-grained sand. Horizon I is decalcified in the Barton on Sea section, but in the Ramnor Inclosure Borehole, it yielded a small coral, the gastropods *Ancilla*, *Bittium semigranosum*, *Calpytraea*, *?Cerithium*, *Crepidula* with attached oyster, *Euspira*, *?Globularia*, *Globularia* cf. *patula*, *Marginella?*, *Pseudocominella deserta*, *Turritella* (not recorded higher than Horizon H by Burton (1933, p.146)), *Typhis pungens*, *Unitas nassaeformis* and *Volutocorbis ambigua*, the scaphopod *Dentalium bartonense*, and the bivalves *Anomia*, *Calpitaria*, *Cardiocardita sulcata*, *Chama*, *Barbatia*, *Crassatella*, *Cubitostrea plicata*, *Cultellus*, *Glycymerita deleta*, *Ostrea sp.*, and *Pectunculina scalaris*.

The Becton Bunny Member has a basal bed (65.68 to 64.55 m) of gravelly clay with shell debris. The overlying strata are predominantly olive-grey silty and sandy clay that pass up at about 59 m into clayey silt and, near the top of the member, to clayey sand. The member contained the anthozoan *Graphularia*, a bryozoan, the gastropods *Ancilla buccinoides*, *?Calyptraea*, *Euspira ?bartonensis*, and *Sigatica hantoniensis ?Pollia*, *Pollia* cf. *lavata*, *?Ringicula sp.*, and the bivalves *Anomia*, *?Axor compressa*, *?Calpitaria*, *Chlamys sp.*, *?Corbicula*, *Crassatella*, *Cubitostrea plicata*, *Cultellus* cf. *affinis*, *Glycymeris/Limopsis/Glycymerita*, *Linter*, *?Mactra*, *Nucula* cf. *tumescens*, ostreid, *Pterelectroma*, *?Pteria*, tellinid, and a tellinid or mactrid.

Much of the overlying upper sand member of the Becton Sand was not cored; it consists predominantly of very fine-grained sand. No fauna was recorded.

CHAPTER 9

Palaeogene: Headon Formation

In the Southampton district, the Headon Formation can be divided into three. The lower part, here termed the lower Headon Formation, consists dominantly of pale greenish grey, relatively sand-free, commonly shelly clay, medium-grained silt and very fine-grained sand. It is overlain by olive-grey clay, usually extremely silty or sandy, and olive-grey clayey very fine-grained sand or silt with subordinate beds of pale greenish grey clay; this unit is here termed the Lyndhurst Member. Above it the upper Headon Formation is lithologically similar to the lower Headon Formation. These three parts are almost identical to the Lower, Middle and Upper Headon Beds of Forbes (1853). However, Forbes distinguished the Middle Headon Beds by the presence of marine to brackish-water faunas, while the Lyndhurst Member of this account is recognised by its lithological as well as its faunal character.

The Headon Formation crops out in the south of the New Forest in the Southampton district. Outliers are present at Bolderwood and west and south-west of Lyndhurst; the main outcrop extends from south of Lyndhurst to Beaulieu Heath (Figure 37).

Within the district the Headon Formation ranges in thickness up to the 40 m proved in the Ramnor Inclosure Borehole. Even though the highest beds are not preserved, this is almost as great as the 43 m recorded for the full succession in the Isle of Wight. The lower Headon Formation is about 10 m thick; the Lyndhurst Member is 11m thick at Lyndhurst; and up to 19 m of the upper Headon Formation are preserved.

The base of the Headon Formation rests on a palaeosol that is developed on the upper surface of the Becton Sand.

Above this is a basal bed of carbonaceous silt, commonly associated with lignite. The bulk of the lower and upper Headon Formation show little facies variation along their outcrop. The clays and silts commonly contain laminae of silt and very fine-grained sand; many of the laminae are lenticular and micro-faulting is general. There are also thin bands of comminuted shells, though some of the clays are apparently structureless, possibly due to bioturbation. At depth, as in the Ramnor Inclosure Borehole, the clays of the lower unit become sandier, presaging the beds of sand, fresh-water limestone and lignite that are present in the equivalent strata in the Isle of Wight.

The Lyndhurst Member is distinguishable by being appreciably more arenaceous; the clays contain a significant sand content and beds of very fine-grained sand are thicker and more numerous. Most of the sediments are intensely bioturbated, though laminations occur sporadically towards the top of the sequence. The succession is very fossiliferous, thick-shelled bivalves and oysters forming markers at several levels. It varies little in nature within the district, though again lignites and limestones occur to the south in the Isle of Wight, and sand assumes an increasing importance.

The Headon Formation sequences proved in the Lyndhurst area and in the Ramnor Inclosure Borehole, and their presumed correlations with those in the Isle of Wight, are shown in Figure 38. Correlations between the Isle of Wight and the mainland Headon Formation sequences have long been a source of controversy because of the variable nature of the lithological sequences. However, several correlations can be made within the Lyndhurst Member. A basal transgression during which strata belonging to the Brockenhurst

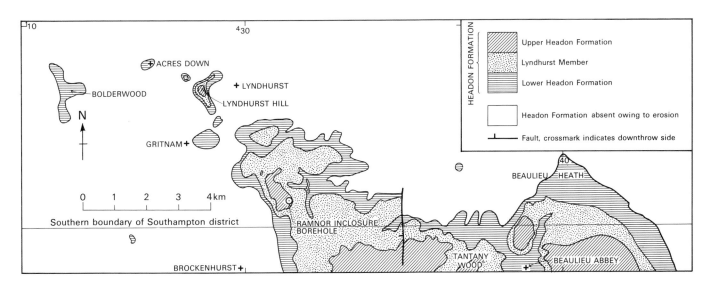

Figure 37 Distribution of the Headon Formation in the Southampton district and part of the Lymington district, showing also the main localities referred to in the text

Zone were deposited, is followed by clayey silts that are overlain by the Venus Bed (see below).

The clay-mineral assemblages of Headon Formation samples from the Ramnor Inclosure Borehole show an up-ward increase in kaolinite content, a trend that continues that of the Barton Group. Kaolinite contents range from 20% to 30%. The assemblage is commonly illite > smectite ≃ kaolinite except from one level high in the upper Headon

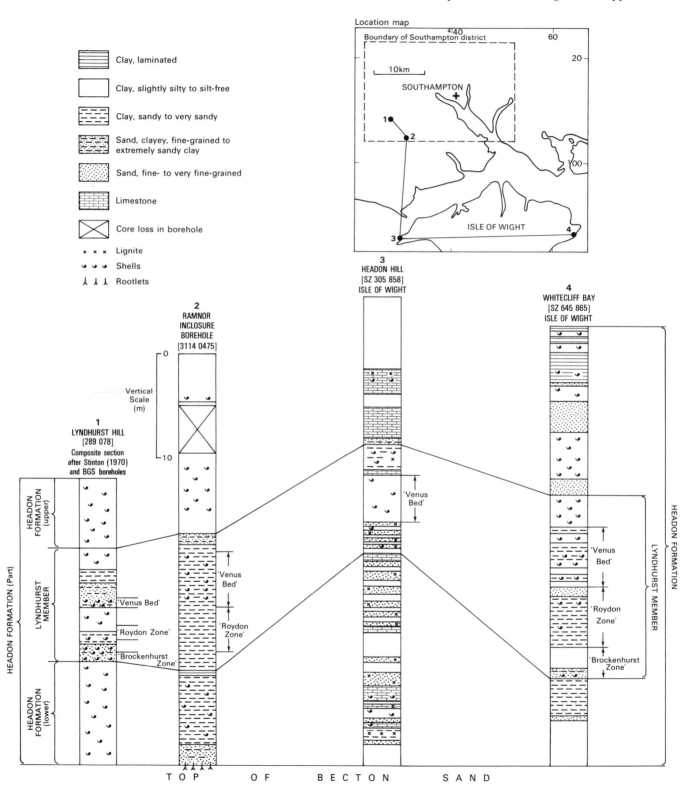

Figure 38 Stratigraphy of the Headon Formation in the Southampton district compared with sequences on the Isle of Wight

Formation in which illite > kaolinite > smectite.

The sand- and silt-grade fractions of the Headon Formation clays consist mainly of subangular quartz ranging in size from $10\,\mu$ to $100\,\mu$. Marcasite is also sporadically present. Fine-grained shell debris is commonly abundant either distributed throughout the clay or concentrated in bands and laminae. A sand-grade residue from near the base of the Lyndhurst Member in the Ramnor Inclosure Borehole consists of poorly sorted angular to subangular quartz ranging in size between 3.8ϕ and 2.0ϕ and common subrounded glauconite in the size range 3.8ϕ to 2.2ϕ. Shell debris and limonitic material are also present.

The sands contain heavy minerals of dominantly Scottish origin, like the underlying Barton Group, but with the addition of heavy minerals of Armorican and Cornubian origin. The proportion of heavy minerals from the latter two sources diminish in the Lyndhurst Member. The sands and silts of the Headon Formation (excluding the Lyndhurst Member) range in mean size from 6.17ϕ to 2.53ϕ with sorting values between well sorted (0.39ϕ) and very poorly sorted (2.28ϕ) with an average of 1.09ϕ. The sands tend to show positive skewness values up to $+0.89$, but some sands have symmetrical grain-size distributions. The sands of the Lyndhurst Member have similar mean size and sorting values to those of the rest of the formation, but have more symmetrical distributions (average skewness $+0.21$).

Much of the Headon Formation is very fossiliferous. The lower and upper Headon Formation contain a mainly freshwater to brackish-water macrofauna. Gastropods recorded from the district include *Australorbis* [*Planorbina*] *sp.*, *Batillaria ventricosa*, *Galba* cf. *longiscata*, *Melanopsis*, *Nystia*, *Pollia labiata*, *Potamaclis turritissima*, *Potamides vagus*, *Stenothyra*, *Tarebia acuta*, and *Viviparus*. Amongst the bivalves, *Corbicula* [*Cyrena*] *obovata*, *Erodona* [*Potamomya*] *plana* and oysters are common, and *Sinodia suborbicularis* and *Polymesoda convexa* have also been recorded.

The macrofaunas of the Lyndhurst Member are generally more marine than those of the lower and upper parts of the formation, but include brackish-water forms that occur throughout the remainder of the formation. The Lyndhurst Member in Hampshire was divided by Keeping and Tawney (1881) into three biostratigraphical units on the basis of their faunal assemblages. They were, in ascending order the 'Brockenhurst Zone', the 'Roydon Zone', and the 'Venus Bed'. The lower two 'zones' were also referred to as the 'Brockenhurst Beds'. In the Southampton district, the Roydon Zone and the Venus Bed have been recognised in the Ramnor Inclosure Borehole and in outcrops around Lyndhurst. The Roydon Zone is characterised by the abundance of *Volutospina* (formerly *Voluta*) *geminata*. Stinton (1970) recorded the foraminifer *Quinqueloculina hauerina* (common); an anthozoan, 22 species of gastropod amongst which *Atys lamarcki*, *Bathytoma hantoniensis*, *Euspira oligocaenica*, *Rimella rimosa* and *Volutospina geminata* were common, 15 species of bivalve, in which *Corbicula obtusa* and *Corbula pisum* were common, 4 species of crustacean, an echinoderm, and 15 species of fish and otoliths from the 'zone' at an exposure [289 078] near Lyndhurst.

The Venus Bed is characterised by *Sinodia suborbicularis* (formerly *Venus incrassata*). At a locality [289 078] near Lyndhurst, Stinton (1970) recorded a foraminifer, 20 species of gastropod, 10 species of bivalve in which *Circe edwardsi*, *Corbicula deperdita*, *C. obovata*, *C. obtusa* and *Trinarcia deltoidea* were common to very common, 2 crustacean species, and 14 species of fish and otoliths.

Foraminifera are largely confined to the Lyndhurst Member; a restricted foraminiferal fauna is present in the upper Headon Formation (Murray and Wright, 1974). Dinoflagellates are also mainly confined to the Lyndhurst Member; freshwater dinoflagellates have been described by Harland and Sharp (1980), from the upper Headon Formation in the Ramnor Inclosure Borehole.

CONDITIONS OF DEPOSITION

Taken together, the brackish to fresh-water nature of the macrofaunas, the lack of foraminifera, the relatively high kaolinite contents, and the presence of a palaeosol resting on the marine Becton Sand, suggest that the lower Headon Formation was deposited in a lagoon behind a beach-barrier sand. In the south-western part of the Hampshire Basin around Christchurch, eastward-flowing rivers deposited sand into the western part of this lagoon. The lenticular lamination commonly seen in the lower and upper Headon Formation suggests gentle winnowing by wind- and storm-generated currents. In the Isle of Wight, contemporaneous fresh-water limestones were deposited in temporary lakes. Figures 39 and 40 show suggested palaeogeographical reconstructions for the lower Headon Formation and the Lyndhurst Member. The base of the Lyndhurst Member represents a rapid marine transgression from the south-east. The Venus Bed marks a gradual regression to more lagoonal conditions which in turn gave way to the fresh- to brackish-water lagoonal deposits of the upper Headon Formation.

The appearance of southerly-derived heavy minerals at the base of the Headon Formation and the diminution of heavy minerals of northerly origin suggest that the open linear coastline of the Becton Sand was replaced by a more irregular coastline. This was probably caused by tectonic activity, possibly involving movement on the Portsdown Anticline, the Isle of Wight Monocline and many similar but smaller structures that occur in the Hampshire Basin. Murray and Wright (1974) reported reworked fragments of lower Headon Formation limestone in the Lyndhurst Member at Headon Hill, Isle of Wight, and Daley and Edwards (1971) noted evidence for contemporaneous activity at even higher stratigraphical levels in the Tertiary.

The position of a north-eastern margin to sedimentation in the Headon Formation is uncertain. During the deposition of the lower and upper Headon Formation it may have been oriented NW–SE in the vicinity of Southampton, close to the Portsdown Anticline, or beyond the anticline in what is now the Weald. During deposition of the Lyndhurst Member the shore retreated north-eastwards and formed a connection with the North Sea.

DETAILS

Acres Down

A small outlier of lower Headon Formation forms a cap beneath gravel on a hill at Acres Down. There are many overgrown small clay-pits [for example 2722 0894] in this outlier in sticky yellow and greenish yellow clay with abundant shells. Reid (1892 MS) recorded 'Cyrena, Ostrea, Cerithium, Melania and Lepidosteus' in one of these.

Lyndhurst Hill

A combination of two piston-sampler boreholes and a section measured in a reservoir excavation [289 078] by Stinton (1970) has enabled the complete Headon Formation sequence to be determined at Lyndhurst Hill (Figure 38). A piston-sampler borehole [2870 0816] showed the following section:

	Thickness m	Depth m
UPPER HEADON FORMATION		
Clay, yellow-stained, grey, silty, with some silt laminae and fine-grained comminuted shell layers	1.95	1.95
Clay, heavily yellow-stained, very shelly, greenish grey, smooth to slightly silty	1.10	3.05
Clay, greyish green, brown-stained, brecciated; top 0.5 m is smooth, shelly, reddish brown clay	0.90	3.95
Clay, greyish green, heavily brown-stained, with bands of comminuted shell debris in the top 0.15 m and silt laminae in the bottom 0.1 m	1.10	5.05
Clay, brown-stained, greyish green, smooth, with shell debris 0.1 m below the top; the basal 0.2 m consists mainly of shell debris	1.00	6.05
Clay, greenish brown, smooth, with some yellow stain and a few silt pods	0.50	6.55
LYNDHURST MEMBER		
Clay, olive-grey, yellow-orange-stained, smooth, with a few shells	0.30	6.85
Clay, olive-grey, smooth, with some yellow and orange stain and scattered shells; reddish brown earthy seam towards the top; more dense comminuted shell debris near the base	0.50	7.35

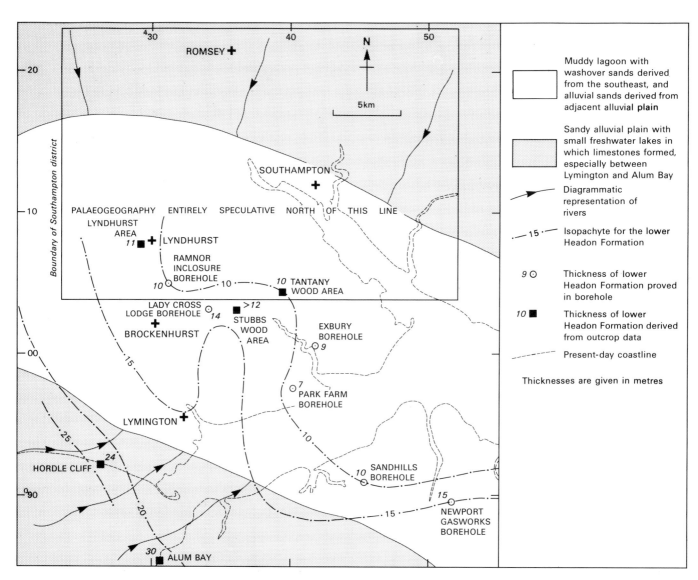

Figure 39 Isopachyte map and possible palaeogeography of the Southampton district and adjoining areas during deposition of the lower Headon Formation

Clay, dark greenish grey, yellow-brown-stained, slightly sandy, becoming sandy downwards, heavily bioturbated with small sand bodies; contains comminuted shell debris and marcasite

	Thickness m	Depth m
Clay, dark greenish grey, yellow-brown-stained, slightly sandy, becoming sandy downwards, heavily bioturbated with small sand bodies; contains comminuted shell debris and marcasite	1.60	8.95
Clay, dark greenish grey, sandy, with some darker bands, and occasional sand layers; some yellow clay layers in the top show micro-faulting; dark grey micaceous sand laminae occur near the base	1.00	9.95
Clay, dark olive-grey and greenish grey, laminated, with medium grey fine-grained sand laminae	0.70	10.65
Sand, pale to medium grey, fine-grained, with occasional clay laminae	0.40	11.05
Clay, greenish grey, extremely sandy, to clayey sand with fragments of thick-shelled bivalves	0.90	11.95
Sand, pale greenish grey, very clayey, fine-grained, to extremely silty clay with many fragments of thick-shelled bivalves	1.10	13.05

Samples from 5.05 and 8.95 m yielded the colonial alga *Pediastrum*, and a sample from 13.05 m yielded a fauna which is diagnostic of the Venus Bed. It included the gastropods *Cantharus labiatus*, *Euspira vectensis*, and *Uxia elongata*, and the bivalves *Sinodia suborbicularis*, *Trigonodesma lissa*, and *Trinacria deltoidea*. The ostracods included *Cytheretta porosacosta*, *Eocytheropteron wetherelli*, *Paijenborchella brevicosta* and *Pterygocythereis pustulosa*, all belonging to Keen's (1978) Assemblage V, also characteristic of the Venus Bed.

Another piston-sampler borehole [2886 0794] extended the section downwards; at 11.85 m it contained a molluscan fauna characteristic of the Brockenhurst Beds. The gastropods included *Calyptraea sp.*, *Cantharus labiatus*, and *Euspirus vectensis*, and the bivalves included *Corbula subpisum*, *Nemocardium* cf. *hantoniense*, *Tivelina sp.*, and *Venericardia deltoidea*.

The Roydon Zone and Venus Bed were recorded by Stinton (1970) in the reservoir excavation.

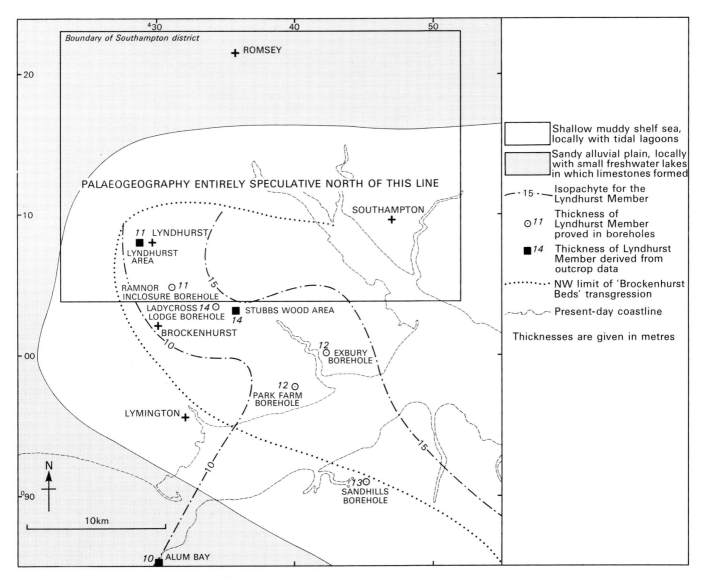

Figure 40 Isopachyte map and possible palaeogeography of the Southampton district and adjoining areas during deposition of the Lyndhurst Member (Headon Formation)

Ramnor Inclosure Borehole

The Headon Formation was penetrated in the Ramnor Inclosure Borehole between ground level and 40.4 m depth. The base of the Lyndhúrst Member was at 30.0 m and the base of the upper Headon Formation at 17.5 m depth. A condensed graphic log is shown in Figure 38, and a lithological log is given in Appendix 1. The base of the lower Headon Formation is marked by an 0.1 m-thick bed of clayey sand which rests sharply on the Becton Sand. The remainder of the lower Headon Formation consists of 10.3 m of greenish grey sandy clay with many bands of comminuted shell debris. Gastropods recorded include *Australorbis* [*Planorbina*] *sp.*, *Batillaria ventricosa*, *Galba* cf. *longiscata*, lymnaeids, ?*Melanopsis*, *Potamclis*, and *Viviparus*; bivalves include *Corbicula obovata*, oysters, and *Erodona plana*. Turtle fragments were also recorded. The Lyndhurst Member consists predominantly of dark greenish grey to olive-grey silty to slightly silty bioturbated clay, and clayey very fine-grained sand. It rests with a sharp base on the lower Headon Formation. The member is very shelly; the gastropod fauna includes *Atys lamarcki*, *Bonellitia sp.*, *Calyptraea* cf. *aperta*, *Clavilithes sp.*, *Crenilabium sp.*, ?*Colwellia flexuosa*, *Conorbis alatus* var. *hemilissa*, *Euspira headonensis*, *Euspira oligocenica*, *Gibberula vittata*, *Hemipleurotoma laeviuscula*, *Murex hantoniensis*, planorbids, *Pollia labiata*, *Potamides vagus*, *Rimella rimosa*, '*Scaphander*' *sp.*, *Turricula transversaria*, *Viviparus*, *Volutospina geminata* (at 24.76 m), and *Volutospina* cf. *spinosa*. The bivalves include an arcid, *Cardita* cf. *deltoidea*, *Cardita simplex*, *Chlamys sp.*, *Corbicula obovata*, *Cubitostrea plicata*, *Erodona plana*, *Garum rude*, *Linter curvirostris*, lucinid, *Musculus*, ?*Nemocardium hantoniense*, *Ostrea* cf. *velata*, *Panopea intermedia*, *Sinodia suborbicularis*, *Pterelectroma media*, tellinid or mactrid and *Thracia* or *Lyonsia*. The other fauna includes *Ditrupa plana*, crustacean remains, foraminifera, otoliths, and a shark tooth.

The upper Headon Formation consists predominantly of pale to dark greenish grey slightly silty to silty clay, commonly with silt laminae and comminuted shell beds. A few thin beds of very fine-grained sand are present. The rests with a sharp base on the Lyndhurst Member. The following gastropod fauna was recorded: *Melanopsis*, *Nystia*, *Pollia labiata*, *Potamides vagus*, *Potamaclis turritissima*, ?*Rissoina*, *Stenothyra*, *Tarebia acuta*, and *Viviparus*. Bivalves included *Corbicula obovata*, *Erodona/Potamomya plana*, oysters, *Sinodia suborbicularis*, and *Polymesoda convexa*.

A roadside section [3013 0590] beside the main Lyndhurst to Brockenhurst road shows 2.5 m of brownish green smooth clay with a 0.1 m-thick orange-brown clayey sand 1.5 m below the top. The basal 1 m contains abundant gastropod and bivalve debris, including *Sinodia suborbicularis*, and probably correlates with the Venus Bed.

Tantany Wood

A piston-sampler borehole [SU 3666 0371] sited on the lower Headon Formation outcrop showed the following section:

	Thickness m	Depth m
HEADON FORMATION		
Clay, sandy to very sandy, greyish yellow-orange-stained	1.95	1.95
Sand, greenish grey, very clayey, to extremely sandy clay with strong orange-yellow stain and some limonitic material	1.00	2.95
Clay, pale greenish grey, heavily yellow-stained, smooth to slightly silty, with some shell debris	1.00	3.95
Silt, pale buff, passing rapidly to dark greyish green smooth to slightly silty clay with some brown staining. Greyish brown carbonaceous clay is present 0.08 m below the top and a comminuted shell band just above this	1.80	5.75

A sample from 5.75 m yielded the freshwater alga *Pediastrum*. Uphill from this piston-sampler hole, seismic shot holes and other piston sampler holes penetrated the Becton Sand, lower Headon Formation and Lyndhurst Member. One of these [SU 3631 0356] proved the following sequence (thicknesses are approximate):

	Thickness m	Depth m
Drift (gravel wash)	1.5	1.5
LYNDHURST MEMBER		
Clay, yellow-brown, sticky	1.5	3.0
Clay, brown and greenish grey, sticky, becoming sticky greenish grey clay with much bivalve debris	3.0	6.0
Clay, brownish olive-grey, with some chocolate-brown clay at around 6.7 m	3.1	9.1
LOWER HEADON FORMATION		
Clay, pale greenish grey	7.7	16.8
BECTON SAND		
Sand, brownish yellow	1.2	18.0

Beaulieu Abbey

An old clay-pit [SU 3940 0265] contains green shelly clay with *Corbicula obovata* and *Sinodia suborbicularis*. This fauna indicates the Venus Bed.

CHAPTER 10

Structure

The relatively gentle folds that affect the Tertiary and Cretaceous rocks of the district can be seen in seismic sections to be related to horst and graben structures in the older Mesozoic rocks; these structures were probably controlled by major faults in the Variscan basement. A contour map of the base of the Tertiary, based on seismic and borehole data, shows the most structurally complex zone to extend from Swanwick in the south-east to Nomansland in the west (Figure 41). In the Tertiary rocks this zone consists of a complementary anticline and syncline with sinuous axial traces. The anticline is asymmetrical and has a relatively steep northern limb with dips up to 7° and a southern limb with dips of only 0.8° to 2.5°. The fold axes appear to bifurcate in the northern part of the district (Figure 41). This structure appears to be a north-westerly continuation of the Portsdown Anticline, which in the Portsmouth area trends WNW–ESE. The base-Tertiary contours suggest that these structures may not be continuous but may be made up of several *en-échelon* anticline–syncline pairs which, taken together, have a WNW–ESE trend.

In the southern part of the district a number of very gentle anticlines and synclines are present with axial trends between E–W and ESE–NNW (Figure 41). The maximum dip is 2.5°, with the overall dip to the south. A gentle NE–SE-trending syncline in this area contains the outcrop of the Headon Formation; it is probably the north-westward continuation of the Bembridge Syncline of the Isle of Wight. Other small folds with probable NW–SE trends were recorded in the Palaeogene in the Fawley Tunnel (Curry and others, 1968).

Examination of seismic sections established that many, if not all, of the folds in the Tertiary rocks can be related to faults that show large displacements in the pre-Aptian rocks (Figure 41). These faults mostly strike between NNW and WSW; a few strike NW. They appear to have a complex history; pre-Aptian movements along them usually show downthrows to the south, but Palaeogene to Miocene downthrows, although very much smaller, are mostly to the north. As a result, the post-Aptian Cretaceous and Tertiary rocks have not fractured, but drape across the faults to form anticlines with relatively steep northern limbs. Elsewhere in southern England, the Isle of Wight, Purbeck and Hog's Back monoclines are much larger versions of the same type of fold. In these monoclines there is evidence of horizontal transport northwards due to compression, in addition to the draping effect.

In southern England, many of these faults, including those beneath the Southampton district, may have been inherited from faults in the Variscan basement. At outcrop in southwest England, this basement shows two dominant fault trends, E–W and NW–SE. The latter commonly cut the former. Although in southern England the evidence from the NW–SE-trending faults indicates that their main movements were dextral shears, it is probable that they acted as block faults during periods of crustal tension. Interference between these fault trends may have been responsible for the change in trend of the Portsdown Anticline in the district, and it is possible that a major basement fault, the so-called Bembridge-Bray Fault, causes the deflection of the anticline; the fault may pass to the north-east of Southampton Water.

The NW–SE trend of the isopachytes for many of the Palaeogene formations in the Hampshire Basin—for example those for the Selsey Sand (Figure 28)—suggest that tectonic structures influenced sedimentation. The Bembridge Syncline and its associated folds have this trend, and Daley and Edwards (1971) have suggested that they controlled sedimentation in the Bembridge Marls and Limestone in the Isle of Wight. Drummond (1970) suggested that similar structures controlled the thickness of Cretaceous sediments in Dorset. The only E–W-trending fault in the Hampshire Basin that is thought to have influenced Tertiary sedimentation is the major concealed fault thought to underlie the Purbeck and Isle of Wight monoclines (Plint, 1982).

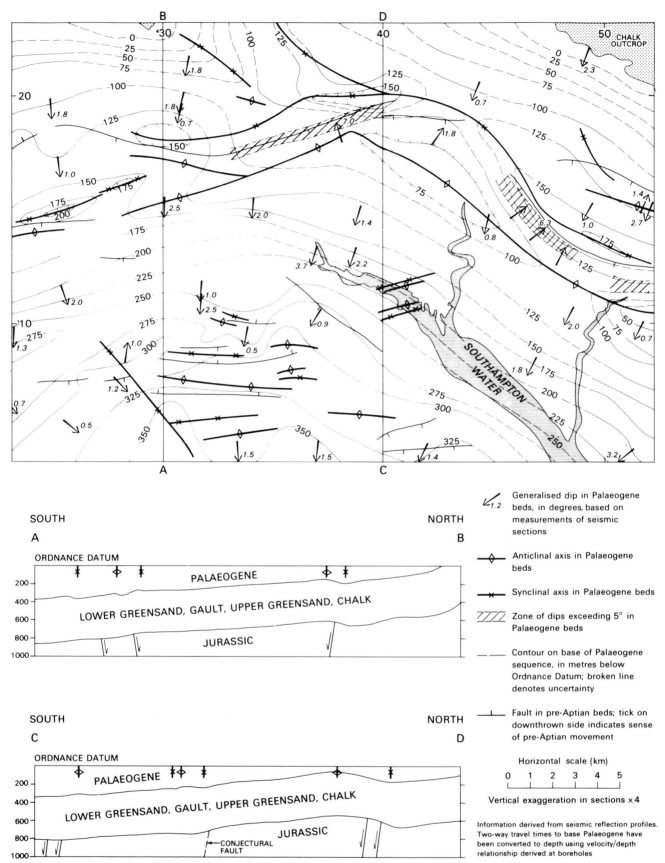

Figure 41 Structural map and sections of the Southampton district, based on seismic and borehole data

CHAPTER 11

Quaternary

The Quaternary era saw many oscillations of climate. During several of the colder episodes extensive ice-sheets pushed southwards across England, but they did not reach into the Hampshire Basin, and so there are none of the till-sheets that elsewhere prove valuable in unravelling the Quaternary sequence. Nor have any of the Raised Beaches that might provide alternative datum-planes been identified with certainty. Instead there is a range of fluvial deposits, including Older River Gravels, River Terrace Deposits, Buried Channel Deposits and Alluvium, broad coastal spreads of Estuarine Alluvium, and extensive though thin spreads of Head. Apart from those belonging to the most recent (Flandrian) stage of the Quaternary none of these has yet yielded fossils within the district. In consequence the placing of these deposits within the presently accepted British framework can only be speculative. Their ages in relation to one another are, however, reasonably certain, and they are enumerated in stratigraphical order in Table 1.

CLAY-WITH-FLINTS

Clay-with-flints is a term used to described reddish brown clay containing unabraded flints, lying unevenly on or filling pipes in a chalk surface. It is generally considered to represent partly the insoluble residue of chalk and partly material from former Tertiary deposits, especially the Reading Formation (Loveday, 1960). Solifluction has probably affected the Clay-with-flints at most localities.

In the Colden Common area, patches of reddish or orange-brown to buff, smooth to sandy clay with abundant angular flint fragments overlie the Chalk on south-facing dip-slopes, along valley sides, and near the boundary with the Reading Formation. Around Hensting [495 220], the Clay-with-flints can be divided into an upper unit of orange-brown to buff, silty clay with flints, and a lower unit of reddish brown, smooth clay with flints. Elsewhere in the district, the deposits consist of orange-brown, flinty sandy clays that weather to yellow-brown. Owing to solution of the underlying chalk, the base of the Clay-with-flints is highly irregular. Although generally only between 0.5 m and 1.0 m thick, it infills solution pipes that penetrate up to 11 m of chalk.

Details

Exposures in the Clay-with-flints are mainly confined to chalk-pits. One of these [4988 2228] in the Hensting valley, exposes brown sandy clay and sandy clay with angular flints that forms a thin capping to, and penetrates up to 11 m into the Chalk. A silage-pit [5191 2208] near Marwell House, revealed up to 1.0 m of orange-brown sandy clay with abundant flint fragments resting on an irregular surface of rubbly chalk. The clay passes laterally into 0.2 m of brown loam with flint and chalk fragments.

Table 1 Quaternary deposits of the Southampton district, showing their conditions of deposition, and the suggested climatic stages in which they were deposited

Deposit	Conditions of deposition	Climatic stage
Alluvium and Calcareous Tufa	Low-energy fluviatile conditions in rivers and lakes	Flandrian
Estuarine Alluvium	Estuarine deposition	
Buried Channel Deposits	Brackish-water to marine; intertidal and salt-marsh sedimentation in outer part of estuary; transgressing northwards at higher levels onto fresh-water clay, silt, peat and calcareous tufa in inner part of estuary	
Buried gravel terraces in Southampton Water (not shown on the map)	High-energy fluviatile, possibly in braided rivers	Devensian
River Terrace Deposits and some Head	Mainly high-energy rivers, possibly fed from glacial melt waters; some low-energy fluviatile clay and loam on some gravel terraces	Pre-Devensian
Head Gravel; and some Head (not shown on the map)	Solifluction in periglacial climate	
Older River Gravels	High-energy fluviatile, possibly in braided rivers	
Clay-with-flints	In situ remanie and solifluction	

OLDER RIVER GRAVELS

The river gravels of the district include spreads in the west that lie at high levels (up to 129 m above OD), and do not appear to relate to the modern rivers: these deposits were formerly called the Plateau Gravels, but are here termed Older River Gravels. Their lithologies, their planar surfaces, and their apparent slight seaward fall suggests that they are fluviatile in origin, and they appear to have been laid down on erosional shelves. Their height so near the present coastline suggests that they are of considerable antiquity, but they contain no fauna and even their assumed Quaternary age is unproven.

The Older River Gravels consist mainly of subangular flint with lesser amounts of well rounded flint and minor amounts of hard, fine-grained, grey sandstone (sarsen) and vein-quartz in a clayey sand matrix. Analyses of the sand fractions from similar gravels in the Fordingbridge area have shown the coarser grades to be flint-rich and the fines to be quartz-rich (Kubala, 1980).

Five older terraces, ranging from 89 to 129 m above OD, have been recognised. Their geographical extent is, however, so restricted that it is not generally possible to determine the precise amount of fall of their surfaces, particularly since solifluction is widespread around the edges of the spreads. In the adjoining Ringwood district to the west, Kubala (1980) has identified 6 surfaces ranging from 85 to 127 m above OD.

The gravels vary in thickness between 1 and 5 m. Some of the small hills in the Lyndhurst area are capped by up to 1 m of clayey gravel or gravelly clay, but in the more extensive outcrops thicknesses are mostly between 2 and 3 m, and can be up to 5 m.

Features indicative of a periglacial climate, such as cryoturbation structures, are common in the gravels. Kubala (1980) reported planar bedding, cross-bedding, poor sorting and high fines contents in the Ringwood district but no undisturbed exposure was seen in the present district. These sedimentary features suggest a fluviatile or fluvio-glacial origin. No far-travelled stone has been recorded from the gravels and it is unlikely that they were derived from an ice-front.

Details

Gravels in Older Terrace 5 at Piper's Waight, Nomansland, were proved to be about 2.5 m thick in boreholes. One borehole [2471 1654] showed the following sequence that is believed to be typical of the area: peat 0.2 m, resting on 1.6 m of loose, fine-, medium- and coarse-grained gravel with a matrix of coarse-grained sand and patches of stiff brown silt. The gravel rests on 0.8 m of brown and pale green silt containing scattered gravel-sized flints. Nearby, disused pits [250 165] contain up to 1.5 m of pale grey gravel with angular and rounded flints.

A borehole [c.243 143] at Fritham House, in Older Terrace 4, penetrated 0.1 m of green sandy clay which rested on 1.1 m of pale green clay and gravel. The terrace forms the extensive plateau that slopes gently from around 121 m above OD near Fritham Lodge [2420 1460] in the north to around 115 m above OD in the southern part of Janesmoor Plain [2450 1320].

Boreholes and cuttings for the Bratley diversion [2371 1003 to 2382 1049] of the A31 trunk road revealed 2.8 to 3.8 m of Older Terrace 2 deposits. A typical section proved in one of the boreholes [2378 1037] consisted of 0.6 m of greyish brown, fine- to coarse-grained sand and fine- to coarse-grained gravel on 2.4 m of dense, brown, clayey, fine- to coarse-grained gravel. The gravels exposed in the cuttings have a wavy base, probably caused by cryoturbation.

A section [2656 1058] in a disused gravel-pit in the same terrace in the SE part of Stoney Cross Plain shows 2 m of yellowish brown gravel with rounded to subangular flints set in a matrix of reddish brown, very clayey sand that contains a lens of reddish brown, very clayey sand 0.15 m thick and 6 m long.

HEAD GRAVEL AND HEAD

The deposits classified as Head within the district are mostly weathering products derived from the solid and older drift deposits that have moved downslope by a combination of solifluction and downwash. They probably also include, at most localities, a proportion of *in situ* weathering material (regolith). A thin skin of Head, commonly <1 m thick, overlies most of the Tertiary formations of the district, but has not been shown on the 1:50 000-scale map. On the Tertiary outcrop, the Head is typically a yellowish brown to orange-brown, silty clay or clayey sand, commonly with scattered angular flints.

Lobes of clayey gravel adjacent to outcrops of Older River Gravels are shown on the map as Head Gravel, and have been derived from the Older River Gravels by solifluction and downwash. The lobes consist typically of flint gravel in a matrix of yellowish brown and grey, clayey sand and sandy clay and have been derived from the Older River Gravels by solifluction and downwash.

Details

Longcross Plain – Stoney Cross Plain

On the west side of Longcross Plain [245 158 to 235 149] lobes of Head Gravel extend from the base of the Older River Gravels at c.120 m above OD downslope to the 107 m contour. Small exposures [2426 1569] show 1.5 to 2.0 m of flint gravel with a matrix of yellowish brown sandy clay. Lobes of clayey gravel are present below the edges of the Older River Gravels outcrop on the north side of Stoney Cross Plain [250 125 to 268 122], and similar lobes are present on the southern side of the gravel plateau [249 111 to 255 110].

Calmore area

An outcrop of Head Gravel, comprising clayey gravel and sand, extends southwards from near Hillstreet [341 158] to blanket the east-facing slopes of Tatchbury Mount. The deposit falls from 45 m above OD in the west to c.15 m above OD in the east, and is thought to have been derived from a former terrace gravel. The following roadside section [3358 1461] typifies the deposit:

	Thickness m
TOPSOIL	
Soil, dark brown, clayey, sandy, flinty	0.2
HEAD GRAVEL	
Sand, orange, brown, and yellow, red-mottled, gravelly; 0.1 m clayey gravel at the base	0.6
Clay, grey, plastic, sandy, red-stained at the top, containing small disrupted masses of green sand	0.5
Sand, orange and yellow, clayey, coarse-grained, with flint pebbles, becoming clayier towards the base	1.4

Allbrook – Fair Oak

In the Allbrook to Fair Oak area there are patches of Head that consists mainly of orange-brown, clayey sand with scattered angular and rounded flint pebbles. Away from good exposures these are not readily distinguishable from the local weathered solid formation. In Allbrook Brick-pit [4522 2147] the deposit is 1.0 m thick, and in a sand-pit [4652 2033] at Burrow Hill it is up to 3.0 m thick. The deposit ranges from 0.3 to 2.0 m in thickness in a sand-pit [4976 1840] at Fair Oak and consists of sandy clay with flints overlain by blocky, grey, sandy clay without flints which, in turn, is overlain with an erosional contact by sandy clay and clayey sand with scattered flints.

RIVER TERRACE DEPOSITS

Extensive spreads of River Terrace Deposits occur along the Test and Itchen. Eleven terraces have been provisionally recognised, their surfaces ranging from 91 m above OD in the north to OD at Southampton Water: another 3 terraces now lie beneath the sea (p.83). They all appear to fall only very gently downstream, paralleling the thalweg of the present rivers.

The eleven terraces have been numbered on the basis of their heights and outcrop distribution (Figure 42), though their relative heights do not necessarily reflect their relative ages. The 7th to 11th terraces have only limited outcrops on high ground north and NE of Southampton Water and west of Romsey. The 11th Terrace overlaps in height with the Older River Gravels. The 3rd to 6th terraces are preserved widely between Warsash and Nursling, east of Romsey, and also in the Beaulieu Heath and Fawley areas. The 1st and 2nd terraces are the most extensive, occurring along the upper part of Southampton Water and along the valleys of the Test and Itchen.

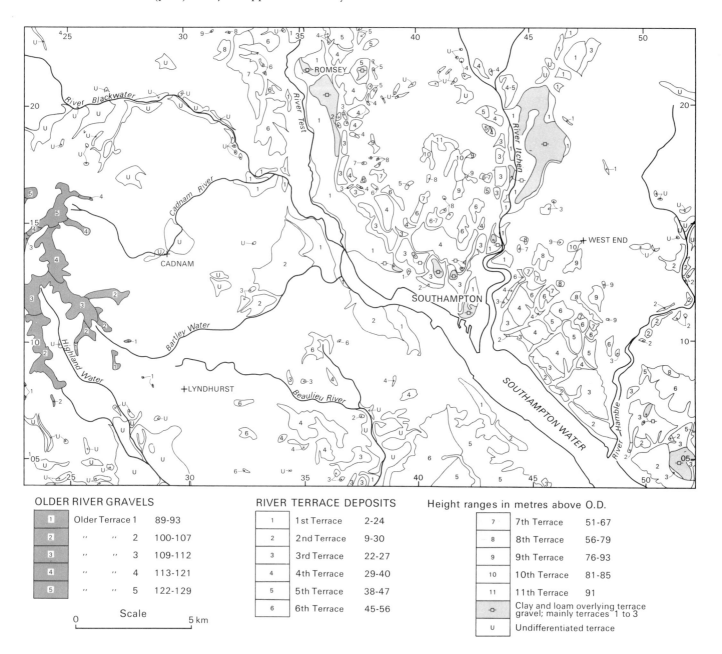

Figure 42   Distribution of Older River Gravels and River Terrace Deposits in the Southampton district

The deposits are very variable in thickness. On the south-western side of Southampton Water the 5th and 6th terraces are commonly 3 to 5 m thick, though 12 m were recorded near Holbury; the 4th Terrace deposits range from 4 to 7 m; around Hook the 3rd Terrace gravels are generally 4 m thick, with an overburden of up to 1.5 m of clayey and sandy silt, but they are commonly only 3 to 4 m thick; near Swaythling the 1st Terrace deposits vary from 1 to 5 m.

The deposits are similar in composition to the Older River Gravels. They consist dominantly of gravels made up of subangular to subrounded flints, with a few well rounded ones. A considerable amount of sand-grade components is also present, mostly as well rounded quartz grains and subangular flints. The five highest terraces have an appreciable clay content. Cross-bedding, usually of the trough variety, is common, mostly forming units up to 0.3 m thick, though units of up to 0.8 m occur near Woolston. In the Holbury area current directions of 242° to 340° are indicated by the cross-bedding. Channels and mud clasts are also present (Keen, 1980).

Poorly sorted, clayey and sandy silts and silty clays overlie the 1st, 3rd, 5th and 6th terraces widely, and some of the other terrace gravels at more scattered localities. Those on the lower two of these terraces have been mapped as 'Loam and clay'; the 1899 edition classifies them as 'brickearths'.

All the terrace deposits above the 2nd are affected to varying degrees by cryoturbation. This is particularly true of the higher ones, but the 'Loam and clay' on the 5th and 6th terraces is deeply involuted into the underlying gravel, and even the 3rd Terrace gravels have their bedding violently disrupted in places.

Because the terraces have thalwegs very similar to the present alluvium they presumably formed when the sea-level was higher than it is today, and the 6th Terrace could well grade into the Portsdown Raised Beach (Ap Simon and others, 1977) of believed pre-Anglian age.

The terrace deposits may represent a considerable span of Quaternary time, but they yield no fossils other than a few mammalian bones (Shore, 1905). The widespread cryoturbation shows that at least one intensely cold stage followed the deposition of all the terraces except possibly the lowest two (or that all these higher terraces were deposited in periglacial conditions). A little to the south, at Stone Point [SZ 456 985] on the Solent, a brackish-water deposit has yielded pollen and molluscs indicative of the Ipswichian interglacial, Brown and others, 1975. It is both underlain and overlain by gravels but, although these have been suggested to equate with the 1st Terrace, their relationship to the terraces of the Southampton district is far from clear. Palaeolithic stone implements are common in the lower terraces, mostly in the 1st to 4th terraces, and the Acheulian affinities of some of these again suggest an Ipswichian age.

Details: Undifferentiated terraces

River Blackwater

Exposures in a small pit [2700 2006] near Giles Lane, Plaitford, show 1.6 m of yellowish brown flint gravel with a matrix of yellowish brown, medium- to coarse-grained sand and some lenticular sand beds, one 0.1 m thick and 1.2 m long. Another small pit [2881 2004] shows 1.8 m of angular and rounded flints in a matrix of brown clayey sand, with some lenticles of similar sand.

Cadnam River

Gravel in a matrix of brown and grey, sandy silty clay, was proved in boreholes [2953 1396 to 3010 1449] near Cadnam to average 1.35 m thick (range 0.6 to 2.3 m), beneath 0.3 to 0.9 m of soil.

Brockenhurst to Brinken Wood to Balmer Lawn

A gravel-resource borehole [2706 0653] at Brinken Wood showed 0.5 m of very clayey gravel, overlain by 0.8 m of sandy silty clay and underlain by Chama Sand. Farther south-east, however, another gravel-resource borehole [2897 0401] proved 4.3 m of fine- and coarse-grained gravel and sand overlying Becton Sand. Around Balmer Lawn, just south of the district boundary, in the extreme south-eastern outcrop of the deposit, the gravel is only 2 m thick and is very clayey with an overburden of sandy clay about 0.8 m thick.

Details: 3rd to 11th terraces

A gravel-pit [3298 2151] in the 7th Terrace at Squabb Wood, Shootash, exposed up to 2.2 m of brownish yellow to grey, homogeneous, compact gravel of angular to rounded flints in a matrix of pale yellowish brown and reddish brown, medium- to coarse-grained, clayey sand. Well developed involutions of bands of sand and gravel were seen nearby.

Boreholes [4040 1801 to 4059 1801] in the 11th Terrace at Chilworth proved 1.7 to 2.4 m of gravel in a matrix of brown sandy clay. Cuttings and boreholes [4191 1721 to 4195 1720] for the M27 motorway at Bassett showed between 2.8 and 5 m of reddish brown, yellowish brown and orange-brown flint gravel of the 10th Terrace with brown sandy clay matrix and some lenticular sand beds.

Bursledon area

A foundation excavation [4790 1089] near Lowford, Bursledon, showed strongly cryoturbated gravels and laminated sands of the 8th Terrace. In one part of the excavation orange and grey mottled, extremely sandy clay, 1.5 m thick, rested on yellow, clayey, sandy gravel. The trend of the involution structures in the deposit was apparently E–W.

Netley Hill

Test-pits [4806 1164] in the 9th Terrace at Netley Hill showed 1.4 m of red sand and gravel with some blue gravelly clay resting on Wittering Formation. The presence of clay lenses and the very irregular contact of the gravel with the Wittering Formation, indicates that the gravel is probably highly cryoturbated.

Romsey to Lordshill

The following section was recorded in a gravel-pit [SU3633 2324] in the 5th Terrace at Abbotswood near Romsey:

	Thickness m
Highly contorted gravel with involutions and inclusions of the underlying bed	0.12
Clay, orange-brown and pale greenish grey, extremely sandy, containing flint pebbles up to 30 mm across	0.20–0.90
Gravel, mainly fine- and medium-grained, with a matrix of orange-brown clayey medium- to coarse-grained clayey sand	1.30

Temporary excavations [3849 1604] in the 4th Terrace at Lord-shill showed 0.4 m of orange-brown, gravelly, extremely sandy clay resting on orange-brown extremely sandy clay with scattered very small flint chips, 0.8 m thick but thinning to 0.1 within 5 m, on 0.9 m of orange-brown clayey gravel. A nearby borehole [3846 1601] penetrated 1.8 m of reddish brown, sandy, clayey silt with abundant gravel and cobbles on 4.5 m of medium dense, fine- to coarse-grained gravel with cobbles.

Coxford, Shirley, City Centre area

Much of the city of Southampton is built on the 3rd to 6th terraces. It is in places difficult to separate the individual terraces in the built-up area; in addition, many of the gentle slopes that separate the terraces are underlain by thick gravel wash. A borehole [3902 1430] near Coxford proved about 5 m of brown, sandy gravel belonging to the 3rd Terrace, overlying Wittering Formation. However, another borehole [3886 1440] only 200 m NW, proved 7 m of brown clayey sand with subordinate flint gravel, resting on Wittering Formation.

A borehole [4005 1424] in the 4th Terrace at Shirley showed the following section overlying Wittering Formation:

	Thickness m	Depth m
Made Ground	0.46	0.46
RIVER TERRACE DEPOSITS (4th Terrace)		
Clay, soft, orange-brown, sandy, with scattered gravel	1.83	2.29
Gravel, coarse-grained, and sand	3.20	5.49
Gravel, with some sand and increasing clay content with depth	1.22	6.71

A borehole [4226 1268] in the 3rd Terrace at Bellevue near Southampton city centre, proved 2.2 m of medium-grained gravel and sand resting on 2.4 m of blue, sandy clay with gravel.

The highest gravels in the Southampton Common area are those of the 6th Terrace. They are highly variable in thickness and in composition. A test-pit [4069 1499], NW of Southampton Common, exposed 2.3 m of orange, silty, sandy gravel, but a borehole only 35 m to the SE showed 0.6 m of orange, silty, sandy, gravelly clay resting on Tertiary deposits.

Chandler's Ford area

Cuttings [4378 1913] for the Chandler's Ford bypass in the 4th Terrace revealed about 2.5 m of flint gravel with a matrix of orange-brown and grey, extremely sandy clay and extremely clayey, fine-grained sand.

Woolston – Bursledon – Hamble-Chilling

In the Woolston to Netley area the gravels of the 4th Terrace have been extensively worked. The following section was exposed in a disused pit [4500 1135] near Woolston:

	Thickness m
RIVER TERRACE DEPOSITS (4th Terrace)	
Sand, yellowish brown and grey, laminated, fine-grained, containing a lens of brown sandy gravel and gravelly sand with cross-beds dipping SE	3.0
Gravel, yellowish brown, sandy	3.0

Another disused gravel-pit [4570 0980] in the same terrace exposes 3 m of orange-brown gravel with occasional cobbles up to 10 cm across. This gravel also contains sand layers. To the east of this [4608 0975], the gravel is overlain by 0.5 to 0.8 m of yellowish brown silty clay.

Two trial boreholes, [4561 1181 to 4561 1186] in the 6th Terrace showed a change from 1.9 m of buff, silty, sandy gravelly clay on Wittering Formation to 2 m of very silty, clay overlying at least 0.8 m of sandy gravel within a distance of only 50 m.

A road cutting [4777 1024] in the 6th Terrace at Lowford, Bursledon, exposes up to 1.5 m of orange-brown, sandy gravel with a highly cryoturbated base and many involution structures that involve the underlying Tertiary strata.

A gravel-pit [4788 0874] at Hamble displays the following section:

	Thickness m
RIVER TERRACE DEPOSITS (5th Terrace)	
Clay, extremely sandy, orange-brown, with stringers of scattered flint pebbles	1.5
Sand, orange-brown, poorly laminated, clayey	1.0
Gravel	1.0

In a disused pit [5012 0560] in the 3rd Terrace at Warsash 1.5 m of Made Ground overlies 1.8 m of orange flint gravel which in turn overlies Marsh Farm Formation. Another pit [5126 0510] in the same terrace at Hook exposed 1.3 m of orange-brown silty clay resting on 3.65 m of orange sandy gravel with a few cobbles up to 5 cm across. Below this is 4.8 m of orange-brown gravel with cobbles up to 5 cm across resting on Selsey Sand.

Around Chilling, the 3rd Terrace gravel is capped by a considerable thickness of loam. A borehole there [5164 0438] proved 3 m of compact to hard, greyish brown, very silty, fine-grained sand or fine-grained sandy silt overlying at least 1m of gravel. Exposures in a nearby, partly back-filled gravel-pit [509 048] showed the gravel to be about 4 to 5 m thick with an overburden of between 0.5 m and 2 m of red-brown, clayey, fine-grained sand with small flint fragments.

Beaulieu Road Station – Beaulieu Heath – Dibden Purlieu – Hardley

A mineral-resource borehole [3480 0675] near Beaulieu Road Station proved the following succession overlying Becton Sand:

	Thickness m	Depth m
RIVER TERRACE DEPOSITS (4th Terrace)		
Clay, sandy with flint pebbles at the base	1.5	1.5
Gravel, clayey, sandy, fine- and coarse-grained, mainly flint; the matrix is fine-medium- and coarse-grained sand consisting of quartz and flint	1.0	2.5

A mineral-resource borehole [3942 0439] in the 6th Terrace at Beaulieu Heath showed 5.2 m of sandy gravel, rather clayey at the top, resting on Lyndhurst Member.

A mineral-resource borehole [4050 0620] at Dibden Purlieu proved the following section:

	Thickness m	Depth m
RIVER TERRACE DEPOSITS (6th Terrace)		
Clay, sandy, with sporadic flint pebbles	1.2	1.2
Gravel, clayey, sand	1.9	3.1
BECTON SAND	0.4	3.5

A section [4260 0470] in the 5th Terrace in a disused gravel-pit at Hardley shows crytoturbated mixture up to 2.5 m thick of gravelly clayey sand and sandy gravel overlying red to orange mottled, pebbly, clayey sand. This latter rests irregularly on poorly-bedded, orange and yellow, clayey, sandy gravel which is over 2 m thick.

Much planar and trough cross-bedding is visible in the gravels; it indicates that the dominant direction of derivation was from between west and NW.

Details: 1st and 2nd terraces

Romsey to Nursling

A borehole [3611 2111] through the 1st Terrace at Romsey proved 0.85 m of brown clay with some flint gravel on 3.6 m of compact, slightly clayey, fine-, medium- and coarse-grained flint gravel, silty in the lower half and with cobble-sized flints towards the base. In Romsey, and between Romsey and Lee, clay and loam deposits have been mapped resting on the terrace gravels. A borehole [3655 1907] near Ashfield on the 1st Terrace proved 1.7 m of firm, orange-brown, silty, locally sandy, clay with lenses or bands of sand and occasional stones on 3.1 m of gravel and sand.

The 1st Terrace gravels have been extensively worked in pits [3556 1795 to 3633 1654] between Lee and Nursling, and between [3576 1631 and 368 150]. Sections [3598 1770] in a gravel-pit at Lee showed up to 3.5 m of pale grey to pale brown, roughly-bedded gravel with angular flints dominant in a matrix of brown fine- to coarse-grained sand. Boreholes [3672 1671 to 3692 1520] on the 1st Terrace at Nursling Industrial Estate proved 0.3 to 1.8 m of brown sandy clay and gravelly clay on 2.0 to 5.0 m of fine- to coarse-grained sand and gravel.

Totton to Ashurst area

A borehole [3697 1242] at Totton on the 1st Terrace proved 3 m of compact sand and gravel overlying Tertiary deposits. The 2nd Terrace gravels appear to thin south-westwards from Totton towards Netley Marsh and Ashurst Bridge. Elsewhere [3433 1339] the 2nd Terrace deposits are only 1 to 1.5 m thick and consist of very clayey, sandy gravel with some beds of extremely sandy clay. Between Ashurst Bridge [3435 1232] and Poternsford Bridge [3273 1091] these deposits are up to 1 m thick, and consist of very clayey sandy gravel and gravelly clay.

Wimpson – Marchwood

A borehole [3859 1419] on the 1st Terrace at Wimpson showed 2.4 m of gravelly brown sandy clay overlying 2 m of brown sandy gravel. A nearby borehole [3858 1405] proved 1.7 m of brown sandy clay resting on 4.4 m of dense brown sand with gravel.

A borehole [3939 1138] at Marchwood Power Station showed 0.76 m of Made Ground overlying 4.27 m of fine- medium-, and coarse-grained gravel of the 1st Terrace, which rested on Selsey Sand.

Brambridge – Eastleigh – Swaythling – Weston

A borehole [4699 2209] in the 1st Terrace near Brambridge House proved 1.2 m of sandy medium- to fine-grained gravel with brown silty clay on 1.9 m of sandy, medium- to fine-grained gravel.

At Highbridge, the 1st Terrace was penetrated in two boreholes [4643 2102; 4626 2127] which proved 1.2 m and 1.6 m respectively of coarse-, medium- and fine-grained flint gravel with sand lenses.

Numerous boreholes in the Eastleigh area penetrated gravel and sand in the 1st Terrace with thicknesses varying from 0.9 to 5.6 m. The gravel thickens westward toward the back of the terrace. The terrace is overlain by brown silty clay with a few flints, generally 0.5 to 2.0 m thick. At Chickenhall Farm [466 180], 11 boreholes penetrated an average of 1.2 m of silty brown clay with occasional flints, the range of thickness being 0.63 to 1.98 m.

In the Swaythling area, boreholes [447 169] west of Wide Lane Bridge in the 1st Terrace proved about 3 m of flint gravel with a little sand beneath 0.6 to 0.9 m of topsoil.

Hythe area

South-east of Hythe, a site-investigation borehole [4320 0693] in the 1st Terrace proved the following sequence:

	Thickness m	Depth m
Topsoil with small stones	1.2	1.2
RIVER TERRACE DEPOSITS (1st Terrace)		
Sand, pale brown, slightly clayey, fine-grained, with large pockets of pale grey sand and fine- to medium-grained gravel	2.1	3.3
Clay, firm, mottled light brown, pale grey, silty	0.9	4.2
Sand, fine- and medium-grained, greyish brown, with some gravel	1.4	5.6
Gravel, fine-, medium- and coarse-grained, in a greyish brown clayey fine- and medium-grained sand matrix	2.0	7.6

The lower part of the sequence includes Buried Channel Deposits, but these cannot be differentiated here from the River Terrace Deposits.

Weston – Hamble – Warsash – Hook

A borehole [4459 0970] in the 2nd Terrace at Weston proved grey and brown, silty, sandy clay with some gravel resting on 0.7 m of fine to coarse gravel.

Small cliffs [4677 0700] in the 2nd Terrace at Hamble show 3 m of yellowish brown gravel overlying Selsey Sand. A nearby borehole [4749 0645] showed 5.3 m of fine-, medium- and coarse-grained gravel with fine-, medium, and coarse-grained sand.

Warsash area

Excavations [4948 0565] at Warsash showed the thickness of the 2nd Terrace gravels to be about 1.5 m; hand axes of Middle Acheulean type were recorded by Shackley (1970) from this locality.

The following section was recorded in a gravel-pit [5126 0510] at Hook:

	Thickness m
RIVER TERRACE DEPOSITS (2nd Terrace)	
Clay, orange-brown, extremely sandy, and very clayey sand	1.30
Gravel, orange, sandy, with occasional cobbles commonly up to 5 cm across, and some sand beds	2.35
Gravel, orange-brown, with cobbles commonly up to 5 cm across	1.13
SELSEY SAND	

BURIED CHANNEL DEPOSITS

It is likely that whenever the Quaternary sea-level fell below its present level the rivers of the district cut down so as to grade to it: when sea-level recovered sediment choked the channel. The Test, Itchen and Hamble all overlie buried channels which are presumably composite in age, though this is hard to verify. South-east of the Isle of Wight, Dyer (1975) has established that the base of the 'channel' falls to 46 m below OD.

The channels are flanked by river terraces, now covered by the sea. These terraces represent alluvial sediments that choked an early channel, and were then dissected as sea-level fell again, presumably during the late-Devensian glaciation. Everard (1954) has described gravel terraces at 1.5 and 2.5 m below OD, and Hodson and West (1972) have recorded one at Fawley that is at 21 m below OD. The gravels are known beneath Southampton docks, at Dibden, near Weston and Fawley, and in the Test, Itchen and Hamble estuaries. Their position in relation to the most recently excavated channel suggests that they formed in the Devensian, but before the growth of the late-Devensian ice-sheets.

The latest buried channel cuts through these deposits and is itself partly filled with Flandrian clays, silts, sands, fresh-water marls and subordinate gravels. The oldest deposits are fluviatile, but these are replaced upwards by salt-marsh and estuarine sediments deposited as the sea gradually re-invaded the estuaries when the late-Devensian ice melted. Many sections have been described from excavations in Southampton (Hooley, 1903), Southampton docks (Godwin and Godwin, 1940), and Fawley (Hodson and West, 1972); the latter authors have also dealt with the flora and fauna. A radio-carbon date of 6366 BP has been obtained from shelly deposits at 7.3 m below OD at Fawley Power Station, and another of 3689 BP from peats at 3 m below OD at Fawley (Churchill *in* Godwin and Switzur, 1966)

Details

New Docks area

A section [414 120] examined by Hooley (1903) showed 2.74 m of clay overlying about 1 m of peat on 0.07 m of subangular flint gravel. The peat contained remains of oak and pine, and the bones of numerous mammals including red deer and fox. Estuarine molluscs were found near the base of the clays. The main part of the buried channel lies just SW of the outer wall of the new docks, where a borehole [4095 1139] showed the following section:

	Thickness m	Depth m
ESTUARINE ALLUVIUM		
Mud	3.73	3.73
BURIED CHANNEL DEPOSITS		
Peat	2.05	5.78
Sand, loamy	0.30	6.08
Gravel	0.68	6.76

Fawley area

A site-investigation borehole, probably located near the central part [4879 0379] of the buried channel, proved the following section commencing at 0.45 m below OD:

	Thickness m	Depth m
ESTUARINE ALLUVIUM		
Silt	5.02	5.02
BURIED CHANNEL DEPOSITS		
Peat, black	0.61	5.63
Silt, soft, grey	2.75	8.38
Peat, black	0.30	8.68
Gravel (?Pleistocene)	0.31	8.99

ESTUARINE ALLUVIUM

The Estuarine Alluvium of Southampton Water and associated tributaries consists of mud, silt and sand, all high in organic content, and minor amounts of gravel. The deposits are entirely Holocene in age. The deposit has been mapped up the tributary valleys as far as the upper limit of spring tides. Its lower limit has been taken as the lower limit of spring tides. The deposit forms extensive areas of intertidal mud flats and salt marsh. Much of the outcrop of the Estuarine Alluvium is covered by Made Ground; such areas include Southampton container port complex [385 125] and Fawley Oil Refinery [460 050]. Another extensive area occurs south-east of Hythe between [430 075] and [455 050], where mud flats occur beside salt marsh.

ALLUVIUM AND CALCAREOUS TUFA

The main tracts of Alluvium occur along the valleys of the rivers Test and Itchen; most of the smaller streams are also bordered by narrow alluvial strips. The alluvial plain of the Test is generally around 1 km wide, and is underlain by between 1 and 3 m of peat, clayey peat and brown organic silty clay that rests on 2 to 6 m of flint gravel. The sequence is similar in the valley of the Itchen, where 0.4 to 3 m of peaty deposits overlie 2 to 3 m of gravel. The alluvial sequences of the smaller streams of the district are variable in detail, but typically consist of up to 1.5 m of clayey sand and silty clay, locally with scattered flints, resting on up to 1.5 m of flint gravel.

Valley bogs draining into the Beaulieu River between Lynd-hurst and Dibden Purlieu are underlain by brown organic clay, peaty clay and peat; the peat has been worked in places. These peaty deposits generally rest on a thin bed of gravel.

The Alluvium of the Itchen contains beds of Calcareous Tufa (the 'Shell-Marl' of the 1902 memoir) that form hummocks ('malm-knolls') up to 0.2 m above the level of the peaty deposits on which they rest. The tufa is confined to the section of the valley, north of Bambridge, that crosses the outcrop of the Chalk, which is the source of the calcium carbonate in the tufas. Sporadic occurrences of tufa are also present in the Alluvium farther south in the valley of the Itchen, and also in the peaty deposits of the Test alluvium.

The mapped tufa deposits in the Itchen valley consist of cream to grey, concentrically laminated stem crustations of the freshwater plant *Chara*, set in a variable matrix of fine-grained calcareous debris. The tufas themselves occur as concretionary masses, up to 0.4 m across and with a concentric growth pattern around a central core which is commonly a flint pebble, set in peaty clay or peat. Freshwater bivalves and gastropods and land snails were recorded from tufas of the Test and Itchen by Kemp (1889). None of these came from the Itchen tufas north of Brambridge, but boreholes farther south in the Itchen valley and in the Test valley near Nursling penetrated tufaceous clays with shells.

Details

River Test

A borehole [3550 2223] in the Alluvium north of Romsey proved 0.18 m of topsoil on 1.92 m of soft dark brown peat and very soft dark brown peat with light brown clayey silty sand. This last rested on 0.9 m of pale grey to white weakly cemented calcareous tufa which, in turn, rested on 2.7 m of medium dense coarse- to medium-grained and fine-grained flint gravel.

A borehole [3497 2064] at the river-bridge west of Romsey proved 0.40 m of topsoil and fill resting on 2.50 m of very soft dark brown peat with occasional thin 'chalky' silt layers which rested on 1.95 m of fine, medium and coarse flint gravel that was clayey towards its base.

Site-investigation boreholes for the M27 motorway embankment between Hillstreet and Nursling [3460 1643 to 3756 1632] proved a maximum alluvial thickness of 9.1 m at [3497 1640]. The base of the sequence was at 4.3 m below OD. It consisted of 0.3 m of topsoil, on 2.6 m of soft black peat with 'chalky' (tufa?) layers particularly in the upper levels, on 6.2 m of flint gravel with some grey sand. Thinner drift sequences are present around the present river channel of the Test, where a borehole [3456 1639] penetrated 0.8 m of topsoil on 0.7 m of soft black peat which rested on 3.2 m of flint gravel with some sand. The base of the Alluvium was at 0.2 m above OD. Gravel was extracted for construction of the M27 motorway embankments from pits [3475 1620 to 3540 1620] (now flooded and called Broadlands Lake).

River Itchen

North of Brambridge Park [472 223] mounds of Calcareous Tufa occur sporadically within the Alluvium. A borehole [4750 2321] in this area penetrated 1.22 m of tufa on 2.44 m of clay and peat on 4.27 m of gravel.

A borehole [4656 2153] 230 m NW of Highbridge showed a typical sequence in Alluvium that consisted, in descending order, of 0.2 m of topsoil, 0.4 m of very soft silty peat, 0.7 m of firm grey sandy silty clay with medium- to fine-grained flint gravel and 1.3 m of medium dense, coarse-, medium, and fine-grained gravel. The base of the sequence is at 2.6 m above OD.

Between Bishopstoke and the M27 crossing of the Itchen valley [4670 1896 to 4524 1583], numerous boreholes indicate a general sequence of about 0.3 m of topsoil, on 1.5 to 3.2 m of peat and clayey peat, on 1.1 to 3.5 m of gravel with some sand and traces of silty clay. Some boreholes, [e.g. 4679 1874], proved a thin bed of 'fine gravel-sized cellular calcareous material' (possibly Calcareous Tufa) between the peat and topsoil. In the southern part of that area, shells are reported in some boreholes [4594 1650; 4542 1579] in brown organic silty clays. These clays are 0.7 m thick in the latter borehole and rest on clayey peat.

Boreholes [4502 1593 to 4545 1566] along the line of the M27 east of Swaythling penetrated up to 6 m of Alluvium beneath 0.2 to 0.6 m of topsoil. The Alluvium consists of 1.2 to 3.2 m of soft black peat on 2.1 to 3.2 m of flint gravel with a little sand. In one borehole [4516 1586] the peat, 2.1 m thick, is recorded as containing bands of soft, dark brown, sandy silty clay with many small shell fragments. Boreholes [4529 1575 to 4545 1566] in the eastern half of the valley penetrated 0.5 to 1.0 m of soft, grey and brown, organic silty clay above the peat; in one borehole [4542 1579] the clay is shelly.

River Blackwater – Cadnam River

The alluvial flats bordering these streams are commonly less than 100 m wide. Small exposures in the banks of the Blackwater, e.g. near Landford Lodge [2490 2003] and near West Wellow [2974 2008] generally reveal up to 1.5 m of yellowish brown to reddish brown and grey, very clayey sand and silty clay with scattered flints,

resting on gravel. The base of gravel is rarely seen, but the deposit probably does not exceed 1.5 in thickness.

A borehole [3310 1669] penetrated the Alluvium of the Cadnam River near Wigley and proved it to consist of 1.0 m of brown sandy clay with gravel on 1.2 m of brown gravel with sand. Peaty alluvium of unknown thickness is present at Cadnam Bog [290 154]. Ditch exposures [2938 1574] just north of Crock Hill, Newbridge, reveal up to 1.5 m of dark brown peat and clayey peat overlying 1.5 m of greyish green sand with traces of gravel.

Monks Brook

A borehole [4341 2061] through Alluvium in Chandler's Ford proved, in descending order: 0.3 m of topsoil and fill; 0.5 m of orange, brown and grey mottled, silty, very sandy clay with scattered fine-grained gravel; 0.7 m of soft to firm brown, grey and black, organic silty sandy clay with occasional fine- to medium-grained gravel; and 1.5 m of medium dense, grey, brown and black, fine-, medium-, and coarse-grained, subangular sandy gravel.

LANDSLIP

Landslips are confined to slopes around Romsey and near Bitterne where Wittering Formation laminated clays are overlain by river terrace gravels.

Details

Romsey area

Hummocky ground [345 205] lying between the A31 and A27 roads west of Romsey is underlain by slipped laminated clays of the Wittering Formation. The western margin of the slip lies 100 m east of the outcrop of 7th Terrace gravels. A borehole [3451 2051] in the toe of the landslip penetrated about 5.6 m of brown, yellowish brown and greyish green, extremely clayey, glauconitic sand with scattered angular flints and fragments of brown carbonaceous clay and lignite. Uneven marshy ground [3390 2127 to 3423 2087] north of the A27 road is also interpreted as slipped material.

Landslips near Halterworth [370 215 to 374 219; 3785 2195] involve laminated clays of the Wittering Formation just beneath the base of the Earnley Sand, which is in turn closely overlain by gravels of the 4th and 6th Terraces.

Merry Oak, Southampton

Landslipping has occurred in the vicinity of Gainsford Road and Braeside Road in Merry Oak on a NW-facing slope. Slips were noted during the early 1890s by Whitaker when he was carrying out the first 1:10 560-scale geological survey. Several small scarps oriented NE–SW and N–S were present on the slope at that time. Movements occurred in 1978 and 1979 behind the houses [440 121] on the SE side of Gainsford Road. The bulk of the site rests on gravels of the 4th Terrace that overlie laminated clays with bands and partings of sand (Wittering Formation). Part of the site is underlain by clays of the Wittering Formation overlain by up to 2.5 m of Head and up to 3 m of Made Ground. Dr M. F. Barton (written communication, 1981) considers that the 1979 landslip involved only the Made Ground and Head, and was caused by a rise in the water-table in the Made Ground. This reduced the effective stress in the main body of material and caused positive pore pressures, and a consequential reduction in strength. It is probable that the older land-slips involve Wittering Formation and Head.

MADE GROUND

The Made Ground of the Southampton district can be divided into three. The first is found mainly in the older part of Southampton City and ranges in age from Roman through medieval to modern. It consists mainly of rubble derived from previous buildings and their foundations, and is very variable in thickness. Site-investigation boreholes have proved thicknesses of this type of material of up to 4.5 m, [e.g. 422 114], but thicknesses of 1.2 to 1.5 m are more typical. Highly variable thicknesses of this type of Made Ground also occur on the west bank of the Itchen around and south of Northam. There also, thicknesses can be up to 4 m, but the general thickness is around 1 m.

The second type of Made Ground is that filling worked-out gravel-, sand- and clay-pits. The Made Ground within these pits varies markedly and commonly consists of building rubble mixed with domestic refuse, or of waste and overburden produced during the operation of the pit. In the Aldermoor area, in the northern part of Southampton, boreholes and trial-pits proved an area [3996 1565 to 4025 1577] of up to 4 m of malodorous general household refuse filling an old clay-pit. Disused gravel-pits near Hound, south-east of Southampton at around [455 095], have now been almost completely filled with a variety of types of refuse, including domestic rubbish up to 4 m thick. In the Warsash and Hook area gravel-pits have been backfilled, sometimes with domestic refuse, but in many other cases, particularly south of Hook [510 053], with waste material from gravel production. The original thick loamy soil ('brickearth') has been reinstated to restore the land to agriculture. On the south-western side of the river Test around Hardley [426 045] and Holbury, systematic backfilling of pits has not taken place. One pit [422 042] has, however, been filled with domestic refuse which, according to later drilling, is in places over 3 m thick.

The third type of Made Ground consists of reclaimed land, mainly adjacent to Southampton Water. The two most extensive areas are between Marchwood and Hythe, at around [410 095], and at Fawley Oil Refinery. At Marchwood and Hythe, fill material—mainly river dredgings—has been built out over the Estuarine Alluvium. At Fawley Oil Refinery, where the fill material is probably mainly gravel, the Made Ground has also been built out over estuarine deposits.

The docks complex of Southampton, from the older docks at the mouth of the Itchen upstream to the most recent container docks, are all sited on Made Ground built out over Estuarine Alluvium and Buried Channel Deposits.

CHAPTER 12

Economic geology

SOILS AND LAND USE

The following account of the major soil types of the Southampton district is largely based on the on 1:250 000-scale Soil Map, Sheet 6 of the Soil Survey of England and Wales (1983) and the accompanying booklet (Mackney and others, 1983), together with observations made during the geological resurvey. Kay (1939) surveyed the soils of the 'Strawberry District' of south Hampshire between West End and Hamble.

The most widespread soils of the district, developed mainly on all except the sandiest of the Tertiary formations, are broadly classified by the Soil Survey as surface-water gley soils. Such soils, characterised by prominent mottling above 40 cm depth, are seasonally waterlogged and slowly permeable. The two chief varieties present in the district have a distinct topsoil and are called stagnogley soils; those developed on the Reading Formation and London Clay in the north-east are pelo- (clayey) stagnogley soils; elswhere, typical stagnogley soils—characterised by clay-enriched subsoil—are dominant. In the New Forest, typical stagnogley soils carry mainly deciduous and coniferous woodland, with areas of wet lowland heath; small agricultural holdings are present within the Forest around Fritham, Brook, Bramshaw, and Minstead. Outside the New Forest, the typical stagnogley soils, where not built over, are used mainly for growing permanent and short-term grass, and some cereals; considerable areas of woodland are present on the London Clay outcrop in the north-west of the district.

The second commonest soil type is classed as podzol, characterised by an upper 'bleached' horizon overlying a dark humus-enriched subsoil horizon into which sesquioxides, especially iron, have been carried by leaching. The podzols of the district are mainly included by the Soil Survey in the subdivision stagnogley-podzols, in which the humus-enriched layer is directly underlain by a greyish or mottled horizon. In the northern New Forest, such soils are developed on the heaths north of Bramshaw underlain by sands of the Marsh Farm Formation, and Earnley Sand. Podzols are also developed on the sandy parent materials of the Becton Sand and Chama Sand, which underlie infertile heaths in the southern New Forest between Lyndhurst and Dibden Purlieu. Valley bogs are commonest in this area, occurring in hollows underlain at shallow depth by organic clay and peat. Stagnogley podzols, developed on River Terrace Deposits (5th and 6th Terraces) south of Dibden Purlieu and on the 10th and 11th Terraces near Chilworth consist of naturally very acid loamy soil overlying clayey soil with a bleached subsurface horizon, which have slowly permeable subsoils and are subject to slight seasonal waterlogging. Humose or peaty surface horizons are locally present. Some of the soils are shallow and very flinty (Mackney and others, 1983). Similar soils also occur on the extensive flat heaths underlain by Older River Gravels in the west of the district.

These and other New Forest heaths were formerly covered by woodland which was removed by man, the decline in the quality of the soils being a direct consequence of deforestation and shallow ploughing, which both encouraged leaching of soluble mineral salts from the soil (Tubb, 1968). The heaths would probably be replaced by woodland were it not for browsing and grazing by deer and livestock, together with controlled heath burning.

Other podzolic soils include the humo-ferric podzols of the Soil Survey that are developed on the Whitecliff Sand outcrop between Romsey and Otterbourne, and on part of the Earnley Sand outcrop east of North Baddesley. They are mainly well drained sandy to pebbly soils with a bleached subsurface horizon.

Ground-water gley soils, probably the third most extensive soil class in the district, have strongly mottled or grey subsoils that result from periodic waterlogging from a fluctuating groundwater table. The main type in the district has a clay-enriched subsoil and is termed typical argillic gley soil by the Soil Survey. Such soils are developed at scattered localities in the district on River Terrace Deposits, and consist of coarse and fine loamy permeable soils mainly over gravel. The main occurrences are on undifferentiated River Terrace Deposits flanking the River Blackwater between Hamptworth and Nursling; on scattered terrace remnants (mainly 3rd and 4th Terraces) on the east side of the River Test between Romsey and Nursling; on areas of 1st and 2nd Terrace (mostly built over) around Totton; on undifferentiated River Terrace Deposits at Pollards Moor, Cadnam; and on the 1st and 2nd Terrace north of Marchwood. In the New Forest, an extensive area of argillic gley soil occurs on undifferentiated River Terrace Deposits south-west of Lyndhurst and on the 1st Terrace south-west of Dibden Purlieu.

Other ground-water gley soils, classed as pelo- (clayey) alluvial gley soils, occupy small areas of riverine Alluvium north of West Wellow and overlie Estuarine Alluvium north-east of Totton and south-east of Marchwood.

Other soil types, mainly rendzinas, brown earths, and peaty soils, occupy small areas of the district and are described below. The outcrop of Chalk in the north-east of the district is partly occupied by brown rendzinas—shallow, well drained calcareous, silty soils. Patches of Clay-with-flints on the Chalk are associated with argillic brown earths (see below) that are well-drained, commonly very flinty soils, with silty upper horizons over clayey lower horizons (Mackney and others, 1983). The land is mainly agricultural, predominantly used for growing winter cereals and short-term grass, and for rearing stock.

Brown earths have mainly brown or reddish-coloured subsurface horizons that lack mottled or greyish-coloured (gleyed) horizons above 40 cm depth. Argillic brown earths, the main type in the district, are loamy or loamy over clayey soils with a clay-enriched subsoil. The predominantly sandy Reading Formation in the north-west of the district carries argillic brown earths, well drained loamy and sandy soils used mainly for growing cereals and short-term grass.

Other argillic brown earths of the district are developed mainly on River Terrace Deposits. Well drained silty soils are present on gravelly River Terrace Deposits overlain by variable thicknesses of brown clay and loam ('brickearth'). The main occurrences are on the 4th Terrace east of Romsey; on the 1st Terrace between Romsey and Nursling; on the 1st Terrace around Eastleigh; around Hound on a number of terrace levels; and on the 3rd Terrace south of Hook. These soils are suitable for a wide variety of agricultural and horticultural crops. The 7th, 8th and 9th Terraces west of Romsey and the 1st Terrace near Brambridge carry argillic brown earths, that are mainly well-drained gravelly soils, but associated with seasonally waterlogged soils with loamy upper horizons and clayey lower horizons (Mackney and others, 1983). They are used for growing cereals and grass.

Soils developed on the Alluvium of the River Itchen, and on the Alluvium of the River Test north of c.[350 185] are peaty, locally with Calcareous Tufa, and are used mainly for permanent grass and rough grazing. North of Cupernham, Romsey, the soils are artificially well drained and used for growing nursery plants.

BRICK AND TILE CLAYS

With the closure in 1974 of the Lower Swanwick Brickworks [501 099], clays are no longer dug for brickmaking anywhere in the district. The London Clay and Wittering Formation were the main sources of brick clays, but the Reading Formation, Marsh Farm Formation and Barton Clay have also been utilised to a lesser extent. Of the superficial deposits, the main types used for brickmaking were the clays and loams ('brickearths') found overlying terrace gravel deposits. The industry declined because the Hampshire workings could not compete with the much larger workings in the Oxford Clay of eastern England. Historical and stratigraphical details of disused brick-pits in the district are contained in White (1971) and in BGS files.

GRAVEL AND SAND

Quaternary river terrace deposits are widespread in the district and have been extensively dug for sand and gravel. The Older River Gravels were formerly worked in extensive pits [2493 1114 to 2549 1138] in Older Terrace 3 at Stoney Cross. Older River Gravels east of the Avon valley, immediately west of the present district, were shown by Kubala (1980) to have a mean grading of fines (less than 1/16 mm) 19%, sand (1/16 mm to 4 mm) 25%, and gravel (over 4 mm) 56%. Most of the gravel dug in the district comes from River Terrace Deposits, mainly from the 6th and 7th Terraces west of Romsey, the 4th and 5th Terraces east of Romsey, the 1st Terrace near Nursling, the 3rd and 4th Terraces near Netley, the 2nd and 3rd Terraces near Hamble, and the 5th Terrace near Fawley.

The Reading Formation and Whitecliff Sand are the main sources of building sand, concreting sand, and plastering sand in the district. Grading analyses carried out on samples collected during the resurvey are given in Tables 2 and 3 in which the grain-size classification is that used in Mineral Assessment Reports of BGS. The Portsmouth Sand in the Bitterne area has been worked in small pits, but much of its outcrop is now built over. Its use as building sand is restricted by its fine grain-size. The Becton Sand has also been worked on a small scale, for example near Lyndhurst, but there is no working at present in the district. Becton Sand from a pit [363 085] near Longdown is reported to have been used for glass manufacture.

MOULDING SAND

At present only one pit near Hound [4792 0865] in the Earnley Sand is producing moulding sand within the district. The Chama Sand has also been used in the past as a moulding sand; pits were reputedly worked in the Longdown area about 4 km south of Totton.

CHALK AND MARL

Numerous pits on the Chalk outcrop were formerly the source of agricultural lime for use on the adjacent Palaeogene outcrop. Shelly clays in the Headon Formation were used for marling in the New Forest, probably until early this century. Old marl-pits in the Headon Formation, mostly overgrown, can be seen near Bolderwood [2445 0722], at Acres Down near Lyndhurst [2721 0894], southwest of Lyndhurst [3096 0710], and near Beaulieu [3783 0395].

PEAT

Areas of Alluvium beneath valley bogs in the Denny Lodge area carry peaty deposits which have been worked in the historically recent past. Tremlett (1961) considered that peat cutting had taken place in the northern part [343 055] of the Bishop of Winchester's Purlieu. Peaty deposits in the Alluvium of the rivers Test and Itchen have not been exploited, as far as is known.

HYDROCARBONS

The district lies within an area currently being prospected for hydrocarbons. The nearest operating oilfield is at Wytch Farm, Dorset, 30 km to the south-west, which produced 215 000 tonnes of oil in 1983 (Department of Energy, 1984). The reservoir rocks at Wytch Farm are the Triassic Sherwood Sandstone and the Jurassic Bridport Sands; the oil source rocks are thought to be Jurassic clays. A second oilfield, about 40 km north-east of Southampton at Humbly Grove near Basingstoke, is currently under development (1985). Recent finds of possible commercial importance include that at Horndean, Sussex, 30 km east of Southampton (Yarbrough, 1984).

The reservoir rocks of most interest in the Southampton district are the Sherwood Sandstone and the Bridport Sands; other possible reservoirs occur in the Middle Jurassic limestones. No significant hydrocarbon shows were recorded in the Marchwood and Western Esplanade boreholes, although the Sherwood Sandstone and Bridport Sands there have appreciable porosities and permeabilities. A recent hydrocarbon-exploration borehole at Hoe [3845 1915], between Southampton and Romsey, was dry (Kat, 1983).

The mechanism of hydrocarbon formation, migration, and entrapment has been shown in Dorset (Colter and Havard, 1981) to involve pre-Albian fault movements with downthrows to the south across E–W-trending faults. In the downthrown areas Jurassic source rocks descended to sufficient depths for them to generate hydrocarbons. These fluids then migrated northward across the faults into the Sherwood Sandstone and Bridport Sands which lay at higher structural levels within the fault blocks. Post-Albian movements along the same faults in some cases reversed the relative heights of the source and reservoir rocks on either side of the faults. This type of hydrocarbon structural trap occurs throughout the Hampshire Basin and is the basis of the current exploration activity in the region.

GEOTHERMAL ENERGY

The district lies within an area of high heat flow covering east Dorset and south-west Hampshire. At Southampton, the rate is about 59 milliwatts per square metre (mW/m^2) compared to $40\ mW/m^2$ for more northerly parts of Hampshire. High heat flow combined with the possible presence of aquifers at considerable depth led to the drilling of two boreholes to evaluate geothermal energy resources in the district—one at Marchwood, the other at Western Esplanade near Southampton city centre. The most promising potential aquifer, the Sherwood Sandstone, occurred at shallower depths than had been predicted, but was sufficiently deep to be useful. At Marchwood, pumping tests (Price and Allen, 1982) showed that a pumping rate of 29 litres per second (l/s) was feasible giving a drawdown from 5 m down to 370 m; it was calculated that after pumping for 20 years at 29 l/s, the drawdown would be 550 metres. The temperature of water at the surface was 71.6°C. and the down-hole temperature stabilised at 73.6°C. At the Western Esplanade Borehole (Allen and others, 1983) the borehole was pumped at 19.86 l/s for 33 days with a drawdown to 365 m below ground level. The temperature at surface was 74.9°C. and at

Table 2 Grading analyses of Reading Formation sands from the Sherfield English area

Sample locations	FINES	SAND		
Grid reference of sample is given in square brackets	Less than $^1/_{16}$ mm ($<4\phi$)	$^1/_{16}$ to $^1/_4$ mm (4ϕ to 2ϕ)	$^1/_4$ to 1 mm (2ϕ to 0ϕ)	1 to 4 mm (0ϕ to -2ϕ)
[3050 3384]**	2.0	5.5	91.5	—
[3055 2300]**	6.0	61.0	33.0	—
[2332 2303]*	3.7	53.3	43.0	—
[3059 2284]**	7.0	91.3	1.7	—
[3062 2289]*	1.3	6.7	91.9	0.1
[2301 2237]**	5.3	12.7	81.8	0.2
[3036 2288]**	3.5	12.9	82.5	1.1
[3043 2339]*	3.3	18.7	78.0	—
[3007 2264]**	13.7	85.9	0.4	—
[3024 2385]**	5.3	8.9	85.6	0.2
[3062 2331]*	14.5	10.5	75.0	—
[3050 2240]*	1.6	44.4	53.9	0.1
[3045 2246]*	2.0	31.0	67.0	—
[3037 2255]*	1.3	6.2	92.2	0.3
[3050 2240]*	1.8	57.2	41.0	—
[2824 2274]*	4.0	93.5	2.5	—
[2821 2270]*	1.5	14.5	84.0	—
[2821 2270]*	1.6	20.4	78.0	—
[2819 2280]*	1.8	3.6	94.6	—
[2819 2280]*	13.0	83.5	2.8	0.7
[2819 2280]*	3.3	9.7	85.0	2.0

* Samples taken from sand-pits
** Samples taken from small exposures

1755 m was 76°C. Most of the yield comes from thin beds of medium- to coarse-grained sandstone within fining-upward fluviatile sequences in the Sherwood Sandstone, but these sandstones were only 11 m thick in the Western Esplanade Borehole. Thus quite small fault movements could disrupt the reservoir, as could the rapid facies changes which characterise this type of sedimentation. It is probable that the Sherwood Sandstone becomes thinner and finer grained east of Southampton, thus losing its potential as a geothermal source.

HYDROGEOLOGY AND WATER SUPPLY

The Southampton district lies almost entirely within Hydrometric Area 42, administered by the Southern Water Authority. A very small segment at the extreme western edge of the district is in Hydrometric Area 43, administered by the Wessex Water Authority.

The two largest rivers crossing the district are the Test and the Itchen, both deriving the greater part of their flow from groundwater discharge from the Upper Chalk in areas outside the district. The ratio of maximum to minimum daily mean flows through the year is about 4 for the Test and about 3 for the Itchen, the streams being to this extent self-regulating. Lesser streams comprise the Hamble, the Blackwater (a tributary of the Test), the Beaulieu River and Bartley Water; they derive a large proportion of their flow from catchments floored by Tertiary strata from which there is much greater run-off, and the stream flow is, therefore, more variable.

The mean annual rainfall varies from about 750 mm in the south of the district to more than 900 mm in the north. The annual actual evaporation ranges from 460 to more than 500 mm (Southern Water Authority, 1980).

Much of the water used for public supply is abstracted from the rivers Test and Itchen, but about 13 million cubic metres (m^3) are pumped annually from the Upper Chalk at Otterbourne [467 230]. The most important aquifer is the Chalk; the Whitecliff Sand, Bracklesham Group, and Becton Sand, are of lesser importance.

Groundwater resources of the Chalk depend upon infiltration into the outcrop outside the district. Wells and boreholes are restricted to the northern part of the district where the formation crops out or where the overburden is relatively thin. With an overburden thickness greater than 50 m, the specific capacity of a borehole is likely to be less than one cubic metre per day per metre of drawdown per metre of saturated aquifer penetrated (m/d), whereas with less than 50 m thickness, the value may exceed 3.5 m/d. A borehole [436 109], drilled at Southampton in 1912 to a depth of 335 m, reached the Chalk at a depth of 189 m: its yield was only about 590 cubic metres per day (m^3/d), and the quality was poor. With thin or no overburden, yields of 2000 m^3/d or more can be expected from boreholes of 300 mm diameter. However, the yields of boreholes in the Chalk depend upon intersecting water-bearing fissures, and the random distribution of these leads to considerable variation in yield. Many boreholes have a poor initial yield due to the blocking of fissures by slurry formed during drilling, and development with hydrochloric acid ('acidisation') is com-

mon. The quality of groundwater from the Chalk is generally good. The total hardness, mostly carbonate (temporary) hardness, usually ranges between 200 and 300 milligrammes per litre (mg/l), exceptionally being as much as 400 mg/l. The chloride ion concentration is normally less than 25 mg/l, but increases with greater thickness of overburden; the borehole in Southampton previously mentioned showed a value of 700 mg/l. The use of nitrogenous fertilisers over the Chalk outcrop has led to an increase of nitrates in the groundwater, and values exceeding 10mg/l (as NO^3) have been recorded.

Where sandy strata are present, the Reading Formation can yield up to 200 m^3/d to boreholes, although this may in part be due to recharge of the basal sands from the underlying Chalk. A more usual yield is less than 100 m^3/d, and boreholes may be dry where the sands are thin or absent. Further development of the Reading Formation has been inhibited by the presence of the more permeable Chalk beneath, the latter offering a more reliable source.

Sandy beds in the London Clay at various levels beneath the Whitecliff Sand occasionally provide small yields of up to 100 m^3/d, but natural replenishment is hindered by the enclosing clayey strata, and initial yields often diminish with time. The Whitecliff Sand yields groundwater to boreholes much more readily, but the incoherence of the sands requires the use of properly designed and placed sand screens and filter packs. In the past, under-development of poorly designed boreholes has led to silting with consequent deterioration in yield. Most boreholes in the sands are of 200 mm diameter or less, and yield up to 500 m^3/d. Boreholes of larger diameter have occasionally yielded more than 1000 m^3/d, but the sands are not generally able to support large industrial or public supplies. Shallow wells in the sands are liable to surface contamination and need careful siting. In the deeper boreholes, the total hardness rarely exceeds 150 mg/l, and the chloride ion concentration is usually less than 30 mg/l. Iron is sometimes present in amounts exceeding 0.5 mg/l, giving an unpleasant taste to the water.

The variable lithology of the Bracklesham Group makes it difficult to predict borehole yield. In the area west of Southampton, sandy beds are fairly well developed, and yields may be better there. However, boreholes with little or no yield have been recorded. Boreholes up to 200 mm diameter may yield up to 200 m^3/d, and those over 400 mm diameter have given more than 1800 m^3/d from the sandier strata. Sand screens and filter packs are usually necessary, and poor design and development of these has often led to silting. The ground-water quality is usually quite good, with the total hardness less than 200 mg/l and the chloride ion concentration less than 35 mg/l. Where shallow wells have been polluted, the chloride ion concentration frequently exceeds 50 mg/l. Iron is often present, sometimes in amounts greater than 1.0 mg/l.

The Barton Clay, Chama Sand and the Becton Bunny Member are likely to contain little useable groundwater, although sandier parts of the sequence may yield small supplies. Along the southern edge of the district, the Becton Sand forms a useful and fairly reliable aquifer, with boreholes of 300 mm diameter yielding up to 600 m^3/d. Northwards, yields are less good, and rarely exceed 200 m^3/d. The boundary of the sands, both with the overly-

Table 3 Grading analyses of Whitecliff Sand samples from the Southampton district

Sample locations	FINES		SAND	
Grid reference of sample is given in square backets	Less than $\frac{1}{16}$ mm ($<4\phi$)	$\frac{1}{16}$ to $\frac{1}{4}$ mm (4ϕ to 2ϕ)	$\frac{1}{4}$ to 1 mm (2ϕ to 0ϕ)	1 to 4 mm (0ϕ to -2ϕ)
Hamptworth-Landford				
[2374 1919]**	1.0	10.6	88.4	—
[2497 1944]**	2.8	69.2	28.0	—
[2566 2017]**	0.6	55.4	44.0	—
[2566 2017]**	0.4	41.6	58.0	—
[2553 2029]**	5.0	87.5	7.5	—
[2341 1986]*	2.2	19.8	77.9	0.1
[2366 1907]**	8.6	80.4	11.0	—
[2546 2045]**	1.5	46.5	42.0	—
East Wellow				
[3170 2024]*	2.4	96.9	0.7	—
[3174 2170]**	0.8	94.2	5.0	—
[3117 1975]**	0.8	93.7	5.5	—
[3091 2071]*	1.8	88.2	10.0	—
[3071 2063]*	3.0	96.5	0.5	—
[3091 2071]*	0.4	85.6	14.0	—
[3091 2071]*	0.7	63.3	36.0	—
[3156 2095]**	1.4	87.6	11.0	—
[3156 2095]**	0.5	74.5	25.0	—
[3177 2175]**	3.5	95.1	1.4	—
[3091 2071]*	0.4	45.6	54.0	—
[3070 2067]*	7.6	86.4	6.0	—
Hoe-Chilworth				
[4028 1777]**	2.5	97.2	0.3	—
[3864 1936]**	5.0	94.9	0.1	—
[4025 1803]**	0.6	87.4	12.0	—
[3811 1900]*	0.9	50.1	49.0	—
[3811 1900]*	1.0	73.0	26.0	—
[3811 1900]*	1.6	73.4	25.0	—
[3810 1892]*	0.9	17.6	81.5	—
[3811 1900]*	2.0	27.0	71.0	—
Abbotswood				
[3665 2322]**	2.2	88.3	9.5	—
[3639 2321]**	4.0	89.0	7.0	—
[3653 2323]**	1.6	68.4	30.0	—
[3665 2338]**	13.0	86.5	0.5	—
Ampfield				
[4137 2313]*	3.0	96.7	0.3	—
[3853 2328]**	0.4	86.6	13.0	—
[3816 2292]**	2.2	60.8	37.0	—
[3788 2309]**	2.0	28.0	70.0	—
[3875 2318]*	3.6	53.4	42.9	0.1
[3782 2336]**	1.3	77.7	21.0	—
[4235 2327]**	5.0	94.7	0.3	—
Fair Oak				
[4980 1843]*	0.6	64.0	35.4	—
[5048 1846]*	0.5	70.0	29.5	—
[4965 1834]*	0.5	53.5	46.0	—
[5048 1846]*	0.9	68.0	31.1	—
[4891 1842]*	5.5	18.5	75.6	0.4
Hedge End				
[4821 1295]**	8.0	91.9	0.1	—
[4821 1304]**	5.0	94.9	0.1	—
[4804 1320]**	8.0	91.9	0.1	—
[4788 1329]**	20.0	79.8	0.2	—

* Samples taken from sand-pits
** Samples taken from small exposures

ing Headon Clay and the underlying clayey beds, is commonly marked by a line of seepages and springs. The latter are usually small and individually of little use for supply. The groundwater quality is generally fair, with the total hardness less than 150 mg/l and the chloride ion concentration less than 40 mg/l. Iron is sometimes present in sufficient quantity to give an unpleasant taste to the water.

A number of shallow wells has been constructed in the Headon Formation and, where sandy strata are better developed, yields sufficient for domestic or small agricultural requirements may be obtained. In the more clayey lithologies, yields are very small. Shallow wells in this formation are vulnerable to surface pollution. Yields from Alluvium and terrace gravels are often obtained from the adjacent rivers, and, where the latter are tidal, saline water may enter the well. Older River Gravels and River Terrace Deposits are present over fairly extensive tracts of country around Southampton, and yields of a few cubic metres per day are taken from shallow wells. However, such sources tend to fail after extended dry periods and are particularly vulnerable to surface pollution. The extent of clay and loam capping terrace gravels is limited and their potential small. The Clay-with-flints has no importance as an aquifer, but where it provides an extensive cover for the Chalk, infiltration into the latter may be affected.

APPENDIX 1

Selected cored boreholes

Abbreviated logs of five cored boreholes drilled in the district are given below. The National Grid reference and BGS Registration Number are given for each borehole.

Bunker's Hill Borehole [3038 1498] (SU 31 SW/27), near Copythorne, Cadnam. BGS continuously cored borehole drilled for research by S. P. Thorley and W. H. George using the Geological Survey drilling rig, December 1976 to February 1977. Logged by R. A. Edwards. Macrofaunal determinations by C. King. Surface level approximately 40 m above OD.

	Thickness m	Depth m
BRACKLESHAM GROUP		
MARSH FARM FORMATION		
No recovery (rock-bit drilling)	3.05	3.05
Sand, yellowish brown, fine- to medium-grained, with scattered lignite debris; channelled base	4.57	7.62
Clay, brownish grey, with sand interbeds; sharp base	1.20	8.82
EARNLEY SAND		
Clay, dark greenish grey, sandy, silty, bioturbated; and silt, clayey with patches of glauconitic sand, and a few subvertical sand-filled burrows; interbedded sandy clay and clayey silty sand, with scattered lignite fragments, 10.32–10.59 m	1.77	10.59
Sand, dark greenish grey, clayey, silty, poorly sorted, glauconitic, very fine-grained, with a few clay bands	2.81	13.40
Clay, dark greenish grey, extremely sandy, bioturbated; sandier below 14.0 m; marcasite nodules at 14.25 m	0.44	14.34
Sand, dark greenish grey, silty, ?bioturbated, poorly sorted, glauconitic, fine-grained; irregular clay lenses 14.55–15.00 m; gradational base	1.39	15.73
Sand, greyish green, silty, clayey, bioturbated and burrowed, glauconitic, with some bands of dark greenish grey sandy clay; a few molluscan moulds, including *Caryocorbula*, *Macrosolen* and *Venericardia* in lower 6 m; flint pebbles at the base	0.72	16.45
WITTERING FORMATION		
Sand, greenish grey to yellowish green, fine-grained, sparsely glauconitic, with scattered lignite fragments and lignitic carbonaceous bands; core loss 19.20–19.94 m (driller reports soft sand)	6.58	23.03
Clay, olive-grey, well laminated with 3–4 mm-thick laminae of greenish grey glauconitic fine-grained sand and pale grey fine-grained sand	1.15	24.18
Sand, olive-green, clayey, glauconitic, with olive-grey clay bands	0.12	24.30
Clay, olive-grey, silty, with thin beds and		

	Thickness m	Depth m
lenses of glauconitic clayey sand, and lenses and partings of pale grey very fine-grained sand	2.27	26.57
Sand, pale olive-grey to greenish grey, fine-grained, sparsely glauconitic, with a few thin bands of olive-grey sandy clay	1.70	28.27
Core loss (driller reports soft sand)	1.52	29.79
Sand, greenish grey, clayey, fine-grained, with lignitic debris and bands of olive-grey sandy clay (29.79–29.87 m and 30.00–30.14 m)	0.72	30.51
Clay, dusky yellowish brown, sandy, with sporadic thin beds of greenish grey clayey sand	1.09	31.60
Sand, greenish grey, fine-grained, glauconitic, lignitic debris common at 32.25–32.94 m	0.89	32.49
Core loss (driller reports sand)	0.50	32.99
Clay, dusky yellowish brown, sandy, with rare lenses of pale grey very fine-grained sand	0.77	33.76
Sand, olive-grey to greenish grey, fine-grained, with lignitic bands and sporadic olive-grey clay bands; sharp base	2.13	35.89
Clay, olive-grey, sandy, with rare lenses of pale grey very fine-grained sand, and possible rootlets at 36.15–36.79 m	1.65	37.54
Whitecliff Bay Bed (37.54–38.42 m)		
Clay, brownish black, carbonaceous, smooth to slightly silty, with pyritised wood fragments	0.24	37.78
Clay, brown, smooth to slightly silty	0.19	37.97
Clay, dark yellowish brown, slightly silty, with lignitic fragments; gradational base	0.45	38.42
Clay, brownish grey, with rare 2–3 mm-thick lenses of pale grey very fine-grained sand and silt	2.54	40.96
Clay, greenish grey, with 2–3 mm-thick lenses of very pale grey silt at 41.46–42.00 m and 42.72–42.79 m; sharp base	1.83	42.79
Clay olive-grey and brownish grey, sandy, with rare lenses of pale grey very fine-grained sand below 43.16 m	2.41	45.20
Clay, olive-grey, well laminated, with numerous regular partings of sparsely glauconitic very fine-grained sand	5.83	51.03
Clay, olive-grey, sandy, mostly poorly bedded and bioturbated; laminated at 51.26–51.33 m; 52.99–53.06 m; 53.69–54.00 m; 54.93–54.99 m; 55.45–55.67 m; and 55.92–56.06 m	6.53	57.56
Clay, olive-grey, sandy, interbedded with sand, greenish grey, glauconitic; sharp base	0.44	58.00
LONDON CLAY		
WHITECLIFF SAND		
Sand, greenish grey, fine-grained, moderately sorted, with scattered mica and lignite clasts and bands	8.37	66.37
Clay, olive-grey, sandy	1.37	67.74

	Thickness m	Depth m
Sand, olive-grey, very fine-grained, pebbles at base (possibly basal Division D2 pebble bed)	1.26	69.00
Sand, greenish grey, fine- to very fine-grained, moderately well sorted to well sorted, sparsely glauconitic, with a few clay bands	12.23	81.23

NURSLING SAND

	Thickness m	Depth m
Clay, grey, sandy	0.52	81.75
Sand, greenish grey, olive-grey, very fine-grained, silty, with some clay beds and claystones	3.52	85.27
Clay, olive grey, sandy, silty, bioturbated	1.51	86.78
Sand, very fine-grained, silty; and silt, very sandy, olive-grey, bioturbated, with sporadic thin clay beds; fossiliferous below c.90.7; bed of hard shelly calcareous sandstone with *Glycymeris* (the Glycymeris Sandstone) 97.27–97.66 m; beds of rounded flint pebbles 103.60–103.70 m and 103.81–103.85 m (basal Division C pebble bed)	17.07	103.85
Silt, olive-grey, sandy, clayey; and sand, olive-grey, bioturbated, silty, very fine-grained, with scattered shelly fossils and local concentrations of shelly fossils; gradational base	8.15	112.0

Division B Clays

	Thickness m	Depth m
Clay, olive-grey, silty, with sparsely scattered shelly fossils and sporadic claystones; sharp base with scattered flint pebbles and glauconite (basal Division B pebble bed)	34.12	137.97

Division A clays

	Thickness m	Depth m
Clay, olive-grey, silty, sparsely fossiliferous, grading above c.142 m into olive-grey clayey silty very fine-grained sand and silt; gradational base	13.34	151.31

Basement Bed

	Thickness m	Depth m
Sand, yellowish brown and olive grey, clayey, silty, very fine-grained, glauconitic, bioturbated, with sporadic clay bands and scattered shelly fossils; sharp base	6.03	157.34

READING FORMATION

	Thickness m	Depth m
Clay, red-mottled, nodular	0.62	157.96
Clay and clay-breccia, moderate red- to pale reddish brown-mottled, pale grey, smooth to slightly silty, burrowed in places	5.54	163.50
Core loss (driller reports clay)	0.36	163.86
Clay, pale grey, very slightly silty, burrowed, mottled reddish brown	2.51	166.37
Clay, dark reddish brown-mottled, pale grey, silty to slightly silty, burrowed and ?brecciated	0.84	167.21
Clay, reddish brown-mottled, pale grey, silty, burrowed	1.83	169.04
Core loss (driller reports possibly silty clay)	0.51	169.55
Clay and clay-breccia, olive-brown and pale grey, silty, some reddish brown mottles	1.79	171.34
Clay, olive-brown and dusky red, silty, with calcareous and ?limonitic nodules	0.30	171.64
Clay, greyish red- to dark reddish-brown mottled, pale olive-brown to dusky yellow, silty, with patches of pale grey clay	0.34	171.98
Core loss (driller reports possibly clay)	0.18	172.16
Clay and ?clay-breccia, greyish red to dark reddish brown-mottled, pale olive-brown to dusky yellow, slightly silty, with minor patches of pale grey clay	0.92	173.08
Clay, pale grey, greyish red and dusky red, silty, with dark reddish brown mottles	0.94	174.80
Sand and silt, brownish grey to greyish red-purple, extremely clayey fine- to very fine-grained, red mottled at some levels	1.25	176.05
Clay, greenish grey, sandy to very sandy	0.13	176.18
Clay, dusky red, extremely sandy and silty; clayey silt; and fine-grained sand	0.07	176.25
Sand, pale grey and pale olive-brown, extremely clayey, fine-grained; and silt	0.16	176.41
Silt, extremely clayey; sand, fine-grained; clay, sandy and silty, brownish grey to greyish red-purple	0.09	176.50
Clay, greyish green, silty and sandy, with white calcareous nodules and pale olive-brown mottles	0.11	176.61
Clay, mottled greyish red-purple, dark reddish brown, and greyish green, sandy and silty, with white irregular calcareous nodules	2.0	178.61

Basement Bed

	Thickness m	Depth m
Sand, greyish green, clayey to very clayey and silty, glauconitic; band of oysters at 179.06 m	0.68	179.29
Sand, glauconitic, with scattered angular pebbles and fragments of chalk, on an irregular surface of chalk	0.17	179.46

UPPER CHALK

	Thickness m	Depth m
Chalk, white, fairly hard, containing flints between 181.72 and 182.15 m	6.49	185.95
Final depth		185.95

Shamblehurst Borehole [4927 1456] (SU 41 SE/336), near Hedge End. BGS continuously cored borehole for research drilled by W. H. George using the Geological Survey drilling rig, June 1977–July 1977.

Logged by R. A. Edwards and E. C. Freshney. Macrofaunal determination by C. King; nummulite determinations by M. J. Hughes. Surface level approximately 33 m above OD.

	Thickness m	Depth m

BRACKLESHAM GROUP

EARLEY SAND

	Thickness m	Depth m
No recovery (rock-bit drilling)	3.11	3.11
Sand, dusky yellow and pale olive-brown, extremely clayey	0.38	3.49
Core loss (driller reports soft sand)	2.42	5.91
Sand, pale greyish olive, clayey, silty, very fine-grained, glauconitic, moderately to poorly sorted, patchily orange brown stained; core loss 8.09–8.26 m	3.79	9.70
Sand, dark greenish grey, clayey, silty, very fine-grained, glauconitic, poorly sorted; and clayey sandy silt; core loss 10.55–10.68 m	1.73	11.43
Sand, green, extremely clayey, silty,		

	Thickness m	Depth m

glauconitic, with friable fossils including *Nummulites laevigatus* — 0.15 — 11.58

Core loss (driller reports soft sand) — 2.10 — 13.68

Sand, dark greenish grey, clayey, silty, very fine-grained, glauconitic, bioturbated, very poorly sorted, with friable fossils including *Turritella terebellata* and *Macrosolen* at 14.5–14.7 m; *N. laevigatus* is common throughout — 1.04 — 14.72

Sand, dark greenish grey and dusky blue-green, clayey, silty, very fine-grained, poorly sorted, bioturbated, very glauconitic; large cylindrical burrows common; shells, including *Venericor* common at 15.1–15.3 ; fewer shells below 15.3 m; *N. laevigatus* is present throughout — 1.40 — 16.12

Core loss — 0.56 — 16.68

Silt, dusky blue-green, clayey, sandy, very glauconitic, with impersistent greyish green clay lenticles and common large sand-filled cylindrical burrows — 1.12 — 17.80

Silt, clayey, sandy; and sand, clayey, silty, very fine-grained; greyish green and dusky green, glauconitic, very shelly. *Turritella imbricataria* and *T. terebellata* occur between 17.80 and c.18.05 m; *Turritella* very common between c.18.05 and 18.60 m, with *Venericardia carinata* at 18.32 m, 18.35 m, and 18.50 m; large *Venericor* very common between 18.60 and 18.69 m; *Callista* and rare *Venericor* occur between 20.0 and 20.55 m — 2.75 — 20.55

Sand, olive-grey, clayey, silty, bioturbated, with wood fragments; moulds of *Venericor* and *Venericardia* in upper part — 0.40 — 20.95

WITTERING FORMATION

Clay, olive-grey, silty, with impersistent partings of very pale grey very fine-grained sand spaced at 3–10 mm intervals, penetrated by 10 mm-wide vertical and horizontal burrows filled with clayey sand — 0.42 — 21.37

Core loss — 0.24 — 21.61

Clay, olive-grey, silty, with silt laminae — 0.19 — 21.80

Sand, olive-grey, clayey, fine- to medium-grained, bioturbated, with pods and lenses of olive-grey sandy clay and a few pyrite nodules; lignite fragments and lignitic sand 22.38–22.52 m — 0.72 — 22.52

Clay, olive-grey, with many silt partings, locally lensoid; lignitic debris on some partings — 0.47 — 22.99

Core loss — 1.88 — 24.87

Clay, olive-grey, silty, with patchy areas of olive-grey and brownish grey very clayey sand and a few irregular pyrite nodules — 0.34 — 25.28

Clay, very silty; and silt, clayey; dark greenish grey, with pale grey silt streaks and patches and a few burrows — 0.14 — 25.35

Core loss — 0.90 — 26.25

Clay, dark greenish grey, silty, with small patches of pale grey silt — 1.56 — 27.81

Clay, dark greenish grey, silty, bioturbated, with impersistent very pale grey silt laminae — 0.25 — 28.06

Silt, olive-grey, clayey, bioturbated, with small sand-filled burrows — 0.94 — 29.00

Sand, dark greenish grey, very silty, bioturbated; burrowed lower junction — 0.74 — 29.74

Silt, dark greenish grey, clayey — 0.47 — 30.21

Core loss — 1.74 — 31.95

Sand, pale olive-grey, with lignite fragments — 0.04 — 31.99

Clay, dark greenish grey, extremely silty, with patches and lenticles of clayey sand — 0.23 — 32.22

Whitecliff Bay Bed (32.22–33.20 m)

Clay, dark yellowish brown, slightly silty — 0.06 — 32.28

Clay, olive-grey, slightly silty, with subspherical 1–2 mm patches of very pale grey silt and subvertical pyritised rootlet traces — 0.10 — 32.38

Clay, olive-grey, silty to very silty, with subvertical rootlet traces — 0.92 — 33.20

Clay, olive-grey, silty, laminated, with very thin partings and lenses of pale grey silt and very fine-grained sand, and fairly common small sand-filled horizontal and a few vertical burrows — 9.24 — 42.44

Sand, dark greenish grey, fine-grained, glauconitic, possible low angle cross-bedding at 43.0 m; a few thin clay partings; grain size increases downwards; scattered lignite fragments, larger and more abundant below 46.3 m — 4.45 — 46.69

Clay, greenish grey, very silty, well developed partings and lenses of dark greenish grey and medium grey very fine-grained sand; lamination wavy below 48.0 m; some horizontal burrows — 4.59 — 51.28

Sand, dark greenish grey, fine-grained, with some platy clasts of clay — 0.62 — 51.90

Sand, dark greenish grey, fine-grained, with bands and partings of brownish black lignite, lignitic sand, and lignitic clay — 0.33 — 52.23

Core loss — 0.38 — 52.61

Sand, dark greenish grey, clayey, fine-grained, glauconitic, with up to 5 mm-thick clay bands and scattered lignite fragments — 1.55 — 54.16

LONDON CLAY

Division E

Sand, dark greenish grey, silty, fine-grained, bioturbated — 1.95 — 56.11

Silt, olive-grey, clayey, sandy, bioturbated; upward-coarsening from very silty clay at base; fossiliferous below c.56.4 m; at base, glauconitic horizon filling burrows in underlying unit — 4.74 — 60.85

Division D

Silt, olive-grey, clayey, sandy, bioturbated, sparsely fossiliferous — 8.54 — 69.39

Pebble bed, rounded flints up to 50 mm in clayey fine-grained sand (basal Division D2 pebble bed) — 0.21 — 69.60

Silt, olive-grey, clayey, sandy, bioturbated, with scattered fossils; medium dark grey sandy glauconitic shelly limestone with oysters 71.13–71.34 m; very clayey sandy silt below 78.6 m — 13.77 — 83.37

Pebble bed, scattered rounded flints in glauconitic clayey fine-grained sand; burrowed into underlying unit — 0.08 — 83.45

	Thickness m	Depth m

Division C

Silt, olive grey, very clayey, sandy; locally sandy silty clay; bioturbated, with scattered macrofossils; calcareous nodules 94.35 m — 19.90 — 103.35

Pebble bed, rounded flints up to 30 mm in olive-grey clayey fine-grained sand — 0.05 — 103.40

Division B

Clay, olive-grey, silty to very silty and sandy, bioturbated, with scattered fossils; above c.112 coarsening to sandy silt and sandy clayey silt; sporadic claystones; intra-divisional B1/B2 junction at 129.86 m marked by clay with disseminated glauconite and scattered angular flint grains — 33.50 — 136.90

Division A

Sand, olive-grey, silty, fine- to very fine-grained, with irregular clay flasers and partings, and a few burrows — 4.75 — 141.65

Silt, clayey; and sandy silty clay; olive-grey, bioturbated, with scattered fossils and rare pyritic concretions; gradational base — 6.35 — 148.00

Clay, olive-grey, silty, with scattered fossils; claystone 148.20–148.27 m — 6.60 — 154.60

Clay, olive-grey, very silty, bioturbated, with silt and very fine-grained streaks, burrows and partings; scattered fossils; cementstone 156.16–156.32 m — 3.78 — 158.38

Basement Bed

Silt, sandy, clayey; and silt, sandy; olive-grey; bioturbated, with a few thin clay bands, finely glauconitic, with scattered fossils; sharp base — 3.98 — 162.36

READING FORMATION

Clay, grey, slightly silty and sandy, brecciated and burrowed, with moderate red, dark reddish brown and pale olive-brown mottles — 7.25 — 169.61

Sand, pale grey, extremely clayey, silty, fine- to very fine-grained, mottled moderate red, dark reddish brown and pale olive-brown — 2.32 — 171.93

Silt, and sand, fine-grained; pale olive-brown, indistinctly laminated, with thin clay bands dipping 20° — 2.11 — 174.04

Sand, olive-grey, extremely clayey, fine-grained, with some patches and lenses of clayey sand, small fragments of lignite, and carbonaceous staining — 1.31 — 175.35

Sand, olive-grey, clayey to very clayey, silty fine-grained, with bands and fragments of lignite and carbonaceous clay — 0.91 — 177.06

Clay, silty to extremely sandy and silty; and clay-breccia; greenish grey, burrowed, with intense reddish-brown mottling — 8.77 — 185.83

Clay, greenish grey, extremely silty and sandy, with greyish red purple mottles — 0.22 — 186.05

Basement Bed

Sand and silt, greenish grey, extremely clayey, fine-grained, glauconitic — 0.08 — 186.13

Pebble bed, angular to subrounded flints in a matrix of greyish green glauconitic sand — 0.16 — 186.29

Sand, greyish green and pale olive-brown, extremely clayey, with scattered angular flint pebbles, on an irregular surface of chalk — 0.08 — 186.37

UPPER CHALK

Chalk, white, fairly hard, with scattered flint nodules and grey marly wisps and partings; the topmost 0.36 m with irregular cavities filled with greyish green clayey sand and chalk fragments — 4.97 — 191.34

Final depth — — 191.34

Highwood Reservoir Borehole [4647 1612] (SU 41 NE/200), near West End. Continuously cored borehole drilled for site investigation by G. Stow & Co., August 1979. Logged by R. A. Edwards. Surface level 22.90 m above OD.

	Thickness m	Depth m

BRACKLESHAM GROUP

EARNLEY SAND

Sand, colour-banded orange-brown, greyish green and yellowish green, extremely clayey, with scattered glauconite — 2.19 — 2.19

WITTERING FORMATION

Clay, olive-grey, sandy, with partings and lenses of pale olive-grey fine-grained sand; lignitic material in some partings — 1.12 — 3.31

Sand, pale olive-grey and greenish grey, fine- to medium-grained, sparsely glauconitic, with 1–3 mm-thick lenses of olive-grey very sandy clay — 0.69 — 4.00

Clay, olive-grey, slightly silty, with scattered lenses and partings of grey fine- to medium-grained sand — 1.00 — 5.00

Sand, olive-grey, extremely clayey — 1.00 — 6.00

Clay, as 4.00–5.00 m depth — 2.34 — 8.34

Clay, olive-grey, slightly silty, with rare irregularly developed small pods and lenses of sporadically carbonaceous fine-grained sand — 1.68 — 10.00

Clay, as 2.19–3.31 m depth — 1.30 — 11.30

Whitecliff Bay Bed (11.30–14.65 m)

Clay, yellowish grey to pale olive-grey, smooth to slightly silty, with dark yellowish brown irregular carbonaceous mottles and scattered lignite fragments — 1.20 — 12.50

Clay, olive-grey, slightly silty, with sub-vertical rootlets and irregular small pods and lenses of pale olive-grey very fine-grained sand and coarse-grained silt; rootlets occur to 14.65 m — 2.15 — 14.65

Clay, sandy, with sand partings — 2.35 — 17.00

Clay, sandy, structureless — 1.00 — 18.00

Sand, pale olive-grey, medium-grained; and clay, olive-grey, slightly silty, in subequal proportions — 0.50 — 18.50

Clay, as 2.19–3.31 m depth — 0.50 — 19.00

Clay, dark greenish grey, slightly silty, with scattered lignite fragments — 0.50 — 19.50

Clay, olive-grey, well laminated, with very closely spaced partings and lenses of pale olive-grey fine- to very fine-grained sand with carbonaceous material on some partings — 4.00 — 23.50

	Thickness m	Depth m
Clay, as bed above, but with partings and lenses less intensely developed; gradational increase in sand content below 25 m in the form of bands of dark greenish grey extremely clayey sand, with some sand-filled burrows	2.50	26.00
Clay and sand, interlaminated and thinly interbedded; about two-thirds dark greenish grey clay, one third greenish grey glauconitic fine- to medium-grained sand in laminae and beds up to 15 mm thick	5.50	31.50
Sand, dark greenish grey, clayey, medium-grained, glauconitic, with indistinct clay lenses and scattered lignitic fragments	0.50	32.00
Clay and sand interlaminated, as 26.00–31.50 m depth	1.00	33.00
Sand, dark greenish grey, moderately clayey, fine- to medium-grained, glauconitic; 33.88–34.00 laminated sand forming a passage into the underlying unit by gradational increase in clay content	1.00	34.00

LONDON CLAY

?Division E

	Thickness m	Depth m
Sand, dark greenish grey, clayey, silty, fine-grained, finely micaceous	1.9	35.90
Clay, olive-grey, very sandy, bioturbated; and sand, olive-grey, extremely clayey, fine-grained, with irregular pods of sand; finely laminated clay with very fine-grained sand partings at 37.50–37.56 m; shelly fossils including turritellids at 38.40–40.00 m	4.1	40.00
Final depth		40.00

Ramnor Inclosure Borehole [3114 0475] (SU 30 SW/1) near Brockenhurst. BGS continuously cored borehole drilled for research by S. P. Thorley and W. H. George using the Geological Survey drilling rig, March 1977–May 1977.

Logged by E. C. Freshney. Macrofaunal determinations by J. Cooper and C. King; nummulite determinations by M. J. Hughes and C. King. Surface level (estimated) 52 m above OD.

	Thickness m	Depth m
HEADON FORMATION		
UPPER HEADON FORMATION		
Clay, greyish orange, relatively sand-free, with pale grey bands; some thin bands of fine comminuted shell debris	4.90	4.90
Clay, very silty, laminated, greyish orange; and clayey silt	4.68	9.58
Clay, silty, yellow, with a few shell fragments; comminuted shell bands with some whole bivalve and gastropod shells between 10.0 and 10.21 m, 10.6 and 11.0 m, 11.27 and 11.4 m, and 11.96 and 12.5 m; becoming greenish black to greenish grey with depth; sharp base	7.92	17.50
LYNDHURST MEMBER		
Clay, greenish grey, fairly sand-free, some silt bands below 17.6 m; band of shell debris at 18.27 to 18.38 m	0.88	18.38

	Thickness m	Depth m
Sand, clayey, greenish grey, with shell debris common from 18.48 to 20.3 m and 21.7 to 22.1 m	3.72	22.10
Clay, dark greenish grey, with sand content increasing slightly below 22.83 m; much bivalve and gastropod shell debris particularly between 22.4 and 22.83 m and at 28.5 m; 'Venus Bed' and 'Roydon Zone' at 17.6 to 24.5 m and 24.5 to 30.00 m respectively; their shelly fauna includes *Cardita* cf. *deltoidea*, *Corbicula obovata*, *Volutospina geminata* and *V.* cf. *spinosa*; sharp base	7.90	30.00
LOWER HEADON FORMATION		
Clay, greenish grey, sandy, with many bands of comminuted shell debris; bands of clayey sand between 38.36 and 38.72 m and 38.85 and 39.06 m; shells mostly *Corbicula obovata*, oysters, *Viviparus* and *Australorbis sp.*	10.30	40.30
Sand, clayey, sharp base	0.10	40.40

BARTON GROUP

	Thickness m	Depth m
BECTON SAND		
Silt, olive-grey, laminated, coarsening downwards into greenish grey clayey sand; some lignitic debris and mica between 42.75 and 42.82 m; base taken from geophysical logs in core loss	8.35	43.75
Sand, greenish grey; sharp base	2.01	45.76
Clay, sandy, greyish green, passing down to clayey sand with much mica and rootlets; clay masses and some lignite below 46.1 m; core losses at many levels	8.09	53.85
BECTON BUNNY MEMBER		
Sand, greenish grey, fairly micaceous; clay content increasing downwards; shell debris at 56.22 m; passing into olive-grey sandy clay with scattered bivalve and gastropod shells below 58.88 m, and into clayey sand at about 63.4 m; fauna consists of bivales including *Crassatella*, *Chlamys* and *Nucula*, and gastropods including *Euspira* and volutids	10.7	64.55
Clay, gravelly, flint-rich, with shell debris	1.13	65.68
Sand, gravelly, greenish grey, with shell debris; passing down into greenish grey clayey sand and then into greenish grey clay-free shelly sand with some lignite; most of sand cores lost; clay content increases below 72.39 m to become greenish grey clayey sand with abundant shelly fauna consisting of bivalves, including *Crassatella*, *Chama* and *Cubitostrea*, and gastropods including *Calyptraea* and *Euspira*	12.32	78.00
CHAMA SAND		
Sand, clayey, greenish grey, silty, glauconitic, very shelly and intensely bioturbated; gradual increase in clay content towards the base; fauna includes *Chama squamosa*, *Cardita*, *Crassatella*, *Turritella* and *Volutospina*	7.00	85.00

	Thickness m	Depth m

BARTON CLAY

Clay, dark greenish grey to olive-grey, with highly variable sand and silt contents; generally bioturbated and shelly; *Nummulites rectus* occurs between 118.0 and 127.15 m and *N. prestwichianus* between 132.9 and 134.8 m; very sandy between 127.00 and 132.00 m and mostly very sandy between 140.00 m and the base; abundant shelly fauna of bivalves, mostly carditids and corbulids, and gastropods including *Volutospina* and *Turritella* — 75.00 — 160.00

BRACKLESHAM GROUP

SELSEY SAND

Sand, slightly clayey, glauconitic and very shelly; some patchy calcareous cement; *Nummulites* cf. *prestwichianus* abundant — 10.98 — 170.98

Clay, greenish grey, sandy and silty, to extremely sandy and silty with pale silt bands and laminae; shelly, with common bivalves, gastropods and *N. variolarius* — 2.52 — 173.50

Clay, silty to slightly silty, passing down into clayey silt; very shelly — 2.00 — 175.50

Sand, to silt, clayey, becoming slightly clayey at about 180 m; clay content increases below this to become extremely silty towards the base; much coarse glauconite and some shell material, mainly corbulids and turritellids — 9.50 — 185.00

Silt, clayey, to very fine-grained sand with glauconite-rich patches; becomes highly glauconitic and dark greenish grey below 191.5 m; very shelly with many corbulids and turritellids — 13.92 — 198.92

Clay, extremely silty, dark yellowish brown, to clayey silt with patches of glauconite grains; common shelly fauna includes *Lentipecten corneus* — 3.68 — 202.60

Silt, clayey, sandy, olive-grey and greenish grey with a sparse fauna including corbulids, *Crassatella* and *Lentipecten corneus* — 3.90 — 206.50

Clay, extremely silty, dark yellowish brown, with patches of glauconite; restricted fauna includes *Macrosolen hollowaysii* and turritellids — 1.50 — 208.00

Silt, sandy, clayey, greenish grey — 1.50 — 209.85

MARSH FARM FORMATION

Clay, sandy, olive-grey with pale olive-grey sand laminae — 6.95 — 216.80

Sand, dark greenish grey with yellowish brown clay bands and some lignitic material — 3.79 — 220.59

Sand, olive-grey, almost clay-free with yellowish brown plastic clay seams — 6.61 — 221.2

Sand, olive-grey, with silt and clay bands; mostly uncored; laminated sandy clay near base; brecciated material at base with clasts of yellowish grey clayey silt and green glauconitic sand — 10.41 — 231.61

EARNLEY SAND

Core loss; gamma-ray log indicates probably mainly sand — 15.39 — 247.00

Clay, sandy, olive-grey, with abundant stringers of glauconitic sand; heavily bioturbated, with some lignitic material; yellow, possible sideritic concretions between 250 and 251.6 m and at base — 7.45 — 254.45

WITTERING FORMATION

Core loss; geophysical logs indicate mainly sand with increasing clay content towards the base — 9.55 — 264.00

Core loss; geophysical logs indicate interbedded sand and clay with increasing clay content downwards — 11.38 — 275.38

Clay, olive-grey, sandy, interbedded with greenish grey sand; contains small washouts and scour structures — 2.12 — 277.50

Whitecliff Bay Bed (277.5 – 282.3 m)

Clay, dark yellowish brown, disturbed, slightly sandy, with sand masses; lignites and rootlets common below 277.6 m; slight increase in sand content below 280 m; indistinct banding towards the base — 4.60 — 282.30

Sand, pale olive-grey, with some lignitic debris — 0.20 — 282.50

Core loss, probably clayey sand — 4.99 — 287.49

Clay, olive-grey, sandy, with disrupted pale olive-grey sand laminae; contains several thicker beds of olive-grey laminated clayey sand, some of which are micaceous — 4.78 — 292.27

Core loss, probably mainly sand, but with some clay layers, particularly at the top — 9.59 — 301.86

Sand, almost clay-free, greenish grey, with some lignitic debris; sideritic nodule at 302.85 m; bands of olive-grey sandy clay occur below 302.8 m and become more persistent below 303 m; below 303.45 m olive-grey clay layers become dominant down to 304.55 m where the sand again becomes dominant — 2.92 — 304.78

Rock-bit drilling; geophysical logs indicate sand with some thin clay bands — 6.22 — 311.00

LONDON CLAY

?Division D2

Rock-bit drilling; geophysical logs indicate mainly clay with some sand bands — 7.00 — 318.00

WHITECLIFF SAND

Rock-bit drilling; geophysical logs indicate mainly clay-free sand — 4.00 — 322.00

?Division D1 clays

Rock-bit drilling; geophysical logs indicate mainly clay — 4.78 — 326.78

Clay, olive-grey, sandy, micaceous with some greenish grey sand bodies and some interbedded olive-grey sand; thin claystone layers at 327 m and at 328.38 – 328.43 m — 2.90 — 329.68

Core loss — 1.18 — 330.86

?Division C

NURSLING SAND

Sand, olive-grey, with scattered shell fragments; contains pale olive-grey sand masses between 332.4 and 332.9 m; fauna mainly of bivalves including *Glycymeris*, and turritellids — 4.60 — 335.46

Core loss, probably clayey sand — 2.73 — 338.19

	Thickness m	Depth m
Sandstone, hard, olive-grey, calcareous with many bivalves, mainly glycimerids (Glycymeris Sandstone)	0.74	338.93
Sand, olive-grey, clayey, heavily bioturbated; shell fragments and many flint pebbles (basal Division C pebble bed) at the base	2.14	341.07
Final depth		341.07

Chilling Farm Borehole [5098 0443] (SU 50 SW/26), near Hook, Warsash. BGS continuously cored borehole drilled for research by S. P. Thorley using the Geological Survey drilling rig, December 1984 – March 1985.

Logged by E. C. Freshney and R. A. Edwards. Surface level approximately 13 m above OD.

	Thickness m	Depth m
RIVER TERRACE DEPOSITS (3rd Terrace)		
Uncored; gamma-ray log and samples indicate sand and gravel, fine-grained, yellowish brown, with scattered angular flint pebbles; base taken from gamma-ray log	5.00	5.00
BRACKLESHAM GROUP		
SELSEY SAND		
Rock-bit drilling; gamma-ray log and samples indicate sand, fine-grained, yellowish brown, with ?cavings of sandy gravel	3.50	8.50
MARSH FARM FORMATION		
Rock-bit drilling; gamma-ray log and samples indicate predominantly sand, possibly with a few clay beds or intervals of interbedded sand and clay	6.26	14.76
Sand, pale olive-grey, clay-free to slightly clayey, fine- to very fine-grained, moderately glauconitic; pods of clay and a few burrows; irregular bioturbated thin grey clay laminae and a few lignitic partings at 16.26–16.70 m	1.94	16.70
Clay, brownish olive-grey to olive-grey, with partings, impersistent laminae, and a few thicker beds of very fine-grained sand and silt; finely micaceous; a few thicker sand beds at c.18.5 m; scattered lignitic fragments	2.30	19.00
Clay, brownish olive-grey to olive-grey, with fewer sand partings and beds than bed above	3.07	22.07
Core loss; gamma-ray log indicates sand	3.49	25.56
Clay, olive-grey, laminated with thin silt partings	0.34	25.90
EARNLEY SAND		
Sand, greyish green, silty, slightly clayey, fine-grained, moderately glauconitic; shelly, with bivalves and turritellid gastropods; *Nummulites laevigatus* at 26.4–27.5 m	3.70	29.60
Sand, greyish green to dark greyish green, clayey, silty, fine-grained, glauconitic to very glauconitic, shelly	0.20	29.80
Sand, greyish green to dark greyish green, silty, fine-grained, glauconitic to very glauconitic, bioturbated with patches of very glauconitic sand in a purplish grey clay matrix; scattered shells; common large carditids, and turritellids at 30.7 m; shells absent to rare below c.32.6 m	5.22	35.02
Sand, greyish green, silty to very silty, glauconitic, bioturbated with patches of very glauconitic sand and sandy clay; scattered bivalves and gastropods; carditids common at 36.15 m and carditids and turritellids present at 37 m	1.90	37.00
Sand, greyish green, silty, clayey, fine-grained, glauconitic; extremely shelly with abundant closely packed bivalves and gastropods	1.02	38.02
Sand, greyish green, silty, fine-grained, with scattered shells; casts of fossils in the basal 0.1 m	0.73	38.75
Clay, olive-grey, laminated, with partings of very fine-grained sand and silt	0.20	38.95
Sand, greyish green, silty, clayey fine-grained, scattered glauconite; highly bioturbated and burrowed; scattered bivalve moulds	2.55	41.50
WITTERING FORMATION		
Clay, olive-grey, silty, laminated, with mm-scale lenses and partings of pale olive-grey very fine-grained sand and silt; locally less well laminated silty fine-grained sand with irregular laminae of very silty clay; a few horizontal burrows	4.20	45.70
Silt, greenish grey to pale olive, clayey, sandy, bioturbated, with a few pyritic nodules and burrows	0.30	46.00
Whitecliff Bay Bed (46.00–53.80 m)		
Clay, olive-grey, structureless; hard, conchoidally-fracturing with some polished listric surfaces (locally abundant); patchy marcasite and lignite fragments; claystone nodule at 47.00 m	1.80	47.80
Clay, olive-grey, with sporadic partings of pale olive-grey silt, and a few rootlets	0.60	48.40
Sand, olive-grey, silty, clayey, sparsely micaceous, with rootlets moderately common	0.40	48.80
Clay, olive-grey, silty, sandy, with well developed subvertical black rootlets replaced by marcasite	1.90	50.70
Clay, olive-grey, silty, with irregular partings of silt and silty very fine-grained sand; fewer rootlets than overlying unit	1.05	51.75
Silt, olive-grey, clayey, sandy, with rootlets; gradational base	0.25	52.00
Clay, olive-grey, silty, homogeneous, with abundant polished listric surfaces and many subvertical rootlets; patchy green coloration	1.80	53.80
Clay, olive-grey, silty, with sporadic partings of pale olive-grey silt	0.40	54.20
Sand, olive-grey to greenish grey, silty, fine-grained, bioturbated with clay patches, containing sporadic glauconite and mica;		

	Thickness m	Depth m

at c.54.6 m, yellowish brown clay band with sand-filled burrows — 0.55 — 54.75

Clay, yellowish grey to olive-grey, silty, with patches and pods of silt and very fine-grained sand; sparsely micaceous and marcasitic; subvertical rootlets present above 56 m; a few polished listric surfaces; below c.58.6 m, sand content increases as irregular thin sand beds — 4.75 — 59.50

Silt, clayey, sandy, with irregular clay layers; micaceous; possibly bioturbated below 59.4 m, with irregular clay pods, and burrows — 1.50 — 61.00

Sand, olive-grey, fine-grained, silty, with laminae and thin beds of olive-grey silty clay; lignitic debris and mica on some partings; sand and clay in approximate proportions 60:40; clayey sandy silt, possibly bioturbated, at 62.0 m — 2.30 — 63.30

Sand, olive-grey, silty, fine-grained, mostly structureless, but sporadic irregular lamination with fine-grained lignitic material and mica on lamination surfaces — 0.70 — 64.00

Clay, olive-grey, very silty, with wispy wavy partings and thin lenses of pale olive-grey silt and very fine-grained sand — 1.10 — 65.10

Clay, olive-grey, with planer mm-scale partings of silt with very fine-grained lignitic material and mica; 10 mm-thick brown carbonaceous clay band at 66 m — 1.40 — 66.50

Clay, olive-grey, very silty, with irregular silt laminae — 0.40 — 66.90

Sand, olive-grey, silty, fine-grained, low clay content, sparsely glauconitic and micaceous; bioturbated except where small-scale cross-lamination is picked out by clayey silt bands — 2.80 — 69.70

Sand, as above, containing irregular disrupted clay and lignitic fragments — 0.31 — 70.01

Clay, olive-grey, with scattered lignitic material, horizontal burrows, and possible rootlets — 0.29 — 70.30

Sand, olive-grey, silty, fine-grained, with clay laminae; locally predominantly sand with a few dark brown lignitic and clay laminae, scattered mica and fine-grained lignitic debris — 1.40 — 71.70

Sand, olive-grey to greenish grey, silty, fine-grained, sparsely glauconitic to glauconitic; sporadic silty clay laminae dip 10° – 15° — 0.90 — 72.60

Sand, olive-grey to greenish grey, fine-grained, fairly low clay content, finely micaceous; locally moderately glauconitic, with sporadic banding of glauconite-rich sand with dips up to 17°; a few irregular clay laminae at 75.8 – 76.0 m; flat clay clasts and lignitic fragments at 77.02 – 77.22 m and 77.50 – 78.00 m — 7.50 — 80.10

Sand, pale olive-grey, fine-grained, inter-bedded in subequal proportions with clay, dark olive-grey, wavy-laminated on mm to cm scale — 3.50 — 83.60

Sand, olive-grey to greenish grey, fine-grained, moderately glauconitic; scattered flat clay-pebble clasts; cross-laminated at 84.3 m — 0.90 — 84.50

Sand, as above, with irregular clay laminae — 0.35 — 84.85

Sand, olive-grey to greenish grey, with wavy laminae of silty to very silty clay; locally sand predominates — 0.74 — 85.59

LONDON CLAY

Division D

Clay, olive-grey, silty to very silty, bioturbated, micaceous, bioturbated, with some horizontal sand-filled burrows; small shell fragments below c.87.5 m; a few marcasitic nodules present; pyritised wood fragments at c.91.8 m — 8.16 — 93.75

Pebble bed; black rounded flints up to 20 mm across in extremely sandy silty clay matrix (basal Division D2 pebble bed) — 0.30 — 94.05

Sand, olive-grey, fine-grained (locally medium-grained); top 0.2 m clayey, but remainder predominantly clay-free; sparsely glauconitic; scattered lignitic fragments and sporadic clay laminae; below c.95.5 gradational passage to clayey silt — 1.45 — 95.50

Silt, olive-grey, clayey, bioturbated, locally clayey sandy silt, with a few scattered small white shell fragments — 3.90 — 99.40

Siltstone, pale olive-grey, ?calcareous; shelly, with bivalves and gastropods common — 0.25 — 99.65

Sand, olive-grey silty, very fine-grained, micaceous, with scattered small shell fragments — 1.65 — 101.30

Silt, olive-grey, clayey to very clayey, finely micaceous, bioturbated, sporadic white shell fragments; silt content decreases below c.105.5 m — 4.20 — 105.50

Clay, olive-grey, very to extremely silty, micaceous, a few lignitic fragments; rare shell fragments — 1.75 — 107.25

Pebble bed, black rounded flint pebbles up to 80 mm across in matrix of clayey silt with patches of medium-grained sand — 0.20 — 107.45

Division C

PORTSMOUTH SAND

Sand, olive-grey, fine- to medium-grained, slightly clayey and silty; scattered clay laminae at 109.7 m; band of lignitic fragments at top; locally cross-laminated; sparsely to moderately glauconitic, locally picking out bedding; sand coarser around 109 m with scattered lignitic fragments; silt and clay contents increase below c.109.8 m to give silty fine-grained sand to slightly clayey silty fine-grained sand; locally with patches of medium-grained glauconite and rare fragments of white shell fragments; a few clay layers at c.110.8 m — 4.15 — 111.60

	Thickness m	Depth m
Division C clays		
Clay, olive-grey, silty to very silty, homogenous; passing to silty clay below c.112 m; becoming gradationally siltier below c.115.5 m; sporadic scattered small shell fragments; patch of abundant turritellids at c.115 m, large burrow filled with oyster and other bivalve debris at 117.7 m; passing down into extremely silty clay below c.120 m; large septarian nodule at 120.6–121.15 m	10.40	122.00
Final depth		122.00

APPENDIX 2

List of Geological Survey photographs

Copies of these photographs may be seen in the Library of the British Geological Survey, Keyworth, Nottingham, NG12 5GG and at the British Geological Survey, Exeter Office, St Just, 30 Pennsylvania Road, Exeter, EX4 6BX. National Grid references are given in square brackets; those of general views are of the viewpoints. Dates of photographs are also given. Colour or black and white prints and 35 mm slides can be supplied at a fixed tariff. The photographs were taken by H. J. Evans and C. J. Jeffery.

Recent and Pleistocene

A14245   Gravel of the 1st Terrace of the River Test in Lee Gravel-pit, near Nursling [360 177]. 1979.

A14246   River Terrace Deposits (2nd Terrace) overlying Selsey Sand in sea-cliffs near Chilling [508 038]. 1979.

A14247   Involution structures in River Terrace Deposits (5th Terrace) near Holbury [4260 0477]. 1979.

A14248   Drift deposits overlying Whitecliff Sand at Stubbington Farm Sand-pit, near Fair Oak [4975 1839]. 1979.

A14249   Drift deposits overlying Whitecliff Sand at Stubbington Farm Sand-pit, near Fair Oak [4975 1839]. 1979.

A14250   Older River Gravels (Older Terrace 2) in a gravel pit near Newtown, Minstead [2655 1058]. 1979.

A14251   Possible periglacial flexuring of the base of Older River Gravels (Older Terrace 2) near Fritham Cross [2382 1042]. 1979.

A14252   Detail of possible periglacial flexuring of the base of Older River Gravels (Older Terrace 2) near Fritham Cross [2382 1042]. 1979.

A14253   Older River Gravel plateau feature (Older Terrace 3) near Stoney Cross, with lobes of Head Gravel extending over Barton Clay [258 118]. 1979.

A14254   Plateau surface of Older River Gravels (Older Terrace 3) on Janesmoor Plain, Fritham [246 132]. 1979.

Headon Formation

A14255   Headon Formation overlying Becton Sand in a pit near Little Holbury [4257 0402]. 1979.

Barton Group

A14256   Becton Sand in a pit near Little Holbury [4258 0403]. 1979.

A14257   Cross-bedding in Becton Sand in a pit near Little Holbury [4258 0403]. 1979.

A14258   Clay-lined burrows in Becton Sand in a pit near Little Holbury [4257 0402]. 1979.

A14259   Lucas Castle, near Fritham Cross, an isolated small hill capped by Chama Sand [244 104]. 1979.

Bracklesham Group

A14260   Wittering Formation laminated clay, sand with clay laminae, and interbedded sand and clay at Giles Lane Sand-pit, Plaitford [2735 2002]. 1979. (Plate 5).

A14261   Wittering Formation laminated clays at Swanwick Brick-pit [5045 0966]. 1979.

A14262   Detail of Wittering Formation laminated clays at Swanwick Brick-pit [5045 0966]. 1979.

London Clay

A14263   Feature near Landford formed by Whitecliff Sand [260 205]. 1979.

A14264   Dewatering structures in Whitecliff Sand at Stubbington Farm Sand-pit, near Fair Oak [4975 1839]. 1979.

A14265   'Herringbone' cross-bedding in Whitecliff Sand at Stubbington Farm Sand-pit, near Fair Oak [4975 1839]. 1979. (Plate 3).

A14266   Trough cross-bedded Whitecliff Sand at Stubbington Farm Sand-pit, near Fair Oak [4975 1839]. 1979.

A14267   Conglomerate-filled channel in Whitecliff Sand at Stubbington Farm Sand-pit, near Fair Oak [4975 1839]. 1979.

A14268   Channel infill in Whitecliff Sand at Stubbington Farm Sand-pit, near Fair Oak [4975 1839]. 1979.

A14269   Bands of flint pebbles within Whitecliff Sand at Breach Farm Sand-pit, near Stoke Common [4651 2032]. 1979.

A14270   Normal faulting of flint pebble bands in Whitecliff Sand at Breach Farm Sand-pit, near Stoke Common [4651 2032]. 1979. (Plate 2).

A14271   London Clay scenery near Sherfield English, with feature formed by Nursling Sand [283 222]. 1979.

Reading Formation

A14272   Pebble beds in Reading Formation near Sherfield English [2890 2279]. 1979.

A14273   Cross-bedding in Reading Formation sands near Sherfield English [2764 2298]. 1979.

Economic Geology

A14274   Sand with interbedded flint pebbles being worked beneath a thick overburden of clayey sand Head at Breach Farm Sand-pit, near Stoke Common [4651 2032]. 1979.

Topography

A14275   View from West Wellow Common to Plaitford Common, showing country underlain by Wittering Formation, Earnley Sand, and Marsh Farm Formation [284 187]. 1979.

A14276   Topography in country near Furzley underlain by Marsh Farm Formation [286 161]. 1979.

REFERENCES

ALLEN, D. J., BARKER, J. A., and DOWNING, R. A. 1983. The production test and resource assessment of the Southampton (Western Esplanade) Geothermal Well. *Rep. Inst. Geol. Sci.*, *Investigation of the geothermal potential of the UK.*

ANDERSON, F. W. 1933. The New Docks excavations, Southampton. *Pap. Proc. Hampshire Field Club*, Vol. 12, 169–176.

AP SIMON, A., GAMBLE, C., and SHACKLEY, M. 1977. Pleistocene raised beaches on Ports Down, Hampshire. *Pap. Proc. Hampshire Field Club*, Vol. 33, 17–32.

BIGG, P. J. 1980. Upper Cretaceous foraminifera and age determinations of the Marchwood No. 1 borehole. In Marchwood No. 1 borehole. *Palaeontol. Rep. Inst. Geol. Sci.* [*Unpublished*].

BROWN, R. C., GILBERTSON, D. D., GREEN, C. P., and KEEN, D. H. 1975. Stratigraphy and environmental significance of Pleistocene deposits at Stone, Hampshire. *Proc. Geol. Assoc.* Vol. 86, 349–363.

BRYDONE, R. M. 1912. *The stratigraphy of the Chalk of Hants.* (London: Dulau and Co. Ltd.)

BUJAK, J. P., DOWNIE, C., EATON, G. L., and WILLIAMS, G. L. 1980. Dinoflagellate cysts and acritarchs from the Eocene of Southern England. *Spec. Pap. Palaeontology, Palaeontol. Assoc.*, London, No. 24

BURTON, E. ST. J. 1933. Faunal horizons of the Barton Beds in Hampshire. *Proc. Geol. Assoc.*, Vol. 44, 131–167.

BUURMAN, P. 1980. Palaeosols in the Reading Beds (Palaeocene) of Alum Bay, Isle of Wight, UK. *Sedimentology*, Vol. 27, 593–606.

CHANDLER, M. E. J. 1961. *The Lower Tertiary floras of southern England. 1. Palaeocene floras. London Clay flora (supplement).* (London: Palaeontological Society.)

COLLINSON, M. E., FOWLER, K., and BOULTER, M. C. 1981. Floristic changes indicate a cooling climate in the Eocene of southern England. *Nature, London*, Vol. 291, 315–317.

COLTER, V. S., and HAVARD, D. J. 1981. The Wytch Farm oil field, Dorset. In *Petroleum geology of the Continental shelf of north-west Europe*, 494–503. ILLING, V., and HOBSON, G. D. (editors). (London: Hayden & Son Ltd.)

COSTA, L., and DOWNIE, C. 1976. The distribution of the dinoflagellate *Wetzeliella* in the Palaeogene of north-western Europe. *Palaeontology*, Vol. 19, 591–614.

CURRY, D. 1937. The English Bartonian nummulites. *Proc. Geol. Assoc.*, Vol. 48, 229–246.

CURRY, D. 1942. The Eocene succession at Afton Brickyard, IOW. *Proc. Geol. Assoc.*, Vol. 53, 88–101.

CURRY, D., and KING, C. 1965. The Eocene succession at Lower Swanwick Brickyard, Hampshire. *Proc. Geol. Assoc.*, Vol. 76, 29–35.

CURRY, D., HODSON, F., and WEST, I. M. 1968. The Eocene Succession in the Fawley Transmission Tunnel. *Proc. Geol. Assoc.*, Vol. 79, 179–206.

CURRY, D., KING, A. D., KING, C., and STINTON, F. C. 1977. The Bracklesham Beds (Eocene) of Bracklesham Bay and Selsey, Sussex. *Proc. Geol. Assoc.*, Vol. 88, 243–254.

CURRY, D., ADAMS, C. G., BOULTER, M. C., DILLEY, F. C., EAMES, F. E., FUNNELL, B. M., and WELLS, M. K. 1978. A correlation of Tertiary rocks in the British Isles. *Spec. Rep. Geol. Soc. London*, No. 12.

DALEY, B. 1972. Some problems concerning the Early Tertiary climate of southern Britain. *Palaeogeogr. Palaeoclimatol. Palaeoecol.*, Vol. 11, 177–190.

DALEY, B., and EDWARDS, N. 1971. Palaeogene warping in the Isle of Wight. *Geol. Mag.*, Vol. 108, 399–405.

DIXON, F. 1850. *The geology and fossils of the Tertiary and Cretaceous formations of Sussex* (London: Longman, Brown and Green, and Longman.)

DRUMMOND, P. V. O. 1970. The Mid-Dorset Swell. Evidence of Albian-Cenomanian movements in Wessex. *Proc. Geol. Assoc.*, Vol. 81, 679–714.

DYER, K. R. 1975. The buried channels of the 'Solent River', Southern England. *Proc. Geol. Assoc.*, Vol. 86, 239–245.

EATON, G. L. 1976. Dinoflagellate cysts from the Bracklesham Beds (Eocene) of the Isle of Wight, southern England. *Bull. Br. Mus. Nat. Hist.*, A. Geol. No. 26, 227–332.

ELLISON, R. A. 1983. Facies distribution in the Woolwich and Reading Beds of the London Basin, England. *Proc. Geol. Assoc.*, Vol. 94, 311–319.

ELWES, J. W. 1887. Excavations at Bramshaw, New Forest. *Pap. Proc. Hampshire Field Club*, Vol. 17–20.

ELWES, J. W. 1888. Sections opened on the new railway from Fareham to Netley. *Pap. Proc. Hampshire Field Club*, Vol. 4, 80–83.

EVERARD, C. E. 1954. Submerged gravel and peat in Southampton Water. *Pap. Proc. Hampshire Field Club*, Vol. 18, 263–285.

FALCON, N. L., and KENT, P. E. 1960. Geological results of petroleum exploration in Britain 1945–1957. *Mem. Geol. Soc. London* No. 2.

FISHER, O. 1862. On the Bracklesham Beds of the Isle of Wight Basin. *Q. J. Geol. Soc. London*, Vol. 18, 65–94.

FOLK, R. L. 1968. *Petrology of sedimentary rocks.* (Austin: Hemphill's, University of Texas.)

FOLK, R. L., and WARD, W. C. 1957. Brazos River bar, a study in the significance of grain-size parameters. *J. Sediment. Petrol.*, Vol. 27, 3–27.

FORBES, E. 1853. On the fluvio-marine Tertiaries of the Isle of Wight. *Q. J. Geol. Soc. London*, Vol. 9, 259–270.

FRESHNEY, E. C., BRISTOW, C. R., and WILLIAMS, B. J. 1985. Geology of sheet SZ 09 (Bournemouth-Poole-Wimbourne, Dorset). *Geological report for DOE: Land Use Planning.* (Exeter: British Geological Survey.)

FRIEDMAN, G. M. 1967. Dynamic processes and statistical parameters compared for size frequency distribution of beach and river sands. *J. Sediment. Petrol.*, Vol. 37, 327–354.

GARDNER, J. S., KEEPING, H., and MONCKTON, H. W. 1888. The Upper Eocene, comprising the Barton and Upper Bagshot Formations. *Q. J. Geol. Soc. London*, Vol. 44, 578–635.

GILKES, R. J. 1968. Clay mineral provinces in the Tertiary sediments of the Hampshire Basin. *Clay. Miner.*, Vol. 7, 351–361.

GILKES, R. J. 1978. On the clay mineralogy of Upper Eocene and Oligocene sediments in the Hampshire Basin. *Proc. Geol. Assoc.*, Vol. 89, 43–56.

GODWIN, N., and GODWIN, M. E. 1940. Submerged peat at Southampton. Data for the study of post-glacial history. V. *The New Phytologist*, Vol. 39, 303–307.

GODWIN, H., and SWITZUR, V. R. 1966. Cambridge University natural radiocarbon measurements, VIII. *Radiocarbon*, Vol. 8, 390–400.

HARLAND, R. 1979. The *Wetzeliella (Apectodinium) homomorpha* plexus from the Palaeogene/earliest Eocene of north-west Europe. *Proc. IV Int. Palynol. Conf., Lucknow (1976–77)*, Vol. 2, 59–70.

HARLAND, R., and SHARP, J. 1980. *Phthanoperidinium obscurum sp. nov.*, a non-marine dinoflagellate cyst from the late Eocene of England. *Rev. Palaeobot. Palynol.*, Vol. 30, 287–296.

HAWKINS, H. L. 1946. Field meeting at Reading. *Proc. Geol. Assoc.*, Vol. 54, 164–171.

HODSON, F., and WEST, I. M. 1972. Holocene deposits of Fawley, Hampshire, and the development of Southampton Water. *Proc. Geol. Assoc.*, Vol. 83, 421–442.

HOOLEY, R. W. 1903. Excavations on the site of the Electric Light Works. Southampton, May 1903. *Pap. Proc. Hampshire Field Club*, Vol. 5, 47–52.

HUBBARD, R. N. L. B., and BOULTER, M. C. 1983. Reconstruction of Palaeogene climate from palynological evidence. *Nature, London*, Vol. 301, 147–150.

JAMES, J. P. 1974. Report of field meeting to Lower Swanwick, Hampshire. *Tertiary Times*, Vol. 2, 23–28.

KAT, C. 1983. Oil and Gas Developments in Europe in 1982. *Bull. Am. Assoc. Pet. Geol.*, Vol. 67, 1948–1982.

KAY, F. F. 1939. *A soil survey of the Strawberry District of South Hampshire* (Reading: University of Reading.)

KEEN, D. H. 1980. The environment of deposition of the South Hampshire Plateau Gravels. *Proc. Hampshire Field Club Archaeol. Soc.*, Vol. 36, 15–24.

KEEN, M. C. 1977. Ostracod assemblages and the depositional environments of the Headon, Osborne and Bembridge Beds (Upper Eocene) of the Hampshire Basin. *Palaeontology*, Vol. 20, 405–445.

KEEN, M. C. 1978. The Tertiary—Palaeogene. Pp.385–450 in *A stratigraphical index of British Ostracoda*. BATE, R., and ROBINSON, E. (editors). Bell House Place.

KEEPING, H. 1887. On the discovery of the *Nummulina elegans* Zone at Whitecliff Bay Isle of Wight. *Geol. Mag.*, Vol. 4, 70–72.

KEEPING H., and TAWNEY, E. B. 1881. On the beds at Headon Hill and Colwell Bay in the Isle of Wight. *Q. J. Geol. Soc. London*, Vol. 37, 85–127.

KEMP, D. J. 1984a. Temporary excavations in the Bracklesham Group near Southampton, Hampshire. *Tertiary Res.*, Vol. 6, 87–91.

KEMP, D. J. 1984b. M27 Motorway excavations near West End, Southampton (Hants). *Tertiary Res.*, Vol. 6, 157–163.

KEMP, D. J., KING, A. D., KING, C., and QUAYLE, W. J. 1979. Stratigraphy and Biota of the Elmore Formation (Huntingbridge division, Bracklesham Group) at Lee-on-the-Solent, Gosport, Hampshire. *Tertiary Res.*, Vol. 2, 93–103.

KEMP, J. T. 1889. The tufaceous deposits of the Test and Itchen. *Pap. Proc. Hampshire Field Club*, Vol. 1, 83–89.

KING, C. 1981. *The stratigraphy of the London Clay and associated deposits*. (Rotterdam: Dr W. Backhuys.)

KING, C., and KEMP, D. J. 1980. Exposures in the London Clay Formation of the Gosport Aren (Hants). *Tertiary Res.*, Vol. 3, 71–81.

KING, A. D., and KEMP, D. J. 1982. Stratigraphy of the Bracklesham Group in recent exposures near Gosport (Hants). *Tertiary Res.*, Vol. 3, 171–187.

KING, A. D., and KING, C. 1977. The stratigraphy of the Earnley 'division' (Bracklesham Group) at Copythorne, Hampshire. *Tertiary Res.*, Vol. 1, 115–118.

KNOX, R. W. O'B., and HARLAND, R. 1979. Stratigraphical relationships of the early Palaeogene ash-series of N. W. Europe. *J. Geol. Soc. London*, Vol. 136, 463–470.

KRUMBEIN, W. C. 1934. Size frequency distribution of sediments. *J. Sediment. Petrol.*, Vol. 4, 65–77.

KUBALA, M. 1980. The sand and gravel resources of the country around Fordingbridge, Hampshire: description of 1:25 000 resource sheet SU 11 and parts of SU 00, SU 01, SU 10, SU 20 and SU 21. *Miner. Assess. Rep. Inst. Geol. Sci.*, No. 50.

LOVEDAY, J. 1960. Plateau Deposits of the Southern Chiltern Hills. *Proc. Geol. Assoc.*, Vol. 73, 83–101.

MACKNEY, D., HODGSON, J. M., HOLLIS, J. M., and STAINES, S. J. 1983. *Legend for the 1:250 000 Soil Map of England and Wales*. (Harpenden: Soil Survey of England and Wales.)

MORTON, A. C. 1982. Heavy minerals of Hampshire Basin Palaeogene strata. *Geol. Mag.*, Vol. 119, 463–476.

MURRAY, J. W., and WRIGHT, C. A. 1974. Palaeogene foraminifera and palaeoecology, Hampshire and Paris Basins and the English Channel. *Spec. Pap. Palaeontology, Palaeont. Assoc. London*, No. 14.

NORVIK, M. S. 1969. An analysis of the microfauna and microflora of the Upper Eocene of the Hampshire Basin. Unpublished PhD thesis, University of London.

PLINT, A. G. 1982. Eocene sedimentation and tectonics in the Hampshire Basin. *J. Geol. Soc. London*, Vol. 139, 249–254.

PLINT, A. G. 1983. Facies, environments and sedimentary cycles in the Middle Eocene, Bracklesham Formation of the Hampshire Basin: evidence for global sea-level changes? *Sedimentology*, Vol. 30, 625–253.

PRESTWICH, J. 1847. On the probable age of the London Clay, and its relation to the Hampshire and Paris Tertiary systems. *Q. J. Geol. Soc. London*, Vol. 3, 354–377.

PRESTWICH, J. 1850. On the structure of the strata between the London Clay and the Chalk in the London and Hampshire Tertiary Systems. Part i. Basement-Beds of the London Clay. *Q. J. Geol. Soc. London*, Vol. 6, 252–281.

PRESTWICH, J. 1854. On the structure of the strata between the London Clay and the Chalk in the London and Hampshire Tertiary Systems. Part ii. The Woolwich and Reading Series. *Q. J. Geol. Soc. London*, Vol. 10, 75–170.

PRICE, M., and ALLEN, D. J. 1982. The production test and resource assessment of the Marchwood Geothermal Borehole. *Rep. Inst. Geol. Sci., Invest. Geotherm. Potential UK*. Open-file report.

REID, C. 1902. The geology of the country around Southampton. *Mem. Geol. Surv. GB*, Sheet 315.

REID, E. M., and CHANDLER, M. E. J. 1926. *The Bembridge Flora, Catalogue of Cainozoic plants in the Department of Geology, I*. (London: British Museum, Natural History.)

REID, E. M., and CHANDLER, M. E. J. 1933. *The flora of the London Clay*. (London: British Museum, Natural History.)

SHACKLEY, M. L. 1970. Preliminary note on hand axes found in gravel deposits at Warsash, Hampshire. *Pap. Proc. Hampshire Field Club*, Vol. 27, 5–7.

SHORE, T. W. 1905. The origin of Southampton Water. *Pap. Proc. Hampshire Field Club*, Vol. 5, 1–25.

SHORE, T. W., and ELWES, S. W. 1889. The new dock excavation at Southampton. *Pap. Proc. Hampshire Field Club*, Vol. 1, 43–56.

SOUTHERN WATER AUTHORITY. 1980. *Survey of the existing water use and management*. (Worthing: Southern Water Authority.)

STEAVENSON, A. G. 1957. A tree trunk in Bagshot Sand at East Wellow. *Pap. Proc. Hampshire Field Club*, Vol. 19, 179.

STINTON, F. C. 1970. Field meeting in the New Forest, Hants. *Proc. Geol. Assoc.*, Vol. 81, 269–274.

THOMAS, H. D., and DAVIS, A. G. 1949. The pterobranch Rhabdopleura in the English Eocene. *Bull. Br. Mus. Nat. Hist. Geol.*, Vol. 1, 1–24.

TERWINDT, J. H. J. 1971. Litho-facies of inshore estuarine and tidal-inlet deposits. *Geol. Mijnbouw*, Vol. 50, 515–526.

THOMAS, L. P., and HOLLIDAY, D. W. 1982. Southampton No. 1 (Western Esplanade) Geothermal Well: Geological Well Completion Report. *Rep. Deep Geol. Unit, Inst. Geol. Sci.*, No. 82/3. Open-file report.

TREMLETT, W. E. 1961. Geology of the Matley and Denny Nature Reserve, New Forest. *Pap. Proc. Hampshire Field Club*, Vol. 22, 1–7.

TUBB, C. R. 1968. *The New Forest: an ecological history.* (Newton Abbot: David & Charles.)

WENTWORTH, C. K. 1922. A scale of grade and class terms for clastic sediments. *J. Geol.*, Vol. 30, 377–392.

WHITAKER, W. 1861. The geology of parts of Oxfordshire and Berkshire. *Mem. Geol. Surv. GB.*, Sheet 22 (Old Series).

WHITAKER, W. 1910. The water supply of Hampshire. *Mem. Geol. Surv. GB.*

WHITE, H. J. O. 1912. The geology of the country around Winchester and Stockbridge. *Mem. Geol. Surv. GB.*, Sheet 299.

WHITE, W. C. F. 1971. A gazetteer of brick and tile works in Hampshire. *Pap. Proc. Hampshire Field Club*, Vol. 28, 81–97.

WHITTAKER, A. 1980. Marchwood No. 1 Geological well completion report. *Rep. Deep Geol. Unit, Inst. Geol. Sci.*, No. 80/5.

WHITTARD, W. F., and SIMPSON, S. (editors). 1958. *Lexique Stratigraphique International, Part 3a 12 Palaeogene.* (Paris: Centre National de la Recherche Scientifique.)

WRIGHT, C. A. 1972a. Foraminiferids from the London Clay at Lower Swanwick and their palaeoecological interpretation. *Proc. Geol. Assoc.*, Vol. 83, 337–347.

WRIGHT, C. A. 1972b. The recognition of a planktonic foraminiferid datum in the London Clay of Hampshire. *Proc. Geol. Assoc.*, Vol. 83, 413–420.

WRIGLEY, A. 1934. A Lutetian fauna at Southampton docks. *Proc. Geol. Assoc.*, Vol. 45, 1–16.

WRIGLEY, A. G. 1949. The London Clay at Lower Swanwick, Hampshire. *Bull. Br. Mus. Nat. Hist. Geol.*, Vol. 1, 13–19.

YARBROUGH, S. C. 1984. Oil and gas developments in Europe in 1983. *Bull. Am. Assoc. Pet. Geol.*, Vol. 68, 1433–1466.

INDEX OF FOSSILS

GENERAL INDEX

BRITISH GEOLOGICAL SURVEY

Keyworth, Nottingham NG12 5GG

Murchison House, West Mains Road,
Edinburgh EH9 3LA

The full range of Survey publications is available
through the Sales Desks at Keyworth and
Murchison House. Selected items are stocked by
the Geological Museum Bookshop, Exhibition
Road, London SW7 2DE; all other items may be
obtained through the BGS London Information
Office in the Geological Museum. All the books
are listed in HMSO's Sectional List 45. Maps are
listed in the BGS Map Catalogue and Ordnance
Survey's Trade Catalogue. They can be bought
from Ordnance Survey Agents as well as from
BGS.

*The British Geological Survey carries out the geological
survey of Great Britain and Northern Ireland (the latter as
an agency service for the government of Northern Ireland),
and of the surrounding continental shelf, as well as its
basic research projects. It also undertakes programmes of
British technical aid in geology in developing countries as
arranged by the Overseas Development Administration.*

*The British Geological Survey is a component body of the
Natural Environment Research Council.*

Maps and diagrams in this book use topography
based on Ordnance Survey mapping

HER MAJESTY'S STATIONERY OFFICE

HMSO publications are available from:

HMSO Publications Centre
(Mail and telephone orders)
PO Box 276, London SW8 5DT
Telephone orders (01) 622 3316
General enquiries (01) 211 5656
Queueing system in operation for both numbers

HMSO Bookshops
49 High Holborn, London WC1V 6HB
  (01) 211 5656 (Counter service only)
258 Broad Street, Birmingham B1 2HE
  (021) 643 3740
Southey House, 33 Wine Street, Bristol BS1 2BQ
  (0272) 264306
9 Princess Street, Manchester M60 8AS
  (061) 834 7201
80 Chichester Street, Belfast BT1 4JY
  (0232) 238451
71 Lothian Road, Edinburgh EH3 9AZ
  (031) 228 4181

HMSO's Accredited Agents
(see Yellow Pages)

And through good booksellers